IT'S NOT ROCKET SCIENCE

AND OTHER IRRITATING
MODERN CLICHÉS

Clive Whichelow has written for TV shows and stars such as Rory Bremner, Jonathan Ross, *Spitting Image* and *Smith and Jones* and also for the *Mail on Sunday*, *Express*, *You* magazine and others.

Hugh Murray's TV and radio writing credits include work for Steve Coogan, Punt and Dennis, *Smack the Pony*, *Monkey Dust*, *Smith and Jones* and many others.

IT'S NOT ROCKET SCIENCE

AND OTHER IRRITATING MODERN CLICHÉS

Clive Whichelow
& Hugh Murray

PORTRAIT

Visit the Portrait website!

PORTRAIT Portrait publishes a wide range of non-fiction, including
biography, history, science, music, popular culture and sport.

Visit our website to:
- read descriptions of our popular titles
- buy our books over the internet
- take advantage of our special offers
- enter our monthly competition
- learn more about your favourite Portrait authors

VISIT OUR WEBSITE AT: www.portraitbooks.com

First published in 2007 by Portrait
an imprint of
Piatkus Books Ltd
5 Windmill Street
London WIT 2JA
e-mail: info@piatkus.co.uk

The moral right of the author has been asserted

*A catalogue record for this book is available from
the British Library*

ISBN 978 07499 5159 7

Text design by Goldust Design

Edited by Andrew John

This book has been printed on paper manufactured with
respect for the environment using wood from managed
sustainable resources

Printed and bound in Great Britain by
William Clowes Ltd, Beccles, Suffolk

CONTENTS

INTRODUCTION

Over 50 years ago the film producer Samuel Goldwyn said, 'Let's have some new clichés!' Well we've got shedloads of new clichés – and then some!

Back in the 'good old days' you knew where you were with clichés. They'd been around, it seemed, since the dawn of time! Clichés used to be the comfy old armchairs in the furniture of language. Many were taken straight from the pages of Shakespeare or the Bible ('The spirit is willing, but the flesh is weak' and 'Gilding the lily', for example – although both were misquotations).

But then something happened: mass communication. All of a sudden, phrases that might have happily existed as local slang or the jargon of a small community of workers found themselves whizzing round the world on the Internet or through globally broadcast radio and TV programmes. OK, we've had TV and radio for a long while now, but with multiple channels and digital broadcasting many millions more people now have access to a wider variety of programmes – and clichés.

A phrase such as 'no worries' was not widespread 20 years ago, but is now commonplace. Similarly, the dreaded 'upspeak' or rise in intonation at the end of a sentence that makes every statement sound like a question?

From TV and films we get phrases such as 'going commando' and 'bunny boiler'. And with more and more TV channels come more and more people being filmed at minimal expense saying whatever comes into their little heads. And what usually comes into their heads? Clichés!

Add in radio stations, podcasts, blogs, video cams, chatrooms, texting, mobile-phone calls and so on, resulting in more and more people chatting for more and more of the time. And, if you're chatting more and more of the time, clichés are the handrails on a wobbly walk through language. They provide handy, ready-assembled clumps of conversational inanity.

A cliché can instantly mark you out as a 'hip', 'cool', 'happening' kind of guy or girl, just like all the other 'hip', 'cool', 'happening' guys and girls.

Indeed there must be some people out there who communicate in nothing but clichés!

Potentially a cliché can 'jazz up', 'spice up' or 'sex up' an otherwise dull statement or conversation. It can inject a bit of drama, a dash of humour or a splash of colour.

Clichés aspire to be slick verbal idiosyncrasies, but unfortunately they don't tend to remain idiosyncratic for long – clichés spread 'like wildfire'.

The idea of this book is not to list all clichés in current usage but to identify the newer ones, the young upstarts, which in some cases are barely out of short trousers, and usually in their twenties at most.

So how do we define a cliché? Well, it's always difficult because one person's idiom is another person's hackneyed phrase and yet another person's cliché. One good test is if a phrase induces an inward groan. Many of us despair when we hear someone say they've been doing something '24/7', or cringe when a politician says, 'I'm not ruling anything in and I'm not ruling anything out', or recoil when a sportsman says his easy victory was 'just another day at the office'.

Ultimately, anyone's list of clichés is going to be a personal choice, but we hope that the examples in the following pages will include at least some of your own personal favourites – if 'favourites' is the right word.

In the odd case where a cliché has been around a bit longer than the others it will have been included because it has now reached new levels of universality. The classic case is 'at the end of the day'. It is almost impossible to listen to half an hour of a radio phone-in without hearing this phrase at least once, if not 15 times. It is used in political speeches, playgrounds and supermarkets, in parks, pubs and pop songs. Who knows – maybe it's even been said in space? In 2004 the Plain English Campaign asked its supporters in 70 countries to nominate the phrases they found most irritating – at the top of the list, unsurprisingly, was 'at the end of the day'.

We have also included a few non-verbal clichés, such as gestures and packaging information – nothing, it seems, is cliché-free.

So, this is not some slavishly annotated academic tome, but a fun-filled treasure trove that lifts the lid on the whole Pandora's Box of wall-to-wall clichés that we are now being subjected to 24/7. Oh, and by the way, we know that some readers will be going through these pages with a 'fine-tooth comb' looking for clichés that have unwittingly crept into our comments but our defence will always be that we were using them in an 'ironic' and possibly 'postmodern' way.

Unconvinced? All right! We admit it, we've 'bent over backwards' trying to avoid them but 'at the end of the day' clichés are almost impossible to escape entirely!

Enjoy!

GENERAL CLICHÉS

Many clichés are so common (and so versatile) that they cross boundaries, categories and continents with ease. The following are just some that can be found in social situations, politics, business, sport, show business and probably even places where clichés have previously feared to tiptoe. It's also noticeable how aggressive many of these clichés are.

24/7

A numerical cliché! Once a convenient shorthand for those shops or services that stayed open 24 hours a day, seven days a week, but now a catch-all phrase simply meaning 'all the time'. Some examples: 'He's giving me grief 24/7'; 'She's on my case 24/7'; 'The baby's been crying 24/7 since it was born.' Somehow this innocent little phrase denoting convenient availability has become used almost solely to indicate perpetual irritation.

ABSOLUTELY

When routinely used in place of 'yes' it can begin to grate after a while.

ACCIDENT WAITING TO HAPPEN

Accidents do not have minds of their own. They do not hide behind bushes and leap out on unsuspecting passers-by. If they did we could round them up and never pay insurance policies ever again.

AND THEN SOME

Or, in other words, 'and then some more'.

'And then some' is a slightly truncated, ultra-jolly way of informing someone that they have gravely underestimated the extent of something. The phrase can even be used when the original estimate was couched in completely nonspecific terms such as, 'So I understand you had a few pints to drink last night, did you?' 'And then some!' It is usually best to preface 'and then some' with several moments of snorting, derisive laughter.

ARM CANDY
It sounds like a rather unpleasant form of confectionery but means a pretty girl on the arm of someone as a mere decoration.

AS IF
What power can be invested in two such little words! 'He truly believed the overthrow of "civilisation" would benefit mankind. As if.'

AS YOU DO
An ironic little add-on to a sentence that has just described someone's unusual behaviour. For instance, 'To celebrate his thirtieth birthday he decided to bungee-jump off the Eiffel Tower – as you do.'

AT THE END OF THE DAY
Perhaps the most ubiquitous of all modern clichés.
You'll hear it at bus stops, in boardrooms and
bedrooms – it's even been the title of a film. Some
radio phone-ins have desperately tried banning
the phrase, but to no avail. OK, it is useful, but, for
goodness' sake, try something else for a change!

AT THIS MOMENT IN TIME
It has been pointed out again and again that all
you need to say is 'now' but some people think this
phrase sounds more impressive. It doesn't.

BAD-HAIR DAY
A day when absolutely nothing goes right – and
apparently the worst thing of all that can possibly
happen is that you find you can't do a thing
with your hair. Come on! If your family were
kidnapped and your house burned down just
before you found that you'd been made bankrupt,
surely the fact that your hair was sticking up a bit
on one side would be the least of your worries.
And what about people like Don King? Does this
mean he's having a terrible time every single day?

BALLPARK

'Ballpark figure' has now been shortened to 'ballpark' and has scuttled out of business jargon into general use. 'I'd like to get a second-hand car for about six grand – but that's ballpark.' Substitute the words 'football pitch', 'hockey stadium' or 'velodrome' for 'ballpark' and it makes you realise just what a strange phrase this is.

BASICALLY

This is far from new but it refuses to go away. Listen out for it today and you are almost guaranteed to hear it once, if not several times – perhaps even in the same conversation. Some clichés stick around because they're useful: they can encapsulate a thought in a few words. But 'basically' is meaningless. All it does is sit at the beginning of a sentence, usually a reply, and give the thinker a bit of extra thinking time.

BEEN THERE, DONE THAT, AND GOT THE T-SHIRT

This has been around for quite a while but is still frequently heard. It was probably an accurate enough phrase when used in relation to visiting tourist destinations, but not when applied to, say, getting a divorce.

BIG PICTURE
The Sistine Chapel ceiling? Tom Cruise's latest film? No, it just means 'the whole thing'. 'I'm not interested in all the nitty-gritty detail, just give me the big picture.'

BIG TIME
The big time used to be something to aspire to: 'She's hit the big time', 'He's a big-time operator.' Now it's just as likely to be applied to something negative, for example 'I am in debt – big time'; 'I've really messed up – big time.'

BLING
'Bling' or 'bling-bling' is a slang term for expensive jewellery that emerged from hip-hop culture. Possibly the first artist to popularise the term was rapper B.G., who had a big hit with a track called 'Bling-Bling', which made him a lot of money to buy even more bling. Surely it must have annoyed genuine bad-ass rappers when white middle-class people started using the word or phrase.

BLOWN AWAY
'Blown away' is also a term for being killed, usually by gunfire, so it's quite a strong metaphor for being merely impressed. 'I was blown away by your flower arrangements.'

. . . BRIGADE
The first of many adaptable clichés. Although this was originally a military term meaning a body of troops, it can now be tacked onto other phrases to denote a group of people who are often as far from being trained fighters as it is possible to be, for example 'the politically correct brigade'.

BRING IT ON!
Mucho macho but a toucho naffo.

BROWNIE POINTS
'She's been getting in at 8.30 every morning and getting brownie points from the boss.' Always said with an air of disdain and condescension about some poor soul who's trying to do something positive.

BUNNY BOILER
Taken from the film *Fatal Attraction* and meaning a

woman who is without principle or restraint and who should be avoided – a bit like this cliché.

BUT, HEY!
Would-be hip prelude to self-contradiction. 'I don't usually drink in the lunch hour, but, hey, it's your last day!'

BUT IN A GOOD/BAD WAY
'She dresses very seventies – but in a good way.' A clichéd qualifier that is so imprecise it doesn't really qualify anything very much at all.

Bereavement clichés

It may seem cruel or insensitive to include such a section, but these phrases are often uttered by public figures with no direct connection to the dead person or persons and are said insincerely for effect. If you must come out with a platitude about a recently departed

person, try to make it an original one. It's what they would have wanted.

EXTRAORDINARY DIGNITY

After people have suffered some great tragedy in their lives, they then have to suffer other people constantly commenting that they have shown 'extraordinary dignity'. Perhaps it is assumed that nothing cheers people up after some great tragedy so much as being congratulated on their manners, poise and general bearing.

LOVED ONES

People who have just died, often in some dreadful accident, are referred to as 'loved ones'. 'Several families lost loved ones in the disaster.' How do they know? Who's to say that some families weren't secretly delighted that their selfish, good-for-nothing, womanising Uncle Mick was run over by that runaway traction engine?

NOTHING'S GOING TO BRING HIM/ HER BACK

This is so obvious it hardly needs saying, but they still say it anyway.

OUR HEARTS GO OUT ...

This is the sort of thing politicians say after some dreadful public-transport tragedy, hoping perhaps that a bit of public sympathy from them will result in a reciprocal amount coming back when the future of their position is being examined.

OUR THOUGHTS ARE WITH ...

Similar to above – sometimes said by police chiefs for the same reason.

TRIBUTES ARE POURING IN

When somebody famous dies the tributes 'pour in'. They never trickle, drip or dribble in – even when nobody realised the 'celebrity' was still alive in the first place.

BUYING INTO
Originally an expression denoting literally buying into a business (shares, partnerships and so forth), which now can be applied even when no money changes hands – for instance, 'I don't buy into all this religion stuff.'

CALL ME OLD-FASHIONED, BUT ...
Used immediately before saying something distinctly old-fashioned.

(I) CAN'T BE DOING WITH IT
A syntactical mess of a cliché that could surely be better expressed some other way.

CARBON FOOTPRINT
With 'the environment' high on the 'news agenda' it was inevitable that it would result in a new cliché or two. And here we have one so sparkling and shiny that it may not even be quite a cliché yet, but it is being heard increasingly often in the media and means our impact on the environment through carbon emissions. As environmentalists are always urging us to get out of our cars, not board planes and so on, 'footprint' may not be the best

metaphor to use, but, as we know, logic and clichés sometimes go together like Belgian chocolates and curry paste.

CATCH YOU LATER
It makes 'you' sound like a disease, or at best, an object plummeting to Earth.

-CENTRIC
Suffix meaning 'oriented towards the thing that this suffix has been tagged on the end of', for instance, 'child-centric', 'woman-centric', 'person-centric', 'phallocentric', 'nematode-worm-centric' etc.

CHEERS
Once a mere salutation when drinking but now becoming a multipurpose word that can substitute for 'thank you', 'goodbye' and so on. It will be confusing, though, if, instead of performers saying 'Thank you, and goodnight', they say 'Cheers, and cheers'. Even more confusing if they sign off with a drink in their hand, in which case they'll probably have to say three cheers.

(I NEARLY) CHOKED ON MY CORNFLAKES

Don't people have anything else for breakfast? Why can't they choke on their muesli or eggs-over-easy for a change when they hear that a pop singer has been appointed as a UN ambassador?

CLASS ACT

If you ever get a call from Hollywood asking you to provide a class act for them, they probably don't mean for you to go out and perform a piece of direct political action designed to bring down the bourgeoisie. You would, however, be within your rights to act on the basis of such a misunderstanding.

COULD YOU BE ANY MORE …?

Fill in the gap yourself: 'stupid', 'selfish', 'arrogant'. All negative words, note. Never seems to be used with words such as 'nice', 'helpful', 'intelligent'.

(WE DON'T HAVE A) CRYSTAL BALL

The sort of irritating phrase used by petty officials when refusing to make predictions about a service they are meant to be running. 'OK, there's been a points failure, but when will the next train be arriving?' 'I don't know – we don't have a crystal ball.'

DA-DE-DA-DE-DA

No, not Diane Keaton saying 'La-di-da, la-di-da, la la' in *Annie Hall*, but an indication that the speaker can't be bothered to finish a list. 'So we ordered a new kitchen, and new carpets, and had the decorators in … da-de-da-de-da … got a new bathroom suite …' Often used in boastful pronouncements.

DEAL WITH IT!

Uncompromising, aggressive response to someone refusing to accept a *fait accompli*: 'I may have been the cleaning lady last week, but now I'm your new boss – deal with it!'

DID I MISS A MEETING?

Said whenever some behaviour or attitude suddenly seems to have become accepted as the norm – the presumption being that everyone else in the country must have recently got together and democratically decided on it. If so, it would seem that the organisers of this meeting then failed to circulate the minutes to all of us non-attendees.

DIVA

A diva used to be a term for a famous yet demanding female opera singer. It then became a term for a famous yet demanding female pop singer. More lately it has become a term simply for a demanding female. So now we're not even getting a song to make up for all the demanding behaviour!

DO YOU KNOW ...?

Add the phrase 'Do you know' at the start of your response to the most mundane question you could ever possibly be asked and it really brightens up the conversation. 'Would you like a biscuit?' 'Do you know, I would!' Adding 'Do you know' in this fashion flatters the person you are speaking to with its implicit suggestion that their question was one of unparalleled insight that has completely lit up your day and possibly turned your entire life around.

... DODGER

'Coffin dodger' = old person, 'soap dodger' = 'dirty person', and so on. Make up your own!

DOH!
An often self-flagellating expression of dismay popularised by *The Simpsons*. Usually used ironically and self-consciously.

DON'T ASK
A close relative of 'Let's not go there.' (See separate entry under 'Psychobabble' in 'Social Clichés'.)

DOWN AND DIRTY
If you are prepared to get 'down and dirty', you are either fiercely competitive or a sewage worker or perhaps a fiercely competitive sewage worker.

DREAM ON
Although the exact opposite in literal terms, it's surprisingly close to 'Wake up and smell the coffee'. 'I'm going to go backstage after the concert and get her autograph and ask her out for a date.' 'Dream on!' (possibly followed by 'sucker' or similar word or phrase for added emphasis).

DROP-DEAD GORGEOUS
It's strange that we don't have the phrase 'Drop-dead ugly' – it would seem a more apposite description of an extremity of physical appearance.

DUDE

University of Pittsburgh linguistics professor Scott Kiesling has described the use of the word 'dude' in expressions such as 'Whoa, dude', 'Hey, dude' or 'Sorry, dude' as conferring an 'effortless kinship'. The word's origins have apparently been traced to a Gaelic word meaning a 'foolish-looking fellow'.

DUMBING DOWN

When anything is made easier for people in some field of achievement it's said to be dumbed down. The 'down' part of this phrase seems to be redundant and the nonsensical variation 'dumbing up' has been spotted several times.

Politically correct clichés

This strange, insidious and leaderless cult of political correctness has, by its very nature, obliged people to use the 'correct' terminology in specific situations to avoid giving offence, real or imagined. This has led to a limited vocabulary, which in turn has led inevitably to clichés – often clumsy euphemisms.

... CHALLENGED

Once a politically correct euphemism for 'handicapped' or otherwise physically or mentally disadvantaged, this was taken up by humorists amateur and professional – for instance, 'Vertically challenged' meaning 'short'. Still heard, but rather passé now.

DEFERRED SUCCESS

A completely brilliant phrase that was coined to avoid describing students who had failed their exams. They hadn't failed. They had achieved 'deferred success'. Or, in other words, they had failed.

DIFFERENTLY

As in 'differently able'. This is a commendable attempt to be nice and positive about things. Some, however, might wonder just how many distinct ways there are in which someone can be 'able'. Other uses of 'differently' include 'differently weighted' (fat), 'differently qualified' (unqualified) and 'differently tall' (a dwarf).

GENDER

Instead of being asked on a form what sex you are, you may be asked what gender you are. OK, it helps sidestep the appalling embarrassment involved in using the word 'sex' in public but instead it makes you sound like you're a piece of foreign vocabulary.

HERSTORY

Absolutely stunning. Yes, it's the word 'history' as you must now say it to avoid offending hardcore feminists. Particularly ones who are prone to be a bit 'herstrionic'.

IN DENIAL
Meaning not admitting something such as an uncomfortable truth about oneself or one's 'situation'. It's strange that the 'in' hasn't been put to similar use in other phrases such as 'in admittance'.

INAPPROPRIATE
'Inappropriate' behaviour or language is anything deemed so by these invisible policemen. It can mean 'rude', 'demeaning', 'insulting', 'mildly offensive', 'very offensive' or pretty much anything else.

SPECIAL
As in 'You're not different, you're special!' Unfortunately, the word 'special' here is possibly being used in the sense of 'special' but not a sort of 'special' that anyone would willingly choose.

SPECIAL FRIEND

This is an expression used to describe someone with whom you have an intimate relationship, very possibly involving private wobbly parts. Unfortunately, the phrase is invariably used to explain such a relationship to children who, it is assumed, don't have phrases in their vocabulary to describe such a thing. Even more unfortunately, they do have phrases in their vocabulary to describe such things and these are frequently of a crude and indelicate nature.

WIMMIN

Hardline feminists woke up one morning and found to their horror that the word 'women' contained the dreaded syllable 'men' – their worst enemies. They immediately insisted that from now on they would be collectively known as 'wimmin'.

ENJOY!
A curiously disembodied exhortation to appreciate
something. Let's hope this verb-only sentence
doesn't catch on. Relish! Appreciate! Like!

EXECUTIVE DECISION
When someone says they have made an 'executive
decision', what they mean is they have just had to
make a decision to take a particular course of action
all on their own. The reason they have had to do
this is probably that no one was willing to speak to
them at the time. The phrase 'executive decision'
therefore means roughly the same as 'lonely person's
decision'. The word 'executive' does, however, give
the phrase an air of luxury and opulence. This is
probably quite appropriate, since the decision in
question was probably crap and is therefore going to
result in a large amount of money being wasted.

(THE) F-WORD
Originally used by nervous journalists, broadcasters
and politicians who did not want to be seen
swearing. Has also been adapted for comic effect,
as in 'the M-word' (marriage), the 'C-word'
(commitment) and so on.

FAST-TRACK
Annoyingly slow bureaucratic processes can in certain cases be 'fast-tracked'. This usually happens because someone in authority has a word with the bureaucrats involved and tells them to hurry things up a bit and not take quite so many tea breaks.

FIFTEEN MINUTES OF FAME
Could this be the most inaccurate of all clichés? Andy Warhol said, 'In the future everyone will be famous for 15 minutes.' When he said it, the average career span of a pop star was a couple of years. Forty years on, half the pop stars from the sixties are still around and show no signs of leaving the stage soon. Even the ones who died are still selling records, T-shirts and all the rest. And people whose fame should, by all decent standards, be short-lived – such as certain 'reality' TV stars – are also extending their 15 minutes to year after interminable year.

FOR MY SINS
An expression used by a person to explain that they have to perform some mildly uninteresting action or job as a result of having committed some

presumably correspondingly uninteresting sins, e.g.
'I've got to organise the office Christmas party this
year – for my sins!' It would seem that the sinner
concerned has been condemned to this terrible
punishment by some kind of slightly camp deity.

GENIE IS OUT OF THE BOTTLE

Meaning some sort of trouble that has started and
will be difficult, if not impossible, to stop. It is
surprising that some sort of genie-rights group has
not protested about this cliché. Aren't genies those
nice men in turbans that grant you three wishes?
What's wrong with that? And when did they start
coming out of bottles? *Aladdin and his Magic Bottle*?
'Lamp' if you don't mind.

GET A ROOM

Used when a couple are being overamorous or
flirtatious in public. In other words, 'Go and get
yourself a hotel room, have a nice bit of sexual
intercourse, come back when you've calmed down
a little!'

GET OFF THE FENCE!

Used as a jocular remark to someone who has just

made a forcefully negative statement. 'I can't stand people who smoke, it makes me physically sick; I can't even bear to be in the same room as people who smoke.' 'Come on, get off the fence, say what you really think!'

GET OUT OF HERE!
This is a slightly camp expression suggesting absolute astonishment at some piece of mildly surprising information.

GET OVER IT
Another way of saying 'deal with it' (see separate entry).

GET-OUT-OF-JAIL-FREE CARD
'So, I said to my wife, "If I make a start on those household repairs, you won't mind if I go out for a drink occasionally with the boys?" It's my get-out-of-jail-free card.' From the board game Monopoly, but hasn't been around as long as a phrase in its own right.

(IT'S A) GIRL THING
Meaning that a mere man would not understand

that his partner has, for example, to go and have her shoulder cried on by her best friend who has just been dumped. It's as though 'new men' and equality of the sexes never happened.

GO BALLISTIC
People don't just get very annoyed any more, they 'go ballistic'. 'Ballistic' simply means 'relating to projectiles', so, if taken literally, this means they have turned themselves into a projectile. It must be assumed that on doing so they have then launched themselves into the sky – it seems to be quite a way on from merely 'hitting the roof'.

GO FIGURE
Another way of saying 'I don't understand it.' For example, 'I bought brand-new glasses, put braces on my teeth, and almost completely eliminated my acne, but girls still won't talk to me – go figure!'

GO FOR IT!
An inspirational cliché cried out to galvanise an acquaintance towards what may be a rather trivial goal – for example, 'I think I'll just visit the toilet.' 'OK! *Go* for it!'

GO WITH THE FLOW

'The flow' could mean almost anything – midnight
skinny-dipping, smoking illegal substances,
spreading nasty rumours about work colleagues …
What's a nice phrase like you doing in company
like this?

GOBSMACKED

This ugly verb is believed to have originated in
Liverpool, UK. Perhaps it should have stayed there.
It means surprised, but perhaps to about the power
of ten. And maybe that's the attraction – it gives
an emphasis that's difficult to replicate without
recourse to additional words. If you won a lottery
fortune you would be more than surprised: you'd
perhaps be *utterly* surprised, or totally amazed or
absolutely flabbergasted. But, due to overuse, even
'gobsmacked' is losing some of its power. So now if
you are lucky enough to win a stack of cash, being
gobsmacked may soon not be enough: you may
have to be *completely* gobsmacked. This raises the
question: what is it like to be *partially* gobsmacked?

GOING COMMANDO

That a phrase with such apparently limited

opportunities for usage has become a cliché is remarkable. It means not wearing underwear rather than bravely fighting in a war or completing a gruelling assault course. Thought to have been popularised by the TV series *Friends*.

GOING PEAR-SHAPED
When things go wrong, they go 'pear-shaped' or, alternatively, 'a bit pear-shaped'. What is the matter with being pear-shaped? Particularly if you're a pear?

GREENIE POINTS
A play on 'brownie points', and meaning earning approbation for something that might be considered virtuous by environmental groups.

GROUNDHOG DAY
When you feel as if you're reliving something (from the film of the same name). As baseball player and coach Yogi Berra once said in a different context, 'It's like *déjà vu* all over again.'

GROWING OLD DISGRACEFULLY
In years gone by it was thought to be a good thing if people grew old gracefully. Now this has been

inverted to hilarious effect and some older people
now boast that they are 'growing old disgracefully'.
In reality, the phrase probably means they enjoy a
drink rather than doing anything that is literally
disgraceful.

HANDS ARE TIED
A more virtuous version of 'It's more than my
job's worth'. Sometimes wildly exaggerated to
unintentional comic effect as in 'Our hands are
literally tied.'

HANG
Or 'hang out'. 'I'm going to hang with the guys.'
It has unfortunate 'death row' connotations.

'Up' phrases

The only way is up, according to optimists everywhere, and these days 'up' is indeed the only way with the word 'up' being added to a variety of phrases. The 'up' part of these expressions may often be superfluous, but it provides a bit of emphasis with a tinge of optimistic aspiration.

BIG UP

'Big up' is a phrase of possibly Jamaican origin meaning to boost someone's status. If someone tells you to 'big yourself up' this means that you present yourself in the best possible light. So, for example, 'When you go for your job interview, Malcolm, don't forget to big yourself up a bit. I think you'd make a great supermarket trolley-collection operative.'

FESS UP

If you 'fess up' to something, you admit to it

with a degree of reluctance: 'The youth fessed up to having committed the crime.'

FIRST UP
'First up' could possibly be an abbreviation of 'first up on stage' but is now yet another cliché being used to make everyday office life sound a little more jazzy. For instance, 'First up: item one on the agenda: apologies for absence.'

GIVE IT UP
When an audience is invited to 'give it up', this means that they are being asked to applaud wildly. It does not mean that they are being asked to make a formal commitment to stop smoking immediately in honour of the next act to appear on stage.

LIGHTEN UP
'Lighten up' is the advice frequently given to those of a slightly melancholic disposition by those of a slightly irritating disposition.

LISTEN UP

'Hey, everyone! Listen up!' Yes, adding 'up' is especially useful for anyone who doesn't know what an adverb is. 'Listen up' essentially means 'Listen carefully'. Physically, it is rather difficult to 'listen up' in a literal manner, since this would involve possessing quite oddly shaped ears.

NEXT UP

After 'first up', of course, but has there yet been a 'last up'?

PARK UP

Up where?

REST UP

An invitation to have a rest. The word 'up', however, gives the phrase a confusingly upbeat feel. 'OK, everyone, let's rest up! Let's have a rest – but in a lively and energetic kind of way!'

SEX UP
Derived from the alternative use of 'sexy' and meaning to make more attractive.

UP FOR IT
Perhaps it is derived from having one's name up on a notice-board list for some duty or other, but now, like a lot of clichés, it has multiple meanings such as 'Are you ready for it?'; 'Are you interested in it?'.

UP TO SPEED
'I'm 60 years old – I'm not really up to speed with all this new technology.' 'Speed' is one of those words that have to be quantified if they're to have any meaning. What speed? Two miles an hour? The speed of light? But, then, lack of meaning has never stopped any cliché yet.

WAIT UP
Not in the sense of 'Don't go to bed until I come home' but simply 'wait'.

HANG IN (THERE)

'Hang in', confusingly, is not the opposite of 'hang out', but means 'stick at it'. Often said by somebody comfortably uninvolved in the action, such as a boxing coach.

HAPPY-CLAPPY

This started off as a description of those modern church services that make liberal use of tambourines, guitars and shaking the hands of strangers, but it is now applied to any self-consciously upbeat formal occasion – political conferences, business training days, etc.

HARD-WIRED

'He's got the hunting instinct hard-wired into him.' Unless he's a robot this is highly unlikely.

HAVE A GOOD ONE

A slightly mysterious expression of well-wishing often said by one work colleague to another as they are about to go home. But what does it refer to exactly? What sort of good one is it that you are being advised to go off and have? Evening? Bus journey? Do-it-yourself vasectomy?

HAVE A NICE LIFE
The ultimate extension to 'have a nice day' and often said by the half of a relationship that has just been dumped by the other.

HERO TO ZERO
Well OK, it's neat, it rhymes, but it's now a cliché – deal with it!

HIGH-MAINTENANCE
When someone is described as 'high-maintenance' it means they are a lot of trouble to deal with. It means you're like either a clapped-out old motor car or a beautiful but delicate building – take your choice.

HIT THE GROUND RUNNING
Something we are all expected to do these days when we are given some task to perform of which we have little or no previous experience. Presumably, the phrase derives from an obscure extreme sport that involves both parachuting and sprinting.

HOPEFULLY
It's a funny thing with language that, if enough people get something wrong often enough for

long enough, it becomes right. 'Hopefully' used to mean 'in a hopeful manner' – the classic example being 'It is better to travel hopefully than to arrive' – but over the past few decades it has been used more and more to mean 'with a bit of luck'.

HOW GOOD IS THAT?
You tell us.

I COULD TELL YOU BUT THEN I'D HAVE TO SHOOT YOU

This line is used by people who have just been asked to reveal some closely guarded secret such as 'Has X *really* had cosmetic surgery?' or 'Tell me, what's the recipe for this amazing avocado dip?' People who say, 'I could tell you but then I'd have to shoot you' are suggesting that they are members of some top-secret organisation and that the recipe for their avocado dip is a matter of grave international importance. But, apart from joking, when would anyone genuinely use the expression 'I could tell you but then I'd have to shoot you'? Would anyone ever be so fatally inquisitive they would respond, 'OK. You'd better load up because I really do want to know.'

IF YOU CAN REMEMBER THE SIXTIES THEN YOU WEREN'T REALLY THERE

A pretty good joke when first uttered, but since then it's been uttered utterly too much and, sadly, has become a cliché.

I'M LOVING IT/I'M LIKING THAT

If the thing in question is so overwhelmingly wonderful that it turns your sentence structure into that of a backward three-year-old, then is it really so good?

I'M OUT OF HERE

A rather melodramatic way of saying 'I'm going.' The use of the present tense in the phrase seems to suggest the speaker intends to perform an exit so fast that, by the time their words reach your ears, they've already gone.

IN A SENSE

It seems to indicate that the speaker has weighed something up in their mind before opening their mouth, but no – it's just another device for gaining thinking time.

IN YOUR DREAMS

A cliché similar in tone, effect and words to
'Dream on', and used humorously to quash
unrealistic optimism. As such, 'in your dreams' is
often used as a saucy means to assert the status of
the speaker while belittling the level of fantasy the
addressee is capable of – for example, '*You* want to
go for a drink with *me*? In your dreams!'

IN YOUR FACE

A brutal, no-nonsense cliché of the kind that
is typical in the modern world. It's easy to see
how this can once have been an almost literal
observation – for instance a troublesome person
shouting the odds and putting their angry face into
that of the person on the receiving end of their ire.
But clichés never know their place, and, before you
know it, they're getting into all sorts of areas that
have nothing to do with them. So billboards can
be 'in your face' even if they're a hundred metres
away, as can rock bands, fashions, and anything else
that's even the slightest bit provocative.

IS IT JUST ME OR ...?

People use this phrase to preface some observation

of eccentric behaviour or physical deformity they have recently noted. They are therefore asking, 'Am I the only one to perform this odd behaviour/have this deformity myself or to have observed this odd behaviour/deformity in someone else?' The response is therefore, 'Yes! You are a freak!'

IS THAT THE SAME ...?

A faux-naïf question laden with irony. For instance, 'The mayor is doing his best to encourage more people to use public transport.' 'Is that the same mayor that's just doubled the bus fares?'

... IS THE NEW ...

Brown is the new black, tartan is the new brown, poetry is the new rock 'n' roll, big is the new small, 40 is the new 30, dogs are the new cats, gay is the new straight. Anything you can think of is the new something else you can think of. And vice versa!

IT AIN'T OVER TILL IT'S OVER/FAT LADY SINGS

If anyone ever tells you, 'It ain't over, till it's over,' it is useful to be able immediately to produce an overweight female singer. This will then persuade

the person who believes 'It ain't over, till it's over'
that it is in fact over.

IT COMES WITH THE TERRITORY
A rather grandiose expression suggesting that
the speaker is some kind of frontiersman bravely
staking their claim in a remote, unexplored part
of the world where they have to wrestle regularly
for survival with a family of grizzly bears. Usually
what they're referring to, though, is some slight
irritation experienced in everyday life.

IT'S NOT ROCKET SCIENCE
Well, what is – apart from, er, rocket science? And
what do rocket scientists say to their colleagues
when they can't understand something?

IT'S YOUR CALL
Meaning the responsibility, usually for disputing
something, is being passed to you. 'My beer tastes
fine, but you paid for them, so it's your call.'
Thanks, pal.

I'VE GOT A PROBLEM WITH ...
People don't simply say they don't like something

any more: they say they've got a problem with it. Oddly, it always ends up sounding as if it's the thing or person they have a problem with that is at fault rather than themselves.

JUNKIE

The word 'junkie' is now used by people least likely to be actual junkies to describe anything they do regularly. If someone tells you, 'Oh, yes, I'm a bit of a herbal-tea junkie,' it is very unlikely that they spend their leisure hours tearing open camomile tea bags and mainlining the ingredients.

(THE) JURY'S OUT

Juries usually consist of 12 people, but cliché juries can have unlimited numbers, sometimes millions. For example, 'The jury's still out on what causes climate change.'

KEEP IT REAL

Another phrase of friendly farewell. This is always helpful advice, particularly for those of us who keep ending up lost in a surreal fictional universe when we were just trying to find our way to the bus stop.

Contextual clichés

In certain situations people often seem to fall back on the same old responses, observations and comments. While the words they say may not be clichés in other circumstances, they become so in specific situations. Here are some examples.

CHAMPAGNE SPRAYING

When somebody wins a major sporting event such as a motor race, the organisers will congratulate them and present them with an expensive bottle of champagne. Imagine how they must feel when, every time they do this, instead of enjoying a nice drink, the winner instead shakes the bottle as vigorously as possible before taking somebody's eye out with the cork and letting the bubbly spurt all over the place in a great sticky mess, which they probably hardly ever bother to clean up themselves. Sigmund Freud would surely have had something to say about such a performance.

NEIGHBOURS
If a neighbour spots you mowing the front lawn/trimming the hedge/washing the car there is a good chance he will say, 'When you've finished that can you come and do mine?'

WEATHER
Whenever it's unusually hot people will often refer to 'global warming'. 'Say what you like about global warming, but it looks good to me.'

WHAT'S THE TIME?
When people come up to you in the street and ask, 'Do you happen to know the time?' they will often indicate their wrists as though to helpfully advise you, 'This is roughly whereabouts on your body you might find the information I require.' It has often been wondered whether these same people will point to their crotches when asking, 'Do you know where the nearest toilet is?'

KICK IN

Things don't 'take effect' any more: they 'kick in'. Like many other modern clichés, it has a forceful tone. 'I was all right till those double vodkas kicked in.'

KICKING OFF

Usually meaning the start of a punch-up, or at least a heated argument. 'Let's go out – my parents are kicking off again.'

KNOCK-ON EFFECT

If one thing is done, something rather unwelcome occurs as an unexpected result. For example, you press the wrong key on your home computer and the entire Internet is somehow deleted.

LIFE'S TOO SHORT TO ...

The original phrase was 'life's too short to stuff a mushroom' and used by Shirley Conran in her book *Superwoman*. Since then it's been endlessly adapted and used as an excuse to get out of almost any mildly taxing task.

LIKE I CARE

It's strange that, in this 'caring, sharing' world
of mutual understanding fostered by the
psychobabble brigade and the advocates of
'inclusiveness', a common response to someone
else's viewpoint or problem is this dismissive little
phrase. Or, perhaps it's *because* of it.

-LITE

An all-purpose suffix denoting a pale version of
something more robust. So a failure by courts to get
tough on crime will be dubbed 'punishment-lite'.
The format is taken from those low-fat or low-
alcohol products for the health-conscious.

LITERALLY

These days people claim to have 'literally' done
some quite extraordinary things – for example,
'I literally died'; 'I was literally fuming'; 'I literally
exploded'; 'He was literally talking out of his arse'
– and so on. Especially beloved of football players
and other sportsmen but very common in
general speech.

LOST IT

'She used to be a pretty good boss but she's lost it.'
The 'it' in question is presumably 'the plot', which
is far too many words for us modern people.

LOW-RENT

A poor imitation. 'She warbled on histrionically
like a low-rent Liza Minnelli.'

'Low-rent' is a phrase that you will hear applied
to many things, but very rarely to property –
especially if you live anywhere near a major city.

(NO) MAGIC BULLET

Meaning 'no simple solution' but strangely
incongruous in certain circumstances, e.g. 'There's
no magic bullet for stopping gun crime.' Often
thought to have come from the 'single bullet'
theory in John F. Kennedy's assassination, but
actually comes from German folklore.

MAGICAL MYSTERY TOUR

If anyone is taken on a circuitous route they
compare it to a 'magical mystery tour'. Prior to
1967 this would have simply been a 'mystery tour',
but such is the power of the Beatles, from whose

film this phrase came, that this adaptation seems to have taken over.

MEN IN WHITE COATS

Ice-cream salesmen? Dentists? Cricket umpires? No, silly! When someone appears to be behaving in an irrational manner the cry goes up, 'Send for the men in white coats!' – meaning mental-health staff. These days they're probably dressed in jeans and T-shirts, but that garb wouldn't lend itself to such a vivid and comic image, unfortunately.

MINI-ME

An aspirant to a greater person's persona. For example, 'Dave is the boss's mini-me.'

Popularised by comic Mike Myers and supplanting a previous modern cliché – 'wannabe'.

MISSING YOU ALREADY

Has anyone ever said this seriously? It seems to be exclusively ironic.

MONKEY

The word 'monkey' can be added to almost any other word you like to disparage an entire group

of people – e.g. grease monkey = mechanic, hedge
monkey = tramp. (Also see 'cubicle monkey' under
'Corporate speak' in 'Business Clichés'.)

MULTITASKING

A workplace cliché that's now in general use in
relation to, for example, busy mums who may
be simultaneously cooking dinner, attending to
the baby and cleaning the kitchen. In the work
context, however, multitasking can simply mean
chatting on the phone, bending a paper clip into
an interesting new shape and drinking coffee at
the same time.

MUPPET

A withering description of someone ineffectual
or inconsequential. 'Don't employ him – he's
a muppet.' Derived, of course, from the highly
successful TV series that made global stars of
Kermit, Miss Piggy and more. They became so
successful they are probably some of the last
individuals you'd describe as 'muppets'.

NEW AGE

It's odd that the term 'New Age' is used to

describe therapies such as acupuncture, reflexology and meditation that have often been around for millennia.

NO BIGGY

'No biggy' is probably an abbreviation of the cliché 'no big deal'. If so, then this is a slightly redundant abbreviation that reduces the original phrase by a word but then adds in an extra unnecessary syllable, so you end up no better off.

NO CHANGE THERE, THEN

'He's gone out for a drink with his friends when he knows I was cooking this special dinner for us tonight.' 'No change there, then.'

NO PAIN, NO GAIN

'No pain, no gain' is surely the expression of a modern Puritanical work ethic: if you suffer you will ultimately reap the reward. Everyday experience should, however, tell you that 'pain, no gain' will be just as likely a consequence. At the same time everywhere you look, you will see people who are quite clearly enjoying plenty of 'gain' with no noticeable 'pain'. Obviously, the expression derives from the world of physical fitness, but, as the comedienne Carol Leifer famously said, 'I'm not into working out. My philosophy: no pain, no pain.'

NO WAY
This has been around for so long we almost forget how daft it is. 'Are you going to Maisie's party on Saturday?' 'No way! I can't stand the woman!' The 'way' bit of this phrase is completely unnecessary.

NO-BRAINER
Something that is so obvious one doesn't even need a brain to grasp it – which for some people can only be good news.

NOT
'We've had a great time – *not.*' An extremely irritating one-word cliché that negates whatever has preceded it. Very popular in the 1990s due to the film *Wayne's World*, though thankfully appearing to be falling out of fashion.

Gestures

Not content with using verbal clichés, people now even make gesticulatory clichés.

FACE FANNING

In recent years women have conscripted an odd new recruit into their army of social manoeuvres. This is the rapid fanning of the face with both hands when getting over-emotional. 'I am so thrilled to have won Miss World …' (flap, flap, flap); 'I just want to say thank you to – oh, my gosh …!' (flap, flap, flap).

FLUTTERING HAND ON CHEST

This is a gesture much loved by Chris Martin from the band Coldplay, who can often be seen rapidly patting the upper part of his ribcage during a performance. It means either, 'Hey, I love every single person in the 50,000-seat arena who's come to see us tonight – thanks for all the money' or, 'Ooh, I've got terrible heartburn!'

HAND ON CROTCH

The rappers' delight. Stride around in front of
people in an assertive manner while clutching
as much of your manly parts as you can fit into
one big bejewelled fist. Not only will this make
you look like one bad-ass rapper, it will also
give you an opportunity to check yourself for
any lumps your doctor might find interesting.

HAND-PHONE

Making a phone shape with the hand when
asking someone to ring you. Why? Does
anyone mime typing when they're asking
someone to email them?

LA-LA-LA-LA

Putting fingers in ears and saying 'La-la-la-la'
to indicate not wanting to hear something.
'Between you and me I'm writing my wife out
of my will.' 'La-la-la-la – I'm not listening! I
can't hear you!'

LOSER!

Making an 'L' shape over the forehead with thumb and forefinger and saying 'Loser!' At the moment this seems to be mainly in the domain of schoolchildren. This has become widespread only recently but apparently dates back to the 1994 Jim Carrey film *Ace Ventura: Pet Detective*.

QUOTATION-MARK FINGERS

Making quotation marks in the air by wiggling your fingers at either side of your head. A big favourite with trendy young businessmen in the 1980s but now, thankfully, seems to be out of fashion. Just as well – it always made the perpetrator look as though they were doing rabbit impressions.

SINGLE-FINGER SALUTE

A common and automatic response to any manifestation of authority. Much favoured by heavy-metal bands who have realised that swearing cannot be heard in photographs.

NOT A HAPPY BUNNY
Why 'bunny'? Are bunnies usually in a state of
near delirium? More often than not they're stuck
in a cage munching bits of limp lettuce without
even the scant excitement of some decent
salad dressing.

OH. MY. GOD
The verbal full stops are important, for emphasis,
and this type of phrase doesn't seem to have been
replicated. But, even so, it's. Not. A. Normal. Way.
Of. Speaking.

-OHOLIC
Derived from 'alcoholic' but now adapted to such
words as 'shopaholic', 'chocoholic', 'sexaholic'
without perhaps remembering that there are no
such things as shopahol, chocohol and sexahol.

ON A DAILY BASIS
There are three words too many in this phrase
– can you spot what they are?

ONE … SHORT OF A …
An ever-adaptable cliché used to suggest that

someone or something is slightly inadequate – possibly in the mental-capacity department. For example, 'one sandwich short of a picnic', 'one brick short of a full load', 'one arm short of a juggling act'.

ONE-TO-ONE
One-to-one what? Fistfight? Meeting? Affair? Although this usually means a private, possibly intimate, meeting, it sounds rather clinical and utilitarian.

ORWELLIAN
Often 'Orwellian nightmare'. This always seems to define George Orwell's career in terms of one book: *Nineteen Eighty-Four*. He also wrote stuff about cups of tea and boys' comics and vicars' daughters, you know. So, next time you try to make a really nice cup of tea, don't forget that you're doing something 'Orwellian'.

PLEASE
'Please' is not a cliché on its own (yet), but 'Pur-lease!' is. For instance, 'I cleaned up like you asked me to; I've worked my tail-end off to get

this place looking nice.' 'Oh pur-*lease*! Look at the state of it!'

PROVERBIAL
A dangling phrase that seems to indicate a missing word. You hear it in phrases such as 'He punched me right in the proverbial,' presumably meaning 'mouth', though, as far we can establish, there is no such proverb in any existing reference book.

PUSH THE ENVELOPE
'Push the envelope' is yet another hip and trendy phrase drawn from the exciting world of the stationery-supplies business. People who push the envelope are mavericks and risk takers who live life on the edge and don't care whom they offend with their stationery-propelling tendencies.

QUIETLY CONFIDENT
Or 'smug', as it used to be known.

REALITY CHECK
'Take a reality check' – people sometimes say this if what you're doing or saying seems a bit unconventional or wrong-headed, which may

occasionally be sound advice, but the phrase is a cliché. Take an originality check.

RESPECT
This is now commonly used as a piece of street slang meaning deference. It is not, however, possible to interchange the two expressions. Whatever you do, don't diss your homies for 'not never showin' no deference', or it could seriously undermine your street cred.

RESULT!
As all sports fans know, a result doesn't necessarily mean a good one, though in this cliché the sun always shines, the birds are permanently atwitter and all is well with the world. 'I asked Denise out for a drink and she said "Yes" – result!'

ROCK AND ROLL!
A sometimes ironic exclamation uttered when something patently not part of a rock and roll lifestyle is suggested or mentioned. 'We were wondering if you'd like to come over for lunch on Sunday, then maybe have a walk in the park afterwards?' 'Rock and roll!'

SAD
At one time, 'sad' meant 'unhappy'. Now it doubles as a synonym for words such as 'pathetic' and 'inadequate'.

SEE YOU LATER
People tell you this even when they have no intention whatsoever of seeing you later. The phrase suggests that they will mysteriously appear in your house later that evening when you least expect them. Presumably, they believe this will be a cheering prospect rather than an utterly terrifying one. Abbreviated in text speak to 'CUL8R', which is self-defeatingly longer than ''Bye'.

SELL-BY DATE/USE-BY DATE
Today nearly every food item you purchase has a sell-by or use-by date somewhere on it. The use of the sell-by date has now been extended by our throwaway society to cover not only perishable products but also people and/or celebrities and politicians – although whereabouts on their person the sell-by date is printed is unclear.

SENIOR MOMENT
Meaning doing something wrong due to

advancing years such as forgetting where you've put your spectacles or forgetting where you left your grandchildren. We don't yet have 'junior moment' to describe, for example, wetting your pants or being rude to people without fear of the consequences.

SEXY
At one time 'sexy' applied only to people, but now a new computer can be 'sexy', or a new phone, even an idea. It's got a rather strong whiff of the advertising agency about it.

SHOO-IN
Not a love-in for footwear fetishists, but a candidate for a post where success is guaranteed.

SHOP TILL YOU DROP
This is sometimes viewed, by people going on serious shopping sprees, as a good thing. Can this philosophy be applied to any other pleasurable activities? Eat till you're beat? Booze till you snooze?

SHUTTUP!

Surely not a modern cliché, you cry, and yet
the usage of 'shuttup' has changed recently with
the expression being used in a much more pre-
emptive manner than previously. People are now
told to 'shuttup', or, even better, 'shu'up!', before
they've had a chance to say anything. For example,
'What are you looking at? Shuttup!' 'Shuttup' is
also used as an exclamation with a meaning along
the lines of 'I find what you have just told me
absolutely astounding' – for instance, 'I am joining
a group of Trappist monks!' 'Shuttup!'

SORTED!

An upbeat bit of self-congratulation for some
minor accomplishment. 'I got tickets for the match
on Saturday – sorted!'

TA-DAH! (MUSICALLY)

A rather theatrical phrase that accompanies a
surprise unveiling of something just acquired/
achieved, perhaps against expectations. 'So did you
manage to find a Donald Duck watch for Sam's
birthday?' 'Ta-dah!'

TAKE IT TO THE NEXT LEVEL

There is an element of danger and a thrill of excitement when people tell you they are going to take things 'to the next level' – unless, they say it while you are on an escalator with them, which is presumably the source of the phrase.

TALK THE TALK, WALK THE WALK

Oh, you can talk the talk, but can you walk the walk? In other words, 'Your words may sound good, my friend, but are you capable of following through with real action?'

TELL ME ABOUT IT!

Which actually means 'I already know', so you don't need to tell them about it!

THAT'S THE BEAUTY OF IT

Phrase used by very smug individuals to point out what they think is the best bit in some gadget, system or other utterly unbeautiful thing about which they are enthusing to you at great and tedious length.

Hippie hangovers

The hippie period proper, before it was commercialised, was extremely short, maybe a couple of years, but many of the phrases that came from that alternative worldview are still with us and are now mainstream clichés.

DO YOUR OWN THING
It would be difficult to do someone else's thing would it not?

... FREAK
Not heard quite so much these days, apart from the mildly insulting 'control freak', but can also be tagged onto almost any other word to denote keen affinity: 'camera freak', 'table-tennis freak', 'Chihuahua freak'.

GURU
A spiritual teacher originally, but now tacked onto other phrases to denote an expert – for

instance, a 'health guru', a 'fitness guru', an 'antismoking guru'. Real gurus must have an awful job explaining at dinner parties what they do. 'So, you're a *guru* guru, then?'

HANG-UP
Originally a personal inhibition – 'He's got a hang-up about taking his clothes off' – but now used more generally: 'Society has all sorts of hang-ups about child rearing.'

HASSLE
This is now such a part of mainstream English that we are offered 'hassle-free' mortgages and other such consumer delights. Such a short road from Haight-Ashbury to high commerce.

HYPE
Short for 'hyperbole' but now almost always used in its abbreviated form and meaning the exaggerated promotion of something. One wonders, with many of these phrases, how we ever managed without them.

LOSING YOUR COOL

An adjective adrift without a noun. Cool what?
It has never been discovered. Presumably, the
missing word must be 'demeanour', though
it would be difficult to imagine a spaced-out
hippie using such a long word.

MANTRA

In the 1960s a mantra was a word given by a
guru to a rich rock star to try to keep him off
the drugs for five minutes. The idea was that he
would focus on this word in meditation and reach
a state of 'unknowingness'. In some cases this
didn't take long. Now a mantra is any phrase
that someone repeats over and over again, often
when connected with some cause or ideology
– the sort of thing that prompts people to use
another cliché: 'change the record!'

RIP-OFF

Hippies were ideologically opposed to
capitalism while managing to give most
of their money to multinational record

companies, manufacturers of denim clothes and 'drug barons'. Therefore, anything that involved their putting more cash than necessary into the hands of 'The Man' was a deemed to be a 'rip-off'. This neat little phrase is now a staple of journalists everywhere, being headline-friendly brief.

SPACED-OUT

We all know what it's like to be 'spaced out' but try explaining it.

... TRIP

Often tagged onto the back of 'guilt'. 'He's on a guilt trip because he forgot their wedding anniversary.' Also still used in phrases such as 'ego trip', 'head trip'.

VIBE

'Vibes' was once jazz shorthand for a musical instrument called the vibraphone, but now, thanks to those hairy old hippies, it means 'atmosphere' or 'feelings'. I don't like going to that club, there's a bad vibe'; 'I'm getting good vibes from her.'

WHATEVER TURNS YOU ON

Presumably, a drug reference originally, though also applied to sexual tastes and now anything you want. 'I think I'll have the peanut-butter-and-anchovy sandwich.' 'Whatever turns you on'. The phrase has also been adapted. For example, 'Whatever floats your boat.'

THE REST IS HISTORY

People announce this grandly at the end of some great anecdote about their amazingly important and influential lives.

THE . . . THING

Another adaptable cliché phrase that can be used to jazz up the most mundane of experiences. Ideally the construction should be used for genuinely exotic and unusual activities, such as, 'I see you're heavily into the whole voodoo thing.' Often, though, it is put to use to make less interesting activities sound like arcane and perhaps slightly erotic rituals. For instance, 'Young Duane here is about to perform the making-a-cheese-and-tomato-sandwich thing.'

THERE YOU GO
Uttered by somebody giving you something – such as a shop assistant handing over your purchase. In that instance it's a bit of a casual remark to make to a paying customer, and slightly nonsensical and totally unnecessary.

TOO CLOSE TO CALL
A baseball cliché that has conquered the world.

TOUCH BASE
A quick chat with someone to catch up on things, a phrase that also comes from baseball. Though whether the capacity crowd at a New York Yankees game would appreciate players holding an impromptu meeting in the middle of an important match is another matter.

TRADE-OFF
Meaning a compromise. 'It was a trade-off between

wanting to move out of the city and wanting to be near some decent restaurants.' As is often the case with these emphatic-sounding clichés the second word is redundant.

TREE HUGGER

There was once a vogue for old hippies and others with an empathy for the natural world to hug trees to commune with nature. The term has since been used as a term of derision for anyone who, in the speaker's view, has an extreme and unhealthy affinity with 'the environment' and 'green issues'.

USER-FRIENDLY

Once only applied to computers when they allowed the user to be able to operate them without a degree in information technology, but now can be applied to almost anything that doesn't tax the patience of the user – instruction leaflets, household appliances, etc. Though you would think that all products might be designed with the user in mind, wouldn't you?

WAKE-UP CALL

Everyone's getting them now. A bad test result for

a schoolchild is a wake-up call, a surprise visit from an inspector is a wake-up call for a restaurant, and a nuclear-bomb test by one country is a wake-up call for every other country. And what a wake-up call that would be! A long, long way from 'It's 7.15, Mr Warburton.'

WALKING ON EGGSHELLS

Meaning 'treading carefully', but does it make any sense? 'Jim's so sensitive about his divorce we've been walking on eggshells every time we talk to him.' Since it is impossible to walk on eggshells without damaging them, it would be a silly thing to do deliberately, wouldn't it?

WASTE OF SPACE

A terrible insult. A person who is a 'waste of space' is so utterly useless they are actually a waste of the space they're occupying. But of course there isn't that much of a shortage of space in most of the universe, apart from during the rush-hour.

WATER-COOLER MOMENT

This phrase refers to a moment from a television programme that people find so interesting they

want to talk about it the next day at work to
any colleagues they bump into during a visit to
the office water cooler. The mention of 'water
cooler' in the phrase suggests that the TV show in
question appeals to health-conscious, middle-class
people working in a bright, modern office.
'Cigarette-break moment' wouldn't have quite
the same resonance.

WAY
In phrases such as 'way cool' or 'way common',
the word 'way' means 'very'. In Charles Dickens's
novels, lowlife characters tended to pronounce
the word 'very' as 'wewwy' which therefore both
sounds very similar and has a very similar meaning.
However, no Dickensian figure ever uttered
a phrase such as 'That is wewwy cool and no
mistake, Mr Pumplesniff, my bro.'

WE'RE TALKING ...
'So how may of the jail's population are on the
run?' 'We're talking dozens.' Why does that reply
need the words 'We're talking'?

WHAT GOES AROUND COMES AROUND

This phrase is often used by unruly groups of disaffected youths, to explain for example, why they torched an old person's house just because he told them off for urinating through his letterbox.

WHAT PART OF 'NO' DON'T YOU UNDERSTAND?

'Can I just borrow the car for *one* hour, then?' 'What part of "no" don't you understand?' This cliché can be endlessly adapted but it's still a cliché – and a pretty annoying one at that.

WHAT'S NOT TO LIKE?

Well, this curiously inverted phrase for a start. This simple and oft-heard expression is made up of just a few simple words. Nevertheless they have been arranged into the most extraordinarily irritating linguistic flourish. No one in their right mind speaks like this. If you were in the world's best restaurant, faced with the most tempting menu imaginable, would you ever throw up your hands and wonder, 'What's not to eat?'

WHAT'S *THAT* ALL ABOUT?

This phrase (uttered with heavy emphasis on the word 'that') is used by people who have been subjected to something that they felt was needlessly complicated or of which they couldn't see the point. Usually, however, when people say 'What's *that* all about?' they know exactly what *that* was all about.

WISH LIST

It sounds like one of those documents that people send out before their weddings with lists of what presents to buy them so they don't end up with 14 toasters. With wedding lists there's a fair chance you'll receive a few of the items from your list, but with wish lists of, say, what you'd like to find in an ideal partner, you may end up with the human equivalent of 14 toasters.

YEAH?

For some reason certain people seem to need constant reassurance that the person they are speaking to is still listening – and actually when you hear their conversations you can see why. So they say things like, 'You know what I mean?' and 'You understand what I'm saying?' But with the pace of modern life and the need for short conversations this has been abbreviated to 'Yeah?' at the end of every sentence, or sometimes even halfway through. 'We're going down the road yeah? And we see this guy yeah? And he's stealing this car, yeah …?' And so on. The word 'right?' can be substituted for 'yeah?' or, if you really can't be bothered, you just raise the pitch of your voice at the end of each sentence so it sounds like a question?

YEAH, YEAH, YEAH
Not the chorus to the Beatles' 'She Loves You', but said musically, nevertheless.

'I really like your new hairstyle.' 'Yeah, yeah, yeah. It looks horrible.'

YOU CAN'T TURN THE CLOCK BACK
But you can – that's what those little knobs are for.

YOU DO THE MATH(S)
An invitation to the listener to perform a very basic piece of arithmetic which has been offered by the speaker as an illustration of how clever they've been with their finances. For instance,

'We bought our house for 200,000, now it's worth 210,000. You do the math(s).'

YOU KNOW WHAT I MEAN?
If I don't know what you mean I'll soon let you know – you know what I mean?

YOU NAME IT
'The house was amazing. it had electronically controlled curtains, an indoor pool, a home cinema – you name it.' No, *you* name it – *I've* never been there. 'You name it' really means, 'I've run out of things that I can remember to name.'

YOU'RE ALL RIGHT
An odd response to an offer. 'Would you like a cup of coffee?' 'No, you're all right.' I know I'm all right, but do you want a cup of coffee?

YOU'RE HISTORY
If someone tells you, 'You're history', they are informing you that your services are no longer required and you are therefore about to pass into history. Perhaps other subjects on the school syllabus could be used in a similarly tough manner.

For example, 'You're geography' could be a euphemistic way of telling someone they have a weight problem and are covering a larger than necessary area.

YOUR TAKE
'What's your take on the possibility of extraterrestrial invasion?' Why can't we just ask what somebody's view is? Why 'take'?

YUMMY MUMMY
You sometimes get the feeling that some phrases are adopted only because they rhyme. 'Yummy mummy' simply means an attractive mother and the only reason that we don't have an equivalent phrase for an attractive father is that there is no word for 'handsome' that rhymes with 'daddy'.

MEDIA CLICHÉS

Among the media is the last place we should find clichés – these people are supposed to be creative, for goodness' sake! But when you're churning out grist for the media mill 24/7 you can't avoid them.

Criticism

Critics have a whole language of their own. Who are they trying to impress – other critics? Because the plain fact is that most of us don't have a clue what they're on about half the time – and do they?

ALTERNATIVE

In the 1980s anything artistic, especially in the media of TV and film, that wanted a chance of being accepted by anyone under the age of 30 had to be described as 'alternative'. Somehow this word managed to stand on its own despite being a comparative. It was only when you asked the question 'alternative to what?' that some much-needed light was thrown onto the subject. For example, many old-school comedians claimed that 'alternative comedy' was an alternative to being funny – and in some cases they were right.

ARGUABLY
'Arguably the funniest comedy film this year.'
Isn't any critical position arguable – arguably?

AWARD-WINNING
Which always prompts the question: what award?
Some industries are so awash with awards that it would
almost be an achievement never to have won one.

Everything and everyone these days has won
an award. Think about it. You must have won
something, no matter how trivial, at some stage
in your life. You are therefore entitled to describe
yourself as 'the award-winning _____ [fill in
your name here]' even if in full this should be 'The
Bronze Medallion Life-saving Award winning …'

BACK TO BASICS
Usually meaning that an artist, writer or performer
has drawn back from a disastrous flirtation with
something outside their limited range and has
gone back to the old formula that has always
worked best for them.

BUMS ON SEATS
In the entertainment world it means a successful

production; in the real world it means vagrants in shopping malls.

CAR-CRASH TV
Meaning that, although it's awful, you can't help but watch it. The trouble is that a lot of television now is more 'move along now, sir, there's nothing to see' TV.

COMPELLING
Forcing one to pay attention, unlike this cliché, which has the opposite effect.

CRITICALLY ACCLAIMED
By whom? Everything in these hyperbolic days is critically acclaimed. The reason for this is the vast number of newspapers and magazines reviewing every film, book, TV show and so forth. Even if a newly released film, book or TV show is utter tosh, it will pick up at least one semi-decent review out of the multitude of bad ones simply by virtue of the fact that one of the reviewers will get things hopelessly wrong. Every film, book, TV show in existence, no matter how dreadful, can therefore be legitimately described as 'critically acclaimed'.

CUTTING-EDGE
Your book/film/play is so fabulous it can only be compared to the bottom of a bread knife.

(AN) ECLECTIC MIX
'Eclectic' is one of those words beloved by critics but hardly used by anyone else. 'We went to the supermarket yesterday – there was an eclectic mix of vegetables.'

EYE-POPPING
A graphic way of describing something … well, graphic. 'Shocking' is no longer shocking, and soon, through overuse 'eye-popping' will cease to have any impact and they'll have to come up with a brand-new cliché. Why not start now?

GROUNDBREAKING
Road drills are groundbreaking, but films/books/ plays rarely are. Should be used less frequently.

HAVE A BOX OF TISSUES READY
OK, the film/TV programme is going to be a 'tear jerker' but why don't we have similar exhortations for other genres? 'Have a stretcher ready' for films that are going to frighten the life out of you, for example?

I MADE THAT LAST BIT UP

Critics and comedians alike are quite fond of
this one. It usually follows a flight of fancy
culminating in an outrageous statement that is
probably libellous or slanderous. 'The show was
a shambles from start to finish with fluffed lines,
wobbling scenery and dreadful performances and
ended with the entire cast begging the critics to
tear up their notebooks. I made that last bit up,
by the way.'

IMMORTAL

Strangely, this description is often used when one
is referring to people who are far from immortal
– in other words, dead: the 'immortal' Marilyn
Monroe, Elvis Presley, Charlie Chaplin, etc.

INIMITABLE

In the way that 'immortal' is often used to describe
people who are no longer with us, 'inimitable'
is often used to describe people who are staple
parts of the acts of comedy impressionists, both
professional and amateur – for instance, 'the
inimitable James Cagney'.

METAPHOR

Film critics in particular seem obsessed with 'metaphor'. Nothing can be taken at face value. All films are 'metaphors' for something else. There must be something about spending large parts of your adult life sitting in darkened rooms that makes you yearn for more meaning to your existence.

ON ACID

This is one of those phrases critics resort to when they can't be bothered to think of any adjectives. It usually means 'to an extreme degree' or 'with extra weirdness', or that other old critics' standby, 'surreal'. So a madcap comedy film might be described as being like 'the Marx Brothers on acid'; an impenetrable novel might be 'James Joyce on acid'; and so on. Critics might be better off just going out and buying a thesaurus.

PASS THE SICK BAG

The rather unsubtle phrase used when a critic is confronted by something unbearably mawkish or sentimental.

PICK-AND-MIX COMPARISONS

If there's one thing critics like more than hyphens
or hip-sounding arty phrases it's comparisons
('It's *Jaws* meets *Godzilla* with a soupçon of *Edward
Scissorhands* on acid'). This saves wasting time on
original thought, turns of phrase or even good old
observation. In fact it's laziness meets pusillanimity
with a dash of amateurism.

(A) POOR MAN'S ...

Why an author should be described as 'a poor
man's Norman Mailer' or an actor as 'a poor man's
Kenneth Branagh' is odd. Wealth has nothing to do
with it, seeing that the price of the book or theatre
ticket remains the same. What they are probably
trying to say is 'the easily pleased man's . . .'

POSTMODERN

Once you've got bored with 'modern' stuff, what
on earth do you move on to next? Answer: 'postmodern' stuff. 'Postmodern' stuff can be crazy, far
out and wacky but the main thing it has to be is
'*non*-modern'. This means that, if your friends
ridicule you because your clothes and possessions
seem old fashioned and out of date, you can say,

'No, you're wrong. They're not old-fashioned. They're postmodern.' 'Postmodern' therefore means old stuff plus ironic self-awareness.

PROBABLY
An alternative to 'I made that last bit up'.

SCHADENFREUDE
Meaning 'delight in other people's misfortunes' and mercifully shorter, but we have a funny feeling that critics use words like this only to appear clever. What with '*über*' and '*Zeitgeist*' and 'angst', why not write the whole damn review in German if you're that clever?

SNEAK PREVIEW
Whenever you are shown a clip of a new film or TV show, you are told it is a 'sneak preview'. This suggests that the clip has fallen into your hands from some shady unofficial source and that you are exceptionally lucky to have been singled out to enjoy this 'sneak preview'. Yes, you and every single other person in the entire country with a television set – all sneaking together.

STATE OF THE ART

It's supposed to mean 'the ultimate' or the 'best in the field', but why? 'State' means only 'condition', so 'state of the art' only really seems to mean 'the current condition of' whatever art it's describing, which may not be a good thing.

STUNNING

Reviewers seem to be 'stunned' by new releases in the popular arts exceptionally frequently. One must assume they are constantly lurching around the place in a permanently 'stunned' state as they ricochet from the latest 'stunning' new CD to a 'stunning' new movie to a 'stunning' new book.

SUBTEXT

Most people go to films to be entertained. Critics go so they can scribble long words in the dark to impress us and their fellow critics in subsequent reviews. Most of us are also quite happy to enjoy the storyline without looking for a 'subtext' – that is to say, what the film's really about: usually some big universal issue that the rest of us are too stupid to see. 'So on one level it's about a cute alien that befriends a little boy but the subtext is all about alienation, race, Third World debt and peer-group pressure in a consumer society.'

SURREAL
Anything the reviewer doesn't quite understand.

TESTOSTERONE-DRIVEN/FUELLED
Or what used to be called 'macho'. Why an action film needs to be described in terms of the male sex hormone is anyone's guess.

ÜBER
Used as a trendy prefix for words such as 'babe'. Since it's German for 'super', why don't they just say that?

UNCUT
An expression used to make certain extended television broadcasts sound exciting and potentially outrageous. It actually means that the producers have decided to save money on editing and put out an apparently never-ending and utterly tedious stream of dross.

WACKY

One of those descriptions that can mean almost anything the critic or the reader wants it to mean (for instance, frantic, original, surreal), so it doesn't actually tell you much.

X-RATED

Wasn't the 'X' rating ditched years ago? Even when it was around it was used in some countries as a rating for films with sex, violence, nudity, swearing and so on (which probably covers virtually every film made now). These days, it seems to be used mainly to denote the inclusion of explicit sex.

ZEITGEIST

When critics run out of hip-sounding phrases in English they start raiding the lexicons of other countries. Do German critics keep using phrases like 'It's what's happening, man' instead of *Zeitgeist*?

Newspapers

Newspapers use clichéd words, phrases or images that are often not found anywhere else. It's almost as if there is the real world and the alternative world that exists in newspapers.

CHAOS

Chaos once meant a total breakdown of order, if not of civilisation itself. A state of 'total chaos' seemed to suggest mass looting, mobs of crazed peasants roaming around the place setting fire to everything in their path and holding impromptu public executions. These days chaos usually refers to slightly more-irritating-than-usual travel problems.

COCKTAIL OF DRUGS

When people overdose they are often said to have taken a 'cocktail of drugs' – where do they get the recipes? Can you buy some sort of 'perfect hostess' set of equipment?

In fatal cases, people are often said to have 'choked on their own vomit', which, as someone once pointed out, may be unpleasant, but it sure beats choking on someone else's vomit.

COMMUNITY
This has been around for a fair old time but is still being stretched to preposterous and inappropriate usage. It may have been once reasonably accurate to describe a group of people as 'the Jewish community' or the 'Asian community', but we now hear about the 'pilot community' or the 'chef community' as if they were living in special enclaves with their own customs and beliefs.

DOTCOM MILLIONAIRE
The sort of shorthand that newspapers love but that doesn't follow any consistent logic. Before the 'Internet boom' businessmen weren't known as 'Inc-dot millionaires' or 'Ltd-dot millionaires', were they? And since when did the full stop or period become known as 'dot'?

DRUG BARONS
Quite why overseeing the sale of crack cocaine should entitle anyone to elevation to the peerage is not clear.

DYSFUNCTIONAL FAMILY

The worst thing that can ever happen to a family is for them to become 'dysfunctional'. It is, however, quite difficult to imagine a family that is fully functional without feeling slightly nauseous. By definition, then, perhaps all families are dysfunctional.

(THE) EMAIL THAT WENT ROUND THE WORLD

A few years ago newspaper bosses were probably shaking in their shoes at the thought of their business being pushed aside by the Internet, but now they have a found it a permanent source of news stories – from online auctions to round-robin jokes. And every so often some poor soul sends an email to someone else telling them they love them or that they're dumping them, and their work colleagues decide that the content is so mawkish/amusing/appalling that they will send it to everyone they know. Just one question: if the whole world and his or her recipient list have seen this story already, why does it need to go in the newspaper?

EYEBROWS RAISED
A reaction to some mildly surprising stimulus.
Eyebrows might be raised if someone makes a
slightly controversial statement. A new provocative
piece of art might be described as 'currently raising
eyebrows' – but to what degree? An internationally
agreed 'eyebrows-raised' gauge should surely be
created as a means to measure such responses in a
more scientific manner.

FIASCO
'Fiasco' simply means 'failure', but this newspaper
favourite has a stronger ring to it and conjures up
images of panicking headless chickens and other
chaotic clichés. Perhaps it's the liberal peppering
of vowels that can be satisfyingly elongated when
spoken. 'Fiasco' is often preceded by 'utter'.

FREEFALL
Share prices don't just go down: they go into
freefall. This, presumably, is just before they open
their parachutes and float gently to the ground.

-GATE
Since the Watergate scandal in the early 1970s,

journalists have believed that the suffix '-gate' means 'slightly shady goings on, particularly in high places'. Thus, over the years the newspapers have made various stories sound a bit more shocking and dramatic by sticking '-gate' on the end of them. Thus we have had the likes of 'Diana-gate' (a.k.a. 'Squidgy-gate'), 'Iran-gate', 'Camilla-gate' and 'Zipper-gate'. The odd thing is, though, that, when journalists had a diamond-studded excuse to tack 'gate' onto the Clintons' alleged scandal, Whitewater, they instead chose to call it the 'Whitewater affair'.

GONGS

A popular term for an award, and it is spreading from use in the UK and Australia to the rest of the world. Yes, after a blubbering winner at one of the world's several billion annual awards ceremonies has thanked everyone from their parents to their gynaecologist they are then presented not with an award but a gong. If you believed the awards-show commentators, each winner is presented with a dirty great, six-foot-in-diameter bronze gong plus one of those big cotton bud things to bash it with. Wouldn't it be ironic if the only awards ceremony

where you didn't get a gong was the annual awards
of the Official World Gong Bashers' Association,
where the lucky winners were instead presented
with a full size set of tubular bells?

IT'S OFFICIAL!
Very rarely let out on its own without the
accompanying exclamation mark, this prefaces a
story based on some report or other that may not
have any special authority at all. For example, 'It's
official! Most men don't know how to operate the
washing machine, says a survey commissioned by
Razzle Dazzle washing powder.'

LIKE A WHO'S WHO
'The launch party was like a who's who of show
business.' Oh, let's hope not. Thousands of 'celebrities'
giving potted histories of their lives and telling us
their hobbies are 'daydreaming' and 'writing haikus'.

MEDIA STORM
Or, in plain English, a controversy. But, like weather-
men, newspapers thrive on storms; their lives
would be dull without them. So, if they can 'big it
up', they're happy.

MELTDOWN

Newspapers love their apocalyptic words and phrases: 'crisis', 'doomsday scenario', 'catastrophic', etc. But usually they overstate the case and turn it into nonsense. And thus, these days, governments, institutions, traffic systems and so forth seem to go into 'meltdown' more often than the inside of a volcano.

(THE) MOTHER OF ALL ...

To face the 'mother of all battles' was once a terrifying threat made against Western forces. And so 'the mother of all' has entered the language as an adaptable cliché to describe the most fearsome of all possible situations. Isn't this a terrible insult to mothers, though? Shouldn't the 'mother of all traffic jams' be quite a pleasant one where someone brings you round some orange squash and chocolate biscuits while you're stuck in your car?

NEAR-MISS

Not a description of a sex-change operation gone disastrously wrong, but that of two vehicles (usually aeroplanes) that have almost hit each other. It has been pointed out before that the phrase should be 'near hit', but do they listen? Has Bugs Bunny got big ears?

NOT SUITABLE FOR A FAMILY NEWSPAPER

What other sort are there? This phrase is used when a story enters the realms of explicit detail and is the newspaper equivalent of 'Let's not go there.'

OUTED

Originally used in the sense of making someone's homosexuality public, usually against their wishes. Now can be used in almost any other circumstances, such as, 'He's been outed as a toupee wearer.'

PANDEMIC

Newspapers don't just enjoy scaring the pants off us: they have an inflationary scale of disasters with which to terrify the populace. At one time it was enough to threaten an epidemic, now it's always a pandemic – even when the condition is not contagious. A radio commentator was recently heard talking about the 'pandemic of obesity'.

RED-FACED OFFICIALS

Occasionally the newspapers will expose an organisation as having been responsible for some appalling cock-up. If in such cases the newspapers don't immediately have a specific individual to single out and blame, they will describe all the people working for the organisation as being 'red-faced officials', as though every person in the building were wandering around in a permanent state of rosy-cheeked embarrassment.

SAD INDICTMENT
Since an indictment is a formal accusation, usually of a crime, then it's always going to be pretty sad for someone. Why can't we tag a different word onto the front of it for a change – revealing, embarrassing, fierce – or just let it stand on its own?

SERIAL
At one time mainly used in the phrase 'serial killer' but now a multipurpose modifier for all sorts of other phrases for humorous effect, e.g. 'serial adulterer', 'serial dieter'.

SQUEEZE
A word that seems to be used only in print, meaning a girlfriend, usually the most recent of a

long line: 'He turned up at the premiere with his latest squeeze.'

TEXTBOOK
People will proudly announce that something is a 'textbook' case or a 'textbook' example.

TROPHY WIFE
Another of those phrases you don't often hear in the real world, but newspapers and magazines seem to like it. It is usually a wife who is younger and better-looking though considerably poorer than her husband – until she marries him, of course.

WHAT KIND OF MESSAGE ARE THEY SENDING OUT?
'When manufacturers put sexually suggestive slogans on children's clothes, what kind of message are they sending out?' Unless the manufacturers have just entered the communications business they're not sending out any message – they're just manufacturing clothes that are unsuitable for children.

WRONG PLACE, WRONG TIME

When somebody is attacked in a rough area of a city they are said to have been 'in the wrong place at the wrong time'. If you're in the wrong place it's unlikely that it will ever be the right time, and if you're somewhere at the wrong time (i.e. you get attacked) it's hardly the right place.

Z-LIST CELEBRITIES

Hollywood superstars are 'A- list' celebrities; other well-known but less well-paid faces are 'B-list' celebrities; the man who does the weather on your local news bulletin is a 'C-list' celebrity – and so on all the way down to the 'Z-list'. It's lucky the alphabet contains only 26 letters, otherwise this phrase might have suffered an inflationary increase. Some 'celebrities' would struggle to be in the top 26 lists, however many media events they attended.

ENTERTAINMENT CLICHÉS

Even the world of entertainment is not free of clichés. Wherever there's an audience there's a well-worn phrase to make them feel at home.

Comedy

Most comedians apparently turned to jokes because they didn't want to be bullied at school. However, if their jokes weren't very funny, wouldn't that make them even more likely to be bullied?

AIRPORT ROUTINES

Many stand-up comedians find themselves spending lots of time hanging around at airports going from one tour date to another. They will therefore almost inevitably introduce a routine about airports into their acts in order to punish the rest of us by means of a vivid insight into the worst aspect of their job.

'AND THAT WAS JUST ...'

For example, the bar was full of big muscle-bound thugs with tattoos and body piercings – and that was just the women!

AUDIENCE PARTICIPATION
The modern version of capital punishment before a baying mob. Audience participation is usually a good way to get the crowd on your side and to fill your act up if you're a bit short of jokes.

CATCHPHRASES
These irritate comedians almost as much as the rest of us. For some reason when people are assembled in large groups (such as an audience for a comedy show) they will begin to find any repeated phrase hilariously funny. Why not try it yourself? Become a comedian and repeat a meaningless phrase such as 'Mind my asparagus' or 'Ain't that the price of stationery goods', or 'Well I'm a monkey's plumber'. You won't even need any jokes.

DO YOU SEE WHAT I JUST DID THERE?
This phrase is used when a comedian has just made a quite clever but slightly rubbish joke. The comedian follows the joke up with, 'Do you see what I just did there?', thereby giving his/her audience a moment to consider the cleverness of

the jocular construct. At the same time the ironic tinge of the phrase 'Do you see what I just did there?' helps distance the comedian from the joke's essential rubbishness.

HEY, HAVE YOU EVER NOTICED . . . ?

This phrase will be used by a comedian to preface some routine giving their unique insight into going to the supermarket, the behaviour of kids or parents, TV shows or adverts, etc. Yes, we *have* all noticed. But thanks for letting us pay so much to come to the theatre tonight and have the most obvious facts of our existence confirmed.

HIP REFERENCES

Once, comedians wanted you to laugh at them; now they want you to think how clever they are. So they throw in the odd reference to Brecht or Kierkegaard to deflect attention from the quality of their material.

LET ME LEAVE YOU WITH ONE FINAL THOUGHT . . .

I'm about to leave the stage now, so let's hope I at least get a bit of laugh for this next gag.

(THE) RULE OF THREE

'And the third guy says …!' The secret of comedy is supposed to be about surprise, but the genre is full of formulae and conventions such as this.

WHAT A FANTASTIC PLACE THIS IS!

Comedians say this wherever they are. They will also tell every single audience how great they are and how much better than the audience they had last night in some other town or city. Comedians are therefore a bit like a man out on a date.

WHERE ARE YOU FROM, SIR?

Hey, have you ever noticed how comedians seem to have this strange need to go round finding out where every single person in their audience has come from? Why, in all their years in the business, has none of them worked out the answer is always the same: 'From within a fifty-mile radius from this theatre you're appearing in tonight, you numbskull!'

Music clichés

Despite rock music's reputation for unconventionality, its performers rely on the cliché as much as anyone else.

ARTISTS

More and more musicians like to refer to themselves as 'artists', not even 'artistes'. They somehow believe that learning three chords on a guitar puts them on a par with Michelangelo. We hate to break this to you, but …

(THE) BAND SPLIT DUE TO 'MUSICAL DIFFERENCES'

PR spin meaning they all hated each other.

CAMERA POSES

Heavy-metal bands always stick their tongues out or give the finger to the camera, or both. Indie bands always refuse to smile and look at their shoes. Rappers always thrust their hands out in strange positions as if they have chronic arthritis.

COMEBACK
An attempt to relaunch an artist whose career has hit the rocks. This is done after sufficient time has elapsed for the public's memory to fade to the point where they remember only the artist's one decent hit song.

(THE) 'DIFFICULT' THIRD ALBUM
New bands have as long as they want to prepare for their first album, and often have just enough material left over for their second album. Then they're in trouble – unless they possess that rare commodity – talent.

(THE) DUETS ALBUM
Possibly the last hit album made by some musical geriatric in which they get to perform duets of their old songs with some younger singers they've never heard of. The duettists will also probably never even get to meet, since the recording sessions are often done over the phone.

FOR ONE NIGHT ONLY
This probably means they couldn't sell enough tickets for two nights.

HELLO, LONDON!

Or Philadelphia or Sydney or anywhere else. Are rock musicians the only people in the world who introduce themselves to entire cities?

HOLDING UP LIGHTERS AT CONCERTS

Rock venues spend massive amounts of money on phenomenal lighting equipment, and what do those dumb rock stars do? They ask the audience to hold up their cheap plastic cigarette lighters to create a bit of atmosphere.

INTRODUCING THE BAND

During live appearances the star of the show may introduce the guys in the backing band one by one. This provokes a series of ecstatic responses from the crowd, who otherwise wouldn't care who these people were or what they did. This extraordinarily democratic act of sharing the limelight on the part of the lead singer inevitably ends with their telling the crowd, 'And on vocals – there's me!', which then gets the biggest response of all.

(THE) LEGENDARY

Used to describe an artist who hasn't had a successful record out in the last decade.

(THE) LIST OF THANKS ON THE ALBUM COVER

A vast list of all the people an artist must thank for all their help in bringing this latest work of musical genius to its place in the bargain bin. The list will usually include the artist's mum, dad, God, a few people referred to only by their nicknames followed by some meaningless in-joke plus several hundred other names. Whatever happens, the album concerned must not be given any awards or the artist concerned will read the entire list out live at the ceremony.

ONE TWO, ONE TWO

Put a singer or a roadie in front of a microphone and the chances are the first thing they'll say is 'one two, one two'. Come on, be original – even if it's just 'three four, three four'!

(THE) SOLO ALBUM

At a certain point in a band's career (usually when

the public is losing interest in them) the singer decides he wants to do a solo album. Quite why the public should suddenly be interested in a quarter of the band when they're losing interest in the rest of them is a mystery.

THERE'S A LOT OF LURVE HERE TONIGHT!

Only rock stars can get away with this sort of stuff at concerts. Can you imagine Dame Kiri Te Kanawa coming out with this kind of nonsense?

UNPLUGGED

We haven't managed to come up with any new songs, so instead would you just buy all our old songs again, this time played on a couple of acoustic guitars and a mouth organ?

Sport

After gruelling matches or races, sports stars probably just want to have a shower and relax, but in our media-dominated world they have to be interviewed first. Is it any wonder, then, that they fall back on a handful of stock responses?

ANOTHER DAY AT THE OFFICE
Meaning the routine dispatch of an opponent. Though how many office workers do you know who get paid a fabulous salary for a couple of hours' work and an additional fat slab of cash for wearing the right trainers?

(IT'S A) BIG ASK
Sports commentators and players often revert to the language of the nursery. Where will it stop? 'A double burger with extra fries? It's a big eat!'

FOR SURE
Sports stars who don't speak English as their first

language often use this phrase instead of 'yes'. Is it annoying? For sure.

GUTTED
To suffer a particularly annoying disappointment or setback in life. The expression derives from the sense of a particularly annoying disappointment or setback that a fish feels when it's slapped down on a table and has its insides sliced out with a big knife.

HOLD MY HANDS UP
'OK, I'll hold my hands up and admit it …'
No need to hold your hands up, old chum, unless you're under arrest, which, sadly, in the sporting world, is not all that uncommon these days.

(A) HUNDRED AND TEN PER CENT
'I've given a hundred and ten per cent …' (or a thousand per cent or a hundred and one per cent). Why not 'a hundred and seventeen per cent'? It's just as meaningful – or as meaningless.

I FEEL BAD FOR THE FANS
Yes, there are lots of them and they're all now baying for your blood.

KISSING TROPHIES

When sports stars are presented with a trophy they seem to find it hard to restrain themselves from planting a great big smacker on it. Is it because they can't kiss themselves?

SILVERWARE

'It looks like Roger Federer will be taking home the silverware again.' This doesn't mean that you should not invite the great man to your house for fear of his nicking the family heirlooms while you're making a pot of tea, but that he looks favourite to win a tennis trophy.

SNATCHING DEFEAT FROM THE JAWS OF VICTORY

A good joke inversion but now a bit of a cliché.

WE GAVE IT OUR BEST SHOT

How come you lost, then?

WE LET EVERYONE DOWN TODAY

And yet you're being paid more in a fortnight than your fans earn in ten years. What's more, they had to pay for the privilege of coming here today to watch you letting them all down!

WE WERE ROBBED
No. You lost!

WE'RE GOING TO HAVE TO TAKE IT ON THE CHIN
Instead of 'taking it on the chin', why didn't you use the normal method of playing the game today? Then you might have won.

COMMERCIAL CLICHÉS

When someone is actually employed to get you to spend money with their company you'd think they'd at least try to keep you awake while they were talking to you. But, no, they keep you at arm's length with a deadly cliché or two.

Consumers

As if it weren't bad enough being patronised, kept waiting, fobbed off and generally treated like a thundering nuisance by the people who are supposed to be serving you, you will also be treated to a special selection of consumer clichés guaranteed to boil the blood of the most placid of customers.

ALL OUR OPERATORS ARE BUSY

Sometimes pompously elevated to, 'All our sales executives are busy.' This is one we all dread – partly because we know we have just embarked on a wait of Godotian interminability, and partly because we will soon be hearing the sort of dreadful music that could only have been chosen by a committee. This cliché is sometimes accompanied by its near cousin, 'We value your call.'

ARE YOU ALL RIGHT THERE?

At one time, if you were waiting to be served in a shop the assistant would ask if they could help you;

now they are more likely to say 'Are you all right there, sir?' What's the required response? 'No, I'd rather stand over the other side of the shop if you don't mind'.

BEFORE YOU DIE
All of a sudden people are writing articles and books about things you must 'do before you die': 'A Hundred Books You Must Read Before You Die', '1,001 Places You Must Visit Before You Die', '500 Beers You Must Drink ...', etc. You can hardly do any of these things *after* you die, can you? And, if you tried to read all these books, visit all these places, drink all these beers and so forth in such a hurry you might just die because of it.

COURTESY CALL
Someone trying to sell you something, usually over the phone. A greater courtesy would be not to call at all.

NO WORRIES
This phrase is used in social dialogue, but it's particularly annoying when used in a commercial context. For example, 'I'll have a beer, please, and a

gin and tonic.' 'No worries.' What happened to 'yes, sir' or even 'coming up, boss'?

NOT A PROBLEM
A strange one, this. Imagine you're paying some cheques in at the bank. 'I'd like to pay these cheques in please.' 'That's not a problem.' I should hope not!

WE VALUE YOUR CALL
Yet another cliché from call-centre hell. Your call is valued so much that it will not be answered for at least ten minutes.

YOU ARE BEING HELD IN A QUEUE
Another cliché from the lonely wastes of telephone land in the modern world. This one has a slightly sinister edge to it, implying force: 'you are being held …'

YOUR CALL MAY BE RECORDED FOR TRAINING PURPOSES
Yes, you often feel as though your experience at the hands of their operators would be a perfect illustration of how not to do it.

Packaging

Packaging is supposed to be a wrapping that protects products from getting dirty, damp, damaged and so forth, but it seems to have been hijacked by people who write in very small type and have their own little private store of clichés to share with us. Is it really necessary to tell us that everything may contain nuts – even nuts?

BATTERIES NOT INCLUDED
Well, they very rarely are, especially in the case of some toys where the batteries actually cost more than the product.

ENVIRONMENTALLY FRIENDLY
This is such a vague phrase as to be virtually meaningless, but it puts a warm glow of self-satisfaction into most of us who like to feel we're doing our bit without actually changing any of our environmentally unfriendly ways.

LOW FAT

How low is 'low'? When roads signs say 'low bridge' they put an exact height on the sign, too. Why are lorry drivers afforded a level of detail that yoghurt eaters are not?

MAY CONTAIN NUTS

In theory it's possible that almost anything may contain nuts: cakes, meat pies, bottled water, the copy department of the packaging company, but where do we stop? May contain nuclear waste, may contain traces of rodent found running around food factory, may contain false eyelashes, fingernails or other small body parts of packing personnel?

NO ADDED SALT/SUGAR

This may be because the product is already swimming in an effluent of naturally occurring 'baddies'. To take an extreme example: a packet of salt could quite reasonably bear the label 'no added salt' and get away with it.

Restaurants

Restaurant food is fashion with flavours, and the restaurant menu if full of flavour-of-the-moment descriptions of the delights on offer. Here are some of the current favourites:

BED OF ...

Food is now something we must think of as a bit sultry or sexy. Gastronomic delights are served up on a bed of lettuce or a bed of rice as though in readiness for some strange culinary sex act to be performed upon them. In such cases 'on a bed of ...' means 'on some', as in the expression, 'Would you like some salt and vinegar on a bed of chips?'

DRIZZLE

Once a description of a depressingly half-hearted weather condition but now a rather lovely and mouthwatering culinary-based cliché. We now 'drizzle' lemon juice over our cooking, whereas once we just squeezed it. How unsophisticated of us!

ENROBED

This is term often used in the descriptions of expensive chocolates or desserts. Essentially it means 'covered in'. So, while parmesan is busy shaving, the expensive pudding is in the bedroom enrobing itself with chocolate. The use of the word 'enrobed' shows you just how posh the pudding must be.

FLAME-GRILLED/OVEN-BAKED ...

How much better things taste when they have been grilled with genuine flames or baked in an actual oven. The food industry likes to set our mouths watering by weaving in these tantalising details, which let us in on some of the tricks of their trade. And oven-baking really does improve the taste. Try baking something without using an oven. It can be disastrous.

HAND-COOKED

'Hand-cooked' is often used with regard to crisps. The term is, however, misleading. Investigation reveals that the crisps involved have rarely been genuinely hand-cooked. Instead some kind of pan will generally have been used. Insist in future on genuine hand-cooked crisps. You will find them in the packets with an image of the crisp-maker's hideously charred palms on the front.

MEDLEY OF ...

Restaurants will use the phrase 'a medley of' in describing a dish that has several ingredients. For instance, 'It's sea bass served with a medley of tomatoes, chives and roasted chipmunk eyebrows.' In so doing they have confused the worlds of food preparation and musical arrangement. The world of music has now decided to retaliate by stealing the expression 'mash-up', which the posh food industry hasn't been using so much in recent years.

PAN-FRIED

As opposed to ... ?

SHAVED PARMESAN

Generally speaking, if you want to cut cheese briskly into bits by rubbing it against a sharp bit of metal, the process is called 'grating'. For parmesan, however, this simply won't do. Parmesan instead has to be delicately shaved, possibly by a beautiful model in a skimpy black dress. Parmesan, it would seem, is a much more sophisticated type of cheese that shaves, dabs on a bit of aftershave (Pour Le Fromage) and then hits the trendiest nightspots in the company of a couple of cherry tomatoes and an olive.

BUSINESS CLICHÉS

In business it's important that everyone talk the same language. It is often believed that the international language for business is English, but that depends on whether you would apply the term 'English' to the mangled monstrosities and jumbled jargon of the business world.

Corporate speak

The corporate world is a rich and steady source of clichés. It is a world in which cocky young upstarts wish to give an impression of themselves as jazzy, jaunty young things so revolutionary in their thinking that they communicate in a whole new language. The upshot of this is, however, that corporate clichés burn themselves out even more quickly than in any other sphere. For example, any aspiring young business person who tried using the expression, 'Let's run it up the flagpole and see who salutes' today would surely be dismissed immediately and escorted out of the building by security.

BLUE-SKY THINKING
In other words, we must now think in a way that is completely clear and unrestricted. What a pity this voyage into the new regions of human ingenuity has been launched with such a well-worn phrase.

BRAIN DUMP
A jotting down of ideas performed without too much analysis. The concept of a 'brain dump', however, sounds as if either it will be a slightly messy affair or the brain dumper must be some kind of android-like figure. It might also be assumed that a 'brain dump' would require significant resources to accommodate the contents of the human mind. There are, however, individuals within every organisation who can successfully perform a complete brain dump onto a single average-sized Post-it note.

CAFFEINE-FUELLED
In the same way that you can have a gas-fuelled central-heating system, so you can have a caffeine-fuelled meeting. Don't try mixing the two.

CASH COW
The concept of a cow that produces money rather than milk when it has its udders tugged is certainly beguiling, but why do you need it if you have geese that lay golden eggs on your cliché farm?

CUBICLE MONKEY
An office worker, so called because he or she is placed in a cubicle with a computer – presumably in the hope that if the firm has enough 'cubicle monkeys' one of them will eventually type the complete works of Shakespeare.

DUCKS IN A ROW
When you have your work neatly organised and all in order, you will have your 'ducks in a row'. It's a veritable farmyard, this office, isn't it?

FACE TIME
Yuk! Meaning 'meeting face to face' rather than communicating by phone, email, etc. It even makes 'one-to-one' sound quite quaint.

GUESSTIMATE
If you just make a guess it doesn't sound very professional; a 'guesstimate', however, seems rather more dignified. You could say it's a guess with a suit and tie on.

HANDS-ON/HANDS-OFF
If a particular person at work is described as being

'very hands-on', they are the kind of person who likes to get involved with the work that needs doing. 'Hands-on' has also come to suggest someone in authority who is constantly breathing down the necks of his/her underlings and urging them to get on with things. Thus 'hands-off' has come to suggest positive connotations – a boss who lets you get on with things without undue interference. So perhaps the ideal boss is someone who is 'hands-on' (in that they do some real work) but in a 'hands-off' kind of way (they don't interfere).

LEARNING CURVE

Why curve? Sometimes this phrase is preceded by the word 'steep', making it even more odd. Of course, it all comes from the mumbo-jumbo land of graphs and other visual representations that don't have much to do with reality. Usually, any sort of learning that is particularly difficult is more like climbing a mountain – and if you draw your graphs properly they look a bit like mountains, too. Time for a new cliché!

MISSION STATEMENT

Positively swimming, basking and variously

luxuriating in supreme self-importance, this phrase always feels as though it should be written in those big letters made of stone and viewed from beneath like old film posters for epics such as *Ben-Hur* and *El Cid*. All it means is 'a few words about what our company stands for' – and, as the old joke goes, if they stand for this they'll stand for anything.

MOVERS AND SHAKERS
It sounds quite modern, and hip young businesspeople like to use phrases such as this, little realising that this particular one dates back to an 1874 poem by Arthur O'Shaughnessy. Ouch! How trendy does it sound now?

MOVING THE GOALPOSTS
The ultimate frustration in the corporate world, although there is no record of its having actually ever happened during a competitive sporting event.

PAST EXPERIENCE
Business is now full of individuals, especially consultants, who would dearly like to tell you what past experience has told them. Past experience? What other sort of experience is there?

Experience by definition is something that happened to you in the past. The constant use of unnecessary words such as 'past' in 'past experience' is of course one more reason why business meetings go on for so much longer than they need to.

PLAYING HARDBALL

'We're not taking any chances – these guys are playing hardball.' What with 'ballpark', 'touch base' and all the rest, baseball should hang its helmeted head in shame for all the clichés it has bestowed on the language. This one is much favoured by would-be macho business types.

RUN IT PAST

'We'll have to run it past the Marketing Department before we get the OK.'

'Run' may not be quite the right word here. It hints at a swift perfunctory formality that must be observed but in reality may be a lengthy process of multi-department approval that is more of a tortoise-like crawl than a run.

SHOOT THE PUPPY

Similar to 'think the unthinkable' (see the separate

entry under 'Political Clichés'). 'Shoot the puppy' means to consider the most extreme and controversial course of action. It's best to avoid using the phrase, however, since it will probably stun any business meeting into silence for several minutes while those attending solemnly consider the plight of the poor pooch in question.

SUITED AND BOOTED
Dressed up. This phrase isn't exclusive to business circles, but it does have that faint whiff of 1980s yuppie about it, doesn't it?

TALK TURKEY
And what do turkeys say? That's right, 'gobble, gobble, gobble.' Let's not talk turkey, eh?

THINKING OUTSIDE THE BOX
Anyone who is truly capable of thinking 'outside the box' (that is to say unconventionally) should also be capable of writing without using clichés. The phrase comes from a puzzle in which one has to join a 'box' of nine dots with four straight lines without the pen leaving the paper. This is possible only by extending two of the lines outside the 'box' of nine dots.

THOUGHT SHOWER

A latter-day variation on 'brainstorming'. Soon we'll be reduced to having a bit of a 'think drizzle'.

UTILISE

Utilise means use. So why not use 'use' rather than utilise 'utilise'? OK, 'utilise' is in the dictionary, but isn't it really just the word 'use' with two extra syllables squeezed in the middle to make it last that little bit longer? Using words and phrases that are longer than they need to be of course always serves a useful purpose. It makes the person using them seem just that little bit cleverer and more professional than everyone else.

New technology

**New technology has freed us from more
arduous forms of communication, but not,
alas, from clichés. In fact, it's given us a
whole lot of new ones.**

AT THE CLICK OF A MOUSE

Everything's that's available on the Internet is now
said to be available 'at the click of a mouse'. What,
just one click? Have you tried ordering anything
on the Internet lately? Perhaps a more accurate
phrase would be, 'It's available on the Internet after
45 minutes of knuckle-chewing, wall-thumping,
keyboard-smashing bloody frustration, yet another
new password you'll forget within half an hour,
and at least three error messages telling you the
website couldn't be found or you've put in the
wrong password, or you haven't completed the
order form properly or ...'

BUG THAT NEVER WAS

Every so often you will receive an email from
someone you know, copied to everyone in their

address book, warning of a new computer virus coming your way soon. It will wipe your hard drive! It may eat your entire family! There is no known cure! Half an hour later you'll get another, shame-faced, email from your friend telling you that you've all been the victim of a cruel hoax. But you knew that already, didn't you?

CHECK OUT OUR WEBSITE

Some older-fashioned businesses invite us to 'visit' their websites as we might visit, for example, a stately home, but more often than not we are implored to 'check out' people's websites because it sounds a bit groovier and more 'happening'.

EMOTICONS

Yes, those silly little arrangements of punctuation marks that people put in emails to look a bit like a face smiling or being sad because they can't express themselves in words. All right, they're probably fun and harmless enough if you're under the age of 12, but, adults, you will not be taken seriously.

ETAILERS

People who sell online are known as 'Etailers'

– one of those dreadful neologisms that people feel they have to invent. The only problem with these (apart from being ugly and irritating) is that you have to spend so long explaining what it means to the uninitiated that you would have been better off using a proper phrase, such as 'online retailer' in the first place.

FOR QUALITY AND SECURITY PURPOSES, CALLS MAY BE RECORDED

Big Brother strikes again.

'HAVE YOU TRIED TURNING IT OFF AND TURNING IT ON AGAIN?'

This is not only a cliché but also a poor substitute for decent advice on how to deal with your computer problem.

I CAN'T COME TO THE PHONE RIGHT NOW

Why is it necessary to say that? Probably because they've heard other people say it.

I'M ON THE BUS/TRAIN

Despite its being widely recognised as an appalling

cliché, this is still heard frequently. When these people are phoned at home, do they say, 'I'm in the lounge'?

SNAIL MAIL
The oh-so-superior reference to letters that are sent through the conventional mail system. OK, they're a bit slower, but they're not going to be covered in 'emoticons' and trite 'meaningful' quotes at the bottom and demand that everyone's middle name is 'dot', are they?

'TODAY IS THE FIRST DAY OF THE REST OF YOUR LIFE' (AND OTHERS)
Are you irritated to receive emails with little quotations at the bottom? Some people just can't seem to help themselves from adding the wise or witty words of Oscar Wilde or William Shakespeare to the bottom of their otherwise humdrum emails. Is it because they can't think of any wise or witty words of their own?

YOU'RE BREAKING UP
Meaning that the connection is faulty. Was this what Alexander Graham Bell said to his assistant when he made the first-ever telephone call?

Property selling

Certain words and phrases relating to property are only ever seen in sales agents' descriptions – for example, 'equidistant'. Others are so commonplace as to be meaningless, such as 'spacious', 'stunning', 'well-presented', 'attractive', 'rare opportunity' … Here are a few other classic examples of property-speak.

BIJOU
Cramped.

COMPACT
Very cramped.

CONVENIENT FOR LOCAL SCHOOLS
Convenient for several thousand local schoolchildren passing through your front garden; their parents parking their SUVs across your lawn and half a ton of sweet wrappers stuffed through your letterbox every morning and afternoon.

DECEPTIVELY SPACIOUS
Cramped even if you are a midget contortionist.

I COULD SEE YOU IN THIS PLACE
Seeing that this phrase is uttered by the agent while he/she is in the property showing round the potential purchasers, it doesn't require a huge leap of imagination.

IF YOU DON'T SNAP THIS UP, SOMEONE ELSE WILL
In other words, 'Why don't you just get your chequebook out now and let me get on with the rest of my day?'

IN NEED OF MODERNISATION
Which means, 'how this building remains standing is something of a mystery'.

IT'S GOT POTENTIAL
This house is a wreck.

MUCH SOUGHT-AFTER
Sales agents will tell you that every house on their books is 'much sought-after'. If they are all

so 'much sought-after', why are agents necessary? Couldn't you just sell your house to one of the vast hordes of people coming by each day and night seeking it?

ORIGINAL FEATURES
The property benefits from many 'original features'. In other words the place hasn't had any work done on it since 1974.

POPULAR AREA
Yes, of *course* it's a popular area. People live there. They live there because once upon a time someone built some houses there. It is therefore a popular area!

SPECTACULAR VIEW
This property has a spectacular view – well, it would if you removed all the other buildings round it.

THIS ONE'S GOING TO GO QUICKLY
I am still waiting for you to get your chequebook out!

UP-AND-COMING AREA
If you move into this area you will be a bit like a pioneer staking your claim in a wild, lawless territory.

VIBRANT AREA
Probably vibrating with the sound of 500-watt loudspeaker systems, the rumble of riot-squad trucks and sub-machine-gun fire.

(THE) WOW FACTOR
All houses put up for sale these days must have a 'wow factor'. This is often a nice fireplace in the front room or it could possibly be a sacrificial altar in the guest bedroom.

YOU CAN BUILD ON IT
Said even when the property involved already has 36 storeys.

POLITICAL CLICHÉS

Politicians virtually run on clichés, whether verbal, gesticulatory or contextual (kissing babies at election time, for example). Somewhere in a government vault there must be a bumper book of political clichés that is required reading for all aspiring statesmen, and, boy, have they studied it! They also use a fair few business clichés, mixing as they do with 'head honchos' from the world of commerce.

BEGGARS BELIEF

This phrase is often used by opposition politicians
to express their complete astonishment at some
piece of government incompetence. 'This simply
beggars belief,' they will cry while turning a shade
of mauvey russet. The phrase does not, however,
mean that someone has managed to impoverish
the concept of belief itself and turn it into some
pathetic begging figure. Instead, the verb 'beggars'
in this phrase means 'to render inadequate'. So
'beggars belief' means 'belief has been rendered
inadequate'. Which is all very well, but still doesn't
mean anything.

BLACK HOLE

Politicians like to do two things: scare the life out
of us, then rescue us. But sometimes they forget
to do the second bit. 'Black hole' is one of those
expressions they tack onto other words to make
them sound even worse – for instance, 'financial
black hole'. As everyone with even a passing
interest in sci-fi knows, black holes are things from
which nothing can escape – not even light – but

politicians don't let little things like universal laws of physics get in their way, do they?

CHARM OFFENSIVE
Often said by politicians about other politicians when they are being particularly unctuous. Only a politician could come up with an oxymoron with this degree of self-contradiction. What next – fun tax? But let's not give them ideas.

CHILDREN'S CHILDREN
Some phrases exist only in clichés. Have you ever heard anyone – even a politician – say, 'At the weekend we're taking my children's children to the zoo'?

COMPLACENCY
Politicians often accuse one another of being complacent when they should have been constantly vigilant. For anyone in a position of authority, 'complacency' has therefore become a crime apparently greater than serial murder. This is because if people are complacent and allow mistakes to happen, it inconveniences the rest of us. And of course if we're inconvenienced it gets in the way of what we want to do – which is to sit

around, relax, enjoy ourselves and not worry about anything. In other words, to be complacent.

CONSIDER YOUR POSITION
Sack yourself before you're sacked by your boss.

DOING NOTHING IS NOT AN OPTION
Oh but it should be! Perhaps they could start using the reverse phrase: 'Doing something is not compulsory.'

DOOMSDAY SCENARIO
One of several apocalyptic expressions beloved by politicians. Politicians like disasters; the rest of us aren't quite so keen – as we're usually the victims. Like superheroes with ties (or, these days, self-consciously without ties) they are ever-ready to rescue us, the Lois Lanes of perpetual danger, from terrorists, climate change or just plain ol' inflation. But are we grateful?

(LET'S) DRAW A LINE UNDER IT (AND MOVE ON)
You can be pretty sure a politician is in it up to his neck when he wants to do this. Everyone else

wants to investigate it, claim compensation, or sack the politician, but he wants to get out his favourite crayons and draw a line under it.

DREAM TICKET
For normal people a 'dream ticket' would be one to go and see their favourite band, or their favourite football team playing a big match; for a politician it means two politicians (one often being themselves) running for office. Hardly worth going to sleep for, is it?

ELDER STATESMAN
Has-been.

ELEPHANT IN THE ROOM
Not content with having a farmyard full of clichés, politicians have started on the zoo animals now as well. The 'elephant in the room' is the one fact you can't ignore – though they possibly would if the elephant happened to be looking for government funding at the time.

EYE OFF THE BALL
Politicians often talk about having had their 'eye

off the ball' in cases when a problem has arisen. This makes it sound as though they haven't done anything too terrible while suggesting that their dull political work is a bit like a glamorous game of professional football.

(THE) FACTS SPEAK FOR THEMSELVES

Clever old facts, we say.

FEELGOOD FACTOR

Oh, it's so beautifully vague, this one. The 'feelgood factor' is indefinable; it's that strange situation politicians find themselves in when, despite their best (or worst) efforts, they suddenly notice that people are happy and they're not quite sure why. Despite not knowing what it is or where it came from, they naturally claim the credit for it.

(A) FULL AND FRANK DISCUSSION

A rip-roaring, no-holds-barred, stand-up shouting match possibly with fists flying (to use a few more clichés).

GET INTO BED WITH

For a professional group that seems to get

involved in more sexual scandal than any other, politicians seem remarkably fond of phrases that keep reminding of us of the fact. It simply means 'to become heavily involved with' but has the unfortunate effect of conjuring up some fairly unsavoury mental images.

GREASY POLE

Not an abominable racial slur, or even a particularly new cliché, but one that is lovingly preserved by politicians. The greasy pole was originally an attraction at old-fashioned fairgrounds where people would be challenged to climb to the top of a liberally greased pole to retrieve a prize. In politician-speak the allusion is used to denigrate people who will do anything to get to the top. Climbing a real greasy pole probably took some skill, courage and other virtues, and didn't involve stabbing people in the back, taking bribes or whatever else is implied in this cliché.

HAVING SAID THAT

Used just before contradicting themselves and occasionally making a nonsensical statement in the process, such as, 'having said that, dangerous dogs

should be muzzled in public places'. Talking dogs?
Whatever next?

HEADLESS CHICKENS
This is a well-established cliché but a favourite
with politicians, who, with their 'cash cows', 'geese
laying golden eggs', 'ducks in a row', and 'stalking
horses', seem to have a pretty full farm of clichés.

HEARTS AND MINDS
Something politicians are always aspiring to win
– haven't they got any of their own?

I CAN'T COMMENT ON
INDIVIDUAL CASES
The politician's skill at evasion is ever inventive.

I WOULDN'T START FROM HERE
Adapted from the old Irish joke about a tourist
asking for directions. For some reason many
politicians like to think of themselves as being
witty or entertaining – either Churchillian or
vaudevillian, but usually they're not: they're just a
bit embarrassing. This is just one of a formidable
stock of standby jokes, allusions and quotations
that is regularly raided by these serial self-amusers.

IF YOU'VE GOT NOTHING TO HIDE YOU'VE GOT NOTHING TO FEAR

When politicians want to introduce some invasive new security measure such as more surveillance cameras or new security checks at airports they use this phrase. We've all got things to hide – and you'd think politicians would understand this more than most.

I'M ANSWERING IT IN MY OWN WAY

Writhing on the skewer of a difficult question from a pushy presenter, desperate politicians grab for this lifeline. 'I'm answering it in my own way' means, of course, 'I'm not answering it.'

I'M NOT RULING ANYTHING IN AND I'M NOT RULING ANYTHING OUT

An irritating and long-winded way of saying 'I haven't made up my mind.'

JABBING FINGER

Not all clichés are verbal. The experienced politician has in his dressing-up box of political puffery all manner of poses, gesticulations and other self-conscious body language with which to seduce the voters. The jabbing finger can be used accusingly against opponents, admonishingly with a little wag, or it can be used to communicate directly and personally with 'you' the voter. But there's an old saying: 'When you point a finger at somebody you're pointing three at yourself.' Quite.

KEY
Dangling without the support of an article, definite or indefinite, this word always seems oddly adrift in sentences such as: 'The army has more funding than ever before, and this is key ...'

KNEE-JERK REACTION
Politicians like to dismiss the opinions of others as knee-jerk reactions, but perhaps they should stop whacking us with wooden mallets quite so often.

LESSONS MUST BE LEARNED
After any shameful and possibly tragic story has emerged in the news, it will be said that 'lessons must be learned'. Of *course* lessons must be learned. That's the whole point of lessons. Unfortunately, both in the educational sector and in the

shameful-and-possibly-tragic-news-story sector, lessons aren't learned quite as often as they should be. But at least this gives people an opportunity to use the follow-up expression, 'lessons should have been learned'!

LET'S BE ABSOLUTELY CLEAR ABOUT THIS

Politicians constantly express the desire to be absolutely or perfectly clear about things. What politicians actually mean when they use this phrase is, 'I've got a bit confused by the discussion on this point so I'm just going to repeat what I said 15 minutes ago.'

MORAL HIGH GROUND

In the political world an imaginary land like Atlantis, Utopia or Narnia.

NAMING AND SHAMING

Proving that rhyming and timing are also important elements of any political buzz-phrase. Incidentally, it's difficult to imagine being able to shame someone without naming them, though perhaps a few newspaper picture editors might disagree.

NIGHTMARE SCENARIO
Another heart-juddering phrase so beloved of
politicians, but, scary as it is, it must presumably be
slightly preferable to the 'worst-case scenario'.

NO COMMENT
Not especially new and not exclusive to politicians,
but it's as perky as ever, popping up all over the
place wherever politicians and journalists meet.
But is it really necessary? When normal people
have nothing to say they don't say anything, but
politicians just love the sound of their own vices,
sorry, voices, don't they?

NO EASY ANSWERS
When a politician says this he means one of two
things: (a) that he really doesn't have a clue what
the answer is; or (b) he does have an answer but
you're not going to like it very much, because
it probably involves more taxes.

NO MORE MR NICE GUY
Said by politicians when they want to get tough.
It always makes it sound as though there *was* a Mr
Nice Guy to begin with. It also sounds as though the

speaker is something of a Jekyll–and–Hyde character and not to be trusted under any circumstances.

NOT WEARING A TIE

Politicians are so obsessed with image rather than substance they'd conduct interviews standing on their heads in bowls of cold custard if they thought it would get them elected. The latest wheeze is to whip their ties off before they go into a TV studio to be interviewed in the hope that they will look like 'normal people'. They don't: they just look like politicians without ties – and pretty shifty and uncomfortable ones at that.

ON MESSAGE

This daft phrase, meaning to be speaking in accordance with your party's policies, was probably invented because it sounded slightly less dictatorial than 'toeing the party line'.

POWER FIST

Any politician aspiring to appear tough will make his hand into a fist and then use it either as a decorative feature or to bang against the lectern, dispatch box or whatever else is at hand.

RECIPE FOR DISASTER
Take a pound of flesh, a few pounds – or dollars or euros – in expenses, a cup of good cheer, a large serving of ego and a pinch of secretary's bottom.

RIGHTS AND RESPONSIBILITIES
As with 'love and marriage' or a 'horse and carriage', you 'can't have one without the other'. But unfortunately you can. In all three cases.

RING-FENCE
Governments don't just put aside money for specific uses now: they build dirty great, probably electric, fences round it. Not to stop other people getting to it, but to stop themselves. Even they don't trust them.

ROAD MAP
Surely now redundant with the invention of satellite navigation? Though a 'satnav for the Middle East' admittedly doesn't sound quite right. And the choice of 'road map' to describe a peace process is unfortunate – think how many arguments start with two people trying to find their way using a road map.

SAFE PAIR OF HANDS

The singling out of one dull and dependable politician as a 'safe pair of hands' tells you quite a bit about the rest of them.

SINGING FROM THE SAME HYMN SHEET

'On message' with a bit of dignifying religious imagery thrown in.

SOURCES CLOSE TO ...

A cliché much used on news reports to describe the origination point of sensitive political information. Details gleaned from 'sources close to' the Prime Minister or 'sources close to' the President means that the Prime Minister or President didn't necessarily say these things himself. Instead, some official lackey has been set up to tell us what the glorious leader would like to have said but couldn't say in person in case the rest of us didn't like it. 'Sources close to' the Deputy Prime Minister or the Vice President, on the other hand, probably means the Deputy Prime Minister or Vice President himself.

SPIN DOCTOR

You can get a pretty good idea of the state of modern politics by looking at the clichés our politicians use. Originally, a spin doctor was someone who tampered with the ball in say, a game of cricket or baseball, to gain an advantage with the altered spin, but in political terms it's usually a press officer who manipulates truth. And we always thought doctors were there to help us.

STAKEHOLDER

Meaning someone who has a share in something – such as a company, or society in general. Politicians like this word because it's 'inclusive'. If they said 'taxpayer', that might exclude some of their most prominent supporters. Unfortunately, 'stakeholder' also brings to mind those hysterical villagers in horror films who are just about to plunge a wooden stake through the heart of a vampire.

STALKING HORSE

It is very revealing that so many political clichés include animals, often of the farmyard variety. A real stalking horse is one behind which a hunter hides when seeking prey. A political stalking horse is a person put forward to challenge the party leader, only to allow someone else actually to win the challenge. Animals never get up to such dirty tricks on their own.

THINK THE UNTHINKABLE
The problem is that in a politician's seething mind nothing is unthinkable. What they're really trying to say is, 'Think what would be the completely unacceptable by any rational human being.' Also, they overlook the obvious fact that 'thinking the unthinkable' would result in the 'unthinkable' becoming the 'thinkable'.

THIRD WAY
Not left, not right, but somewhere in the middle with all the worst aspects of both left and right. Is there a fourth way? Please?

TICKING BOXES
Not homemade bombs, but adherence to a set of criteria. 'We've ticked all the right boxes on human-rights requirements in the current legislation.'

WATCH MY LIPS

The reason they ask you to watch their lips is so you don't notice what they're doing with their hands.

WE ARE WHERE WE ARE

Always useful when being questioned by a determined interviewer, since it's impossible to dispute this self-evident fact.

WHAMMY

This word seems to have taken over from 'blow' to mean a knock or a setback. It started off as a 'double whammy', found itself through political verbal inflation becoming 'triple whammy', and has gone on to 'quadruple whammy', and 'quintuple whammy' right up to 'octuple whammy'. It seems to have stopped there, partly perhaps because not enough people know the equivalent adjective for 'ninefold' (nonuple). Oddly, it is never seen as simply 'whammy' (apart from here).

WITH RESPECT

Usually used when being interviewed by a probing journalist, and meaning of course, the exact opposite of what it says.

WORST-CASE SCENARIO
The 'case' part of this phrase is redundant.
What's wrong with 'worst scenario'? Indeed, what's
wrong with thinking up something original and
letting this political cliché spend more time with
its family?

SOCIAL CLICHÉS

It's not love or money that makes the world go round: it's clichés! And when we're off-guard, chatting informally, we are probably using more clichés per hour than at any other time. Friends, partners and work colleagues don't care how many times we say 'whatever' because they're probably doing it too. It's just as well there are no cliché police patrolling the streets: we'd all be under permanent house arrest for crimes against the English language.

Personal

These are the clichés we all use in everyday life, whether we're arranging to meet someone ('Can we pencil in the 23rd?') or commenting on the weather ('Nice weather for ducks'). It is possible, with the clever use of clichés, to hold a reasonably long conversation without actually saying anything worthwhile. 'Basically, like, at the end of the day, I'm, like, "whoah!" – know what I mean?'

BLESS!
Once used when talking indulgently about babies/ small children, now almost always ironic – for example, 'She's only read a couple of magazine articles about it, now she thinks she's a fully qualified chiropractor.' 'Bless!'

CHILL
Once the slightly more cumbersome and geographically ambiguous 'chill out', this one, like many clichés, has gone from being specific to being generalised and therefore losing its power

along the way. In rave culture the idea of leaving the throbbing, sweaty and relentless activity of the dance floor for a quiet place of sanctuary to 'chill out' made some sort of sense, but in the context of leaving the front room for a walk round the garden it seems to be a case of unnecessary overemphasis.

DON'T GET ME STARTED

Meaning, 'If we continue along this track of conversation you risk being subjected to my narrow-minded and bigoted viewpoint on this and all related subjects, and I risk dangerously increased blood pressure.'

ER, EXCUSE ME!

Used when indicating that someone has made an unjustified accusation. 'Well you are the fattest person here, aren't you?' 'Er, excuse me – I'm a size ten!' The 'er' is quite important because it gives a dramatic emphasis that would not be there without it.

ER, HELLO?

Used when not making yourself understood to someone you consider of lower intelligence.
'We only crashed because you were over the speed

limit.' 'Er, hello? You were on the wrong side of
the road!' The 'hello' is usually drawn out for
additional emphasis.

GET A LIFE
To which the obvious retort is, 'Get an original
phrase.' 'Get a life' is the instant and unthinking
response from anyone reprimanded for minor
misdeeds – feet on bus seats, pavement cycling,
dropping litter, etc. What, get a life like yours, you
mean? No thanks.

GOOD STUFF
A sickly, soppy phrase that is used to apply to
personal relationships. People will say while
enjoying 'quality time' (see separate entry) with
one another, 'This is the good stuff!' or 'Hey, we're
getting to the good stuff here!' as though they
were gouging their way into the depths of some
exotic fruit.

I DON'T DO ...
Ask someone to be a bit nicer these days and
you may get the reaction 'I don't do nice' – if
you're lucky. Ask someone to apologise and you

may get 'I don't do apologetic' – again, if you're lucky. This is one of those clichés that can be spun and reinvented as much as you like but it's still a cliché.

I'M GOOD
An annoying response to 'How are you?' It seems to imply a degree of self-satisfaction that 'I'm fine' doesn't.

I'M LIKE ...
This is the game of charades of modern dialogue involving a bit of ham acting, a bit of mime, the odd impression and a fair bit of gurning. 'So she accuses me of shoplifting and I'm like ... [*pulls face of complete astonishment*], what?! And then she threatens to call the police and I'm like ... [*pulls another face of affronted surprise*] er, excuse me? And then the security guard grabs my arm and I'm like ... get your hands off me!' Et cetera, et cetera, et cetera!

(IT) SUCKS!
Meaning that the subject under discussion is not very good. This did not stop a vacuum-cleaner

company from once using the slogan 'Nothing sucks like an Electrolux'.

STREET/STREET CRED/STREETWISE

In some quarters, being very 'street' is seen as a good thing. Quite what it means, though, is very hazy. It seems to imply that the person considered very 'street' is lacking in pretension, able to converse in working-class or hip argot, and dresses in urban fashion, or it could mean they are like a lamppost. 'Street cred' is the approbation you receive from people who are very 'street' when you look and behave exactly as they do. Being 'streetwise' is knowing how to avoid trouble if you are foolish enough to venture onto the street without your 'street cred'.

TAKE CARE

A sadly insincere farewell cliché.

Workplace clichés

Somehow, between the business-speak, technical jargon, and computer terminology we all now use, we manage to squeeze just a few more special workplace clichés.

DO LUNCH
Having lunch, especially with someone else, is supposed to be an enjoyable experience. 'Doing' lunch sounds like a perfunctory soulless chore, and perhaps it would be if you were having lunch with the sort of person who uses this expression.

I WANT TO BE MORE PROACTIVE HERE
Intensely irritating phrase in which the speaker seems to be claiming that he or she will have an effect on those around them akin to that of live yoghurt.

LET'S HAVE A CATCH-UP
This is either an invitation to throw a ball

around in the office for a few minutes or, more likely, a summons to a mini-meeting at which the participants will 'catch up' with one another. Although, as any Olympic sprinter will tell you, it is not possible for two people to catch up with each other at the same time.

SACKING CLICHÉS
Bosses just don't have the guts to sack people any more: they 'let them go', they 'downsize', they 'rationalise'. It may make them feel better but it doesn't do much for the person who's just been given 'the bullet', 'the order of the boot' or any of the other 'feel-better' euphemisms bosses use.

TAKE IT EASY
Hip, cool work colleagues like to show just how hip and cool they are when they bid you farewell for the day. So, rather than saying 'goodbye', 'see you' or 'toodle pip', they instead quote the title of the first single released by the Eagles.

WALK
To leave or to walk out in a particularly defiant dramatic manner: 'I've had enough of you talking to me like that. If you don't stop I'm going to walk. Just watch me!' Of course in most circumstances announcing that you're about to walk has very little dramatic resonance – unless, that is, you've just been miraculously cured at Lourdes.

WINDOW
'I'll just see if I have a window for next week.' Why window? In this context of course it means a gap, but it could just as easily be a door, a hole, a bomb crater or a yawning chasm. For some reason it always sounds a bit pretentious.

TALK TO THE HAND
An expression and gesture combined: 'Talk to the hand, because the ears aren't listening' or, alternatively, 'Talk to the hand, the face ain't listening.' In fact the face *is* still listening, so it is possible to carry on making your point. The phrase

is generally believed to be African American in origin, though some claim that 'talk to the hand' derives from kids' TV shows featuring glove puppets such as Kermit the Frog.

TOO MUCH INFORMATION!

Go into too much detail about your recent operation or your toddler's toilet training and you may well be called to an abrupt halt by this traffic cop of a phrase.

WAY TO GO

An expression of encouragement meaning that the speaker is recommending that the person being spoken to should continue to pursue a certain course of action.

WHAT ARE YOU LIKE?

'I got so drunk I fell into a ditch and woke up at six o'clock and got the first bus home.' 'What are you like?!' Well you're like someone who gets drunk, falls into a ditch ...

WHAT ARE YOU ON (AND CAN I HAVE SOME)?

If you do something exceptionally well, or say something exceptionally unconventional, people will often ask, 'What are you on?' and sometimes follow it up with, 'And can I have some?' This seems to be a reference to drug taking, though it appears to imply that you have no innate talent, ability or capacity for original thought without artificial stimulants. A bit of an insult, really.

WHATEVER

Almost completely meaningless, though sometimes used as a substitute for 'et cetera', as in, 'We're having pizza, salad, olives, whatever.' Unlike 'et cetera', it seems to indicate a carelessness and lack of interest in what it is being discussed – would you want someone like that doing your party planning? 'Whatever' is also used as a substitute for 'Who cares?' and often by stroppy children or teenagers. 'If you don't tidy your room, you won't be getting any pocket money this week.' 'Whatever.'

Psychobabble

Everyone these days is an amateur psychologist. We have all been so exposed to the specialist language and jargon of psychology in magazines and newspapers and on TV and radio that we can now analyse, comment upon and even recommend 'coping mechanisms' for all sorts of human problems. It's probably a sign of decadence that we are all so adept at this kind of thing – a sort of psychobabylon.

ANGER MANAGEMENT

Just a new-fangled way of saying 'not losing your temper', but, then, who'd pay half a day's wages to go and learn from an 'expert' how to avoid losing their temper? This sounds far more technical and worthy of specialist fees.

BAGGAGE

For most of us, baggage is what we take with us on holidays; for practitioners of psychobabble it's the combined weight of all our problems, guilt and sordid secrets that we carry round with us all the time and need to offload. It may take several sessions with a psychotherapist to get rid of it all, so it's not just airlines that charge us for excess baggage.

CLOSURE
Despite its clang of finality 'closure' is often seen as the starting point for 'coming to terms' with a 'situation'. It's the psychobabbler's way of saying, 'Get over it.'

COPING MECHANISM
When you're paying someone a sizable pile of money to sort out your problems you feel entitled to a bit of jargon. Just being sat down with a cup of tea and told to 'pull yourself together' won't do. Oh, no, you need 'coping mechanisms', which are strategies with white coats on.

DON'T BEAT YOURSELF UP OVER IT
A phrase that puts an absurd and comical picture into the mind of the person hearing it. Have you ever tried beating yourself up? There's just not enough room to swing a punch.

EMOTIONAL ROLLER-COASTER

A fair enough metaphor with the ups and downs
and all, but has lost all its punch through overuse.

GET IN TOUCH WITH

For example, your inner self, your feminine side,
your inner child, etc.

I CAN SEE WHERE YOU'RE COMING FROM

Why is this phrase so irritating? Is it because it's
verbose or patronising, or because you know that
the speaker is just about to contradict you?

ISSUES

One of those beautifully vague phrases that can
mean pretty much anything you want them to
mean. So it's quite possible for someone to say,
'He's got issues,' for someone else to nod in
agreement, and each to go away with a completely
different idea of what 'issues' the poor man has got.

LET'S NOT GO THERE

A rather overdramatic conversational raising
of the drawbridge that closes a particular track of

discussion. Why can't we just say, 'Let's not discuss that'? However, the phrase 'let's not go there' might be an appropriate response if your partner was suggesting, say, a honeymoon in a war zone.

MINDSET
Meaning 'fixed views or attitudes', but isn't it back to front? Shouldn't it be 'set mind'?

MOVE ON
One of the most common 'coping mechanisms' counsellors will suggest is to move on – in other words, try to forget that you've lost job, your wife/ husband has walked off with the kids, you are feeling suicidal and that now you are being professionally patronised. Try it when your counsellor presents his or her bill. 'Let's not dwell on it, eh? Let's move on.'

PERSONAL SPACE
Have materialism and possession reached such a point that we now own the space we exist in? And how does it work when we move around?

Is our 'personal space' moving with us? 'You're invading my personal space' is just the psychobabbler's way of saying, 'You're in my way.'

PLACE
'I didn't want to talk to anyone – I was in a very strange place then.' It really means 'frame of mind' but 'strange place' makes it sound much more mysterious and important.

(A BIT OF) SPACE
The thing that people experiencing emotional difficulties always tell you they need.
Unfortunately, when they tell you they would like 'a bit of space', what they mean is they would like 'a bit
of space' instead of the space currently occupied by you. It doesn't matter who else is in their space, but that bit of space exactly where you're standing – that's where they'd like 'a bit of space'.

TOUCHY-FEELY
It's impossible to hear this phrase without an unpleasant frisson of slight creepiness.

UNRECONSTRUCTED

For example, 'He's an unreconstructed sexist pig.'
An ugly word that means 'unchanged'. Let's hope
it doesn't mutate into 'unrebuilt' 'unrelived' or
other monstrosities.

Relationships

Of course, it's much harder to avoid clichés in spoken, rather than written, English and we shouldn't be too hard on people employing them in casual conversation, but if we lean on clichés too heavily it's as though our most personal, and what we might wish to be our most meaningful, conversations had been scripted by someone else.

CHEATING

If you happen to have sex with someone other than your partner and then fail to tell them about it, that's OK! It's nothing more than 'cheating'! If you get caught, however, your partner will probably not want to play with you again.

GIVING ME GRIEF

One of those clichés that overstate the case more than a little. Grief is what you might feel when someone close to you has died, not the petty annoyance of someone asking you to put the toilet seat down after using it.

I FEEL LIKE I'VE KNOWN YOU ALL MY LIFE
And that's a good thing?

I WANT TO HAVE YOUR CHILDREN
The ultimate make-your-mind-up line – though try to avoid saying it if you're a man.

I'M THERE FOR YOU
Where? Shouldn't you be here for them?

IT'S NOT YOU, IT'S ME
The classic get-out-of-relationship-free cliché that fans of *Seinfeld* will recall George Costanza claimed to have invented. The sad truth is that, if anyone in real life ever tells you, 'It's not you, it's me,' then it's not them, it's you.

LET'S NOT GET TOO HEAVY
Not a suggestion that you both lay off the burgers and doughnuts, but that you avoid an intense relationship.

QUALITY TIME
Good quality? Bad quality? What does it mean?

SOULMATE
The love of your life. The person you have most in common with on every conceivable level, including the spiritual, physical, intellectual and the what-colour-shall-we-paint-the-bathroom level.

TRIAL SEPARATION
A permanent separation that your partner wants you to believe is going to be only temporary for at least as long as it takes them to get out of the room and away from you.

WE'RE GOOD TOGETHER
That's probably what Hitler and Mussolini thought.

WE'RE PREGNANT
This biologically unlikely claim is often made by ultra-smug couples who wish to inform you that: (a) one of them is up the duff; and (b) their sickeningly mutually supportive relationship is so rock solid it might as well be both of them. Oh we're pregnant are we? That must be why we all suddenly feel like we're about to throw up.

YOU'RE THE BEST THING THAT'S EVER HAPPENED TO ME

Unless you're a total egomaniac, it makes you feel a bit sorry for the person saying it to you.

Lonely-hearts ads

When you place a lonely-hearts advertisement you want to stand out from the rest of the potential lovebirds; you want to communicate your unique appeal. So why do we see the same old descriptions again and again? Here are some examples.

ATTRACTIVE

Remember, newspapers always use phrases like 'attractive brunette' when they can't find anything physically appealing about the person in question.

BUBBLY

This can mean any one of a number of things:

---

unpredictable, excitable, mad as a mop, liable to jump on a table, strip naked and sing rude songs after a couple of drinks.

CUDDLY
Well, we all like a cuddle, but it does tend to make you sound like one of those giant teddy bears that people have to lug home from funfairs when they're proved to be a bit too good at shooting a popgun.

FORTY-SOMETHING
Go on, say you're 47! They'll find out eventually, anyway.

Teenage clichés

Teenagers should be too young to have had their heads filled with clichés but they don't need the 'tried and tested' clichés their parents use – they've got their very own. Sadly, some adults are picking up on the clichés teenagers use and they really should know better because it's, like, just soooo not grown up.

ALL THE TIME
Teenagers say they do something '(like) all the time' to denote an activity they have done very slightly more than once during their brief lives.

AWESOME
A hyperinflationary word of approbation that leaves the speaker with nowhere to go if they should happen to experience anything truly worthy of awe.

COOL
Cool was once a hippie-dippy expression of

the 1960s to express a sense of deep spiritual contentment. Before that it was a be-bop jazz-style expression denoting the ultimate in style, elegance and, well, cool. More recently it has become an unthinking and automatic response to almost any assertion or piece of news whatsoever. For example, 'We're going to my granddad's funeral on Thursday.' 'Cool!' In other words, it has been downgraded from its previous associations with spiritual nirvana or ultimate style to meaning 'OK' or 'Righto!'

DISS
Short for 'disrespect' and used as a verb. 'I hit him 'cos he dissed me.'

GROSS
'Gross' in teenage parlance means anything disgusting, ugly, hideous and in general utterly repulsive. As such it is synonymous with the word 'parent'. Other things that could be termed 'like totally gross' include a plate of steaming green vegetables. Hence the name of the place where you buy them: the gross-er's.

LIKE

A word used to pepper teenage conversation randomly. It serves sometimes to introduce a supposedly vivid but in fact completely detail-less piece of description, such as 'It was, like, totally amazing.' Other times it stands in place of words and phrases of which we can merely dream, 'We were all just, like, "Wow!"' Often 'like' is used to suggest a sense of vagueness and a nonchalant but charming youthful refusal to be tied down to precise detail. For instance, 'I'll only be, like, a few seconds' or 'I'll meet you at, like, eight-ish.' From this usage, however, it is often extended to give an aura of vagueness, even when the detail is extraordinarily precise, 'I'll meet you at, like, eight twenty-seven p.m.'

MEGA

Modern, youthlike way of saying 'big' or 'extremely' or 'very' or 'quite a lot'. 'Mega' can be used to turbocharge an adjective ('That's mega-cool!') or as an adjective in its own right ('That's mega!') or even as an entire sentence ('Mega!') How mega-annoying.

SO

How can this little word be a cliché all on its own? Well, put it into a sentence such as, 'It was so good fun!' and you'll see what we mean. Some blame it on the TV series *Friends*, and with friends like these …

SO NOT

'He is, like, so not funny.' See if you can rearrange these words into a meaningful sentence.

SOOOO …

Not to be confused with 'so', above. In the modern world there are only three emotional reactions that teenagers ever have. These are finding something 'soooo embarrassing', 'soooo amazing' or 'soooo gross'. As you will note, these phrases all belong with an elongated 'soooo', which is a simple and effective alternative to 'extremely', 'excessively' or 'intolerably', none of which would sound quite right coming out of the mouth of a teenager. To express even greater disgust, simply add more 'o's, as in 'The sight of my father in his swimming trunks was soooooooooooooooooooooooooooooooo oooooooooooooooo gross.'

TOTAL/COMPLETE

In teenage-speak the words 'total' and 'complete' will be used to emphasise just how negatively a negative label given to a person asserted to have some negative qualities is meant to be taken. Someone will be a 'total dork' or a 'complete slag'. It is, however, almost unheard of for anyone to be referred to as a 'partial dork' or a '47-per-cent slag'.

WELL

An amplifying prefix that can be tacked onto almost any word of a teenager's choosing: 'well good', 'well bad', 'well fit'. It has an uncomfortable ring of George Orwell's Newspeak about it – though the distinction of being shorter than 'double-plus'.

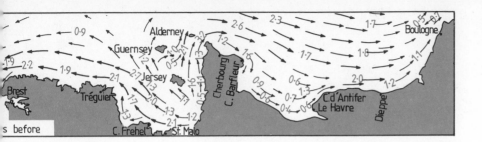

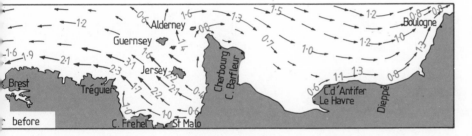

Mean rate of tidal streams in the Channel during the five hours leading up to HW DOVER.

Arrows indicate direction of the stream. The figures give average rate in knots at each point. For Spring rate, add one-third; at Neaps, subtract one-third of the figures shown on each chart.

For greater detail, see Admiralty Tidal Stream Atlases or relevant charts.

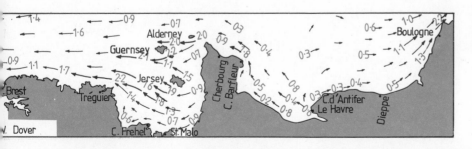

The Shell Pilot to the English Channel

The Shell Pilot to the English Channel

2. Harbours in Northern France and the Channel Islands

Dunkerque to Brest

Captain J. O. Coote, Royal Navy

with plans by
James Petter

A Shell Guide

faber and faber
LONDON · BOSTON

First published in 1985
by Faber and Faber Limited
3 Queen Square London WC1N 3AU
This revised edition first published in 1987

Printed in Great Britain by
Butler & Tanner Ltd, Frome, Somerset
All rights reserved

It is regretted that neither the book's sponsor, nor its author,
nor the publisher can accept responsibility for errors or
omissions, especially those brought about by changes made
by harbour and navigation authorities after the time of
going to press.

The Shell symbol and the name 'Shell' are both trademarks

Although sponsoring this book, Shell UK Ltd would point out
that the author is expressing his own views.

British Library Cataloguing in Publication Data
Coles, Adlard
The Shell pilot to the English Channel.—
2nd ed.
Harbours in Northern France and the Channel
Islands: Dunkerque to Brest
1. Pilot guides—English Channel   2. Harbours
—English Channel
I. Title   II. Coote, J. O.
623.89′2916336   VK839

ISBN 0-571-14988-X

For Antonia

CONTENTS

Indicates that under certain conditions of wind or tide entry may be impracticable or potentially hazardous.

This book is a companion volume to the *Shell Pilot to the South Coast Harbours* which covered those ports between Ramsgate and the Scillies considered suitable for a yacht drawing 2mo to visit. In 1982 it was my privilege to revise that standard work on behalf of Adlard Coles, who first produced it before the War.

I now set out to cover from Dunkerque to Brest, including the Channel Islands. It was tempting to extend the scope of the book a little farther, because there happen to be very attractive deepwater ports just off either end – Ostend and Camaret. The former is a convenient place to leave one's boat, for a brief return to the office or to change crews, because London is a little over three hours away by jetfoil and boat-train. Camaret is the ideal place to wait for the tide to turn at the Raz de Sein or Chenal du Four. It offers pontoon berths and waterfront bistros geared to the tastes of cruising yachtsmen.

With two exceptions all the pictures accompanying the text are hitherto unpublished. They were commissioned by me and taken during the nine-months' field-work period which began in July 1983. After weeks of waiting for the right weather, the whole aerial survey was completed in three days by Malcolm Knight and Graham Adams of Sealand Aerial Photography, Chichester, using respectively a Cessna 172 and a Hasselblad ELM, both about the right speed for the job. Nearly all the sea-level shots were taken by my daughter, Belinda Coote, mostly in the rain during bitterly cold, short winter days. She used an Olympus OM1 with 35–70mm lens and usually 400 ASA film, which literally made light of the discouraging environment. I shot dozens of reels along the whole route, but ended up only being able to claim most of the Channel Islands pictures in Part Four as my own. Credits are given wherever a picture was *not* taken by Sealand, my daughter or myself.

Once again, the simplified harbour plans have been drawn with care and distinction by James Petter of Petersfield.

I am also greatly indebted to friends who have put all or parts of my manuscript to the test of their local knowledge and literacy: Air Vice-Marshal Bill Crawford-Compton, Lt.-Commander Os de Las Casas, Katherine Dorey, Admiral Sir John Fieldhouse, Major-General Jim Gavin, Anne Parker (who also typed the whole book), Baron Danny Pouget, Donald Thompson and Rear-Admiral Sir John Woodward. At every port I found the local harbour masters helpful, if a little uncomprehending in the remoter backwaters of Brittany. Captain Roy Bullen, the Harbour Master at St Helier, was especially patient. So was my wife, without whose help with the research and administration underlying this considerable project it would never have seen the light of day.

Obviously I have been at pains to ensure that the most up-to-date and accurate data have gone to the printers, based on many sources and verified by my own observations. I am indebted to the Controller, HM Stationery Office, the Hydrographer of the Navy, the Service Hydrographique et Océanographique de la Marine (SHOM), the Éditions Cartographiques Maritimes (Navicartes) and Imray Laurie Norie and Wilson Ltd, for allowing me to refer to their charts and publications as part of the source-material where applicable.

At the head of the section on each port I have listed the charts recommended for use with my text and harbour plans as the most reliable guides to safe nagivation. Those shown in brackets are more suitable for making passage to the harbour approaches, rather than for entry or departure.

My aim has been to whet the appetite of the keelboat owner who has not yet discovered the wild, seductive beauty of the whole nor'west coast of France in all its moods. Originally I intended to limit the choice of harbours covered to those which a boat drawing 1m8 could sail right into and, after a brief wait in good shelter, reach an alongside berth. But I soon found that, the major commercial ports apart, I should have been writing a very slim book indeed. So I have included some half-tide stop-overs which I have found to be worth the diversion, as the *Guide Michelin* would put it. The list is entirely subjective, and I make no apologies for its omissions.

No matter how much care and attention are lavished on achieving accuracy, mistakes will emerge or evolve with the passage of time. Hence the cautionary waiver given such prominence by my publisher's lawyers. Please write and tell me if you have any corrections or constructive criticisms: c/o Faber and Faber Ltd, 3 Queen Square, London WC1N 3AU

John Coote
July 1984

Although there have not been so many physical changes along the coast of NW France as those which caused Part 1 (the South Coast Harbours) to be rewritten in its entirety, this new edition affords the opportunity of extending its coverage by adding six new harbours. All of them have limited access, but, barring one, may be of interest to those wanting to look farther afield.

The acknowledgements I made to those who helped me when writing it three years ago need amendment: two of them have moved farther up the Flag List of the Royal Navy; two of them have married (to each other); two new owners have added to the fun I had in revisiting the harbours – David Curling in his Beneteau 32 *Nephele* and Bengy Greenwell in his 42-ft TT Nelson *Dianti*. Moran Caplat updated the ports between the Somme and the Seine and was a convivial shipmate on several cruises elsewhere, during which he filled in some of the unprintable gaps in his witty autobiography, *From dinghies to divas*. Admiral Sir Anthony Morton, winner of the RCC's Founder's Prize in 1985, took a penetrating look at the NW corner of Brittany for me.

I am once again indebted to the same authorities listed in the July 1984 Foreword whose charts and publications were consulted during my research.

Many of the pictures are new, taken by me on a painfully slow learning-curve with a Nikon EM, while James Petter has brought the harbour plans up-to-date with evidently growing expertise.

I should like to thank the handful of readers who took the trouble to write pointing out errors or omissions. I hope many more will do so after sailing with this new book on their chart-tables. Send your letters to me c/o Faber and Faber Ltd, 3 Queen Square, London WC1N 3AU.

John Coote
May, 1987

PART ONE

GENERAL INFORMATION

Terms and symbols, abbreviations, conversion tables, radio
and weather, French–English glossary

CROSS-CHANNEL DISTANCES

Safe navigable routes between breakwaters and/or estuary entrances (in nautical miles)

	NORTH FORELAND	DUNGENESS	BEACHY HEAD	NAB TOWER	NEEDLES	ANVIL POINT	PORTLAND BILL	BERRY HEAD	RAME HEAD	LIZARD	BISHOP ROCK
BOULOGNE	39	25	51	97	125	137	157	196	227	269	318
DIEPPE	90	58	58	91	115	126	144	182	211	246	294
LE HAVRE LV	130	96	75	76	88	94	106	140	165	198	246
GRANDCAMP	158	122	94	78	80	82	89	116	140	175	223
CHERBOURG	164	128	98	66	60	57	60	84	106	141	188
ALDERNEY	180	144	114	74	61	53	49	65	85	118	167
ST PETER PORT	201	165	134	96	83	73	65	70	90	112	157
ST HELIER	219	183	151	113	101	94	87	94	108	130	173
ST MALO	245	209	178	140	127	120	113	117	138	145	183
LÉZARDRIEUX	243	207	175	134	123	113	102	92	100	108	146
MORLAIX	274	238	206	169	149	138	124	106	100	92	123
L'ABER-WRAC'H	300	264	231	195	171	159	146	117	103	84	104
LE CONQUET	325	289	252	216	192	179	161	136	120	98	110
BREST	342	306	269	233	209	196	178	153	137	115	127

Layout The ports covered are dealt with from east to west (Dunkerque to Brest) with the Channel Islands and adjacent coast of France between the Normandy and North-West Brittany sections.

Charts and Conventions Nearly all the 53 ports have their own simplified harbour plans specially drawn for this book to the approximate scale shown on each. These plans should not be relied upon for navigation; they are a simplified version of the best data available from several sources including my own observation. To assist yachtsmen select the best charts available, their publisher and listed numbers are shown at the head of each port. The most suitable are usually of a scale of 15,000:1 or less. The least useful are given in brackets. Their origins are abbreviated as follows:

BA   British Admiralty chart by the Hydrographer of the Navy

Fr   French Navy chart by Service Hydrographique et Océanographique de la Marine (SHOM)

Stan   Stanfords Coloured charts by Barnacle Marine Ltd

Im   Imray Laurie Norie and Wilson Ltd

CG   Carte Guide de Navigation Côtière by Éditions Cartographiques Maritimes (Navicarte)

The last three are the handiest: they have concertina-folds in the manner of road-maps, although Imray will supply theirs unfolded if desired. Those issued by the two navies are delivered with a single fold usually 110 × 50cm (about 43 × 20in). The choice of those to have on board will be determined partly by their scale and legibility, but also on the basis of what individual yacht navigators feel most comfortable with. Familiarity with French Navy charts is not an easily acquired taste for British sailors; there is the language problem, and their style, presentaton and symbols are significantly different.

For planning purposes it is best to have a general chart(s) covering the whole Channel (BA 2675, ImC 10 and 12 or Stan 1 and 2). Then, considering the high cost of charts and their short shelf-life, shop around for what you really need. The price of an unused chart would buy four dozen oysters and a litre of Muscadet in St Vaast, while a full set of Admiralty charts covering the area will cost over £300 at today's prices.

Distances are given in nautical miles (n.m.) and cables (200yds) at sea; in kilometres and metres on land (see conversion table p. 20). The range of lights is shown by 'M' after numerals indicating nominal range in nautical miles.

Heights are given in metres. Against a light's characteristics its height above sea level is given by numerals with the suffix 'm'. Thus 36m 19M is a light 36 metres above sea level with a nominal range of 19 nautical miles. Conspicuous objects ashore may have their heights indicated by numerals in brackets.

Bearings and Courses are True, to which local magnetic Variation should be added ($5\frac{1}{2}$°W. in the Straits of Dover to 8°W. off Brest) and Deviation (if any) applied for ship's magnetic compass readings. Unless otherwise stated all bearings of shore points mentioned in the text are *from seaward*.

Times of High Water For each port the average time difference is given relevant to HW Dover and to the nearest Standard Port (SP). Nearly every port has its own local tide-tables usually available free from a chandlery or HO, which may be more precise. All times are based on GMT or the time prevailing at the SP, expressed as two figures for hours (h.) followed by two for minutes.

Heights above Chart Datum are given in metres and centimetres for Springs and Neaps at Mean High Water (MHW) and Mean Low Water (MLW). To be more precise consult Admiralty Tide Tables, but even then tide levels can vary significantly due to strong winds persisting for any length of time from the same quarter.

Chart Symbols – Lights and Buoys   Some of the characteristics used in this book in two languages:

English	Characteristic	French
F	Fixed	Fixe, Fx, or F
Fl	Flashing	é
LFl	Long Flash	él
Oc	Occulting	Occ
Q	Quick Flashing	Scint or sc
Fl (2) 3s.	Group Flash (2) every 3s.	F 2é (3s)
W	White	b
R	Red	r
G	Green	v
Vi	Violet	vi
Bu	Blue	bl
Y	Yellow	j
B	Black	N
Grey	Grey	Gris
Or	Orange	Or
Iso	Isophase	Iso
Alt	Alternating	Alt
Oc (1 + 2) WG 12s.	Composite Group Occulting 1 eclipse followed by 2 White Green every 12 seconds	F.20.10(12s.)bv
Ø Lts . . . (degs)	Lights in transit	2 Feux à . . . (degs)
RW VS	Red/White Vertical Stripes	

Note that in giving the colours of lights the French use small letters (e.g. 'r', 'v' for RG) but in describing buoys or light structures their colours are indicated by capital letters. Thus an N-cardinal buoy (BY) would be 'NJ' and a BRB isolated danger mark 'NRN'.

Other Abbreviations Used and French Equivalents

TG	Digital Tide Gauge
HM	Harbour Master (Capitainerie)
HA	Harbour Authority (Affaires Maritimes)
HO	Harbour or Marina Office (Bureau du Port)
Y Hbr	Marina (Port de Plaisance)
YC	Yacht Club (Club Nautique, Cercle Nautique)
SC	Sailing Club ('Voile' suffix)
FW	Fresh Water (eau douce)
Fuel	Petrol or diesel (carburant)
Ⓥ	Visitors berths (Apportement visiteurs) or (places réservées au passage)
➞	Right hand edge (le tombant droite)
⟵	Left hand edge (le tombant gauche)
SP	Standard port – for tides.

French–English Glossary (excluding the obvious – *quai*, *jetée, môle, île*, etc)

Navigation Marks

à bâbord	to port
à damier	chequered
à tribord	to starboard
balise	beacon
carré	square
charpente pyl.	lattice tower
cloche (cl)	bell
cyl	round
échelle	scale
épave	wreck
falaise	cliff
flèche	spire
klaxon or typhon	horn
los.	diamond

marques cardinales — cardinal buoys
marques latérales — lateral buoys
phare — lighthouse
radiophare — radio beacon
roche (Rc) — rock
sens conventionel — buoyage direction
sifflet (s) — whistle
tour or tourelle — tower
voy. — topmark

Harbours and Approaches

amer — landmark
anse — bay
asséchage — drying berth
barre — bar
basse mer — low water
bassin à flot — wet basin
bouée — buoy
brise-lames — breakwater
cale — slipway
chenal — channel
darse — basin
digue — mole or breakwater
douane — customs
échouage — beaching
écluse — lock-gates
étale — slack water
flot — flood tide
galets — shingle
grève — sandy beach
grue — crane
jusant — ebb tide
marée — tide
morte eau — Neap tide

mouillage — anchorage
pleine mer — high water
terre-plein — levelled ground
vive-eau — Spring tide

Traffic Signals in use in French Ports With the advent of high-density lights, flags and shapes are gradually being replaced. For most ports other than the major ones, the 'simplified' system is in use. Sometimes, as in opening swing-bridges or lock-gates, ordinary road traffic lights are used, which are self-explanatory.

	SIMPLIFIED SYSTEM		NORMAL SYSTEM	
	DAY	NIGHT	DAY	NIGHT
No Entry	▮ R	● R	● B ▲ B ● B	● R ○ W ● R
No departure	▮ G	● G	▼ B ▲ B ▼ B	● G ○ W ● G
Neither way permitted	▮ R ▮ G	● R ● G	▼ B ▲ B ● B	● G ○ W ● R
Emergency Port shut	● R ● R ● R	● R ● R ● R	SAME	
Port open– Navigate with care	Code Flags	● G ● G ● G	SAME	

Depth and Tidal Signals Shown in a Few Major Ports

	DAY		NIGHT	
Tide Rising	▲	B	●	G
			○	W
High Water	⊠	W B cross	○○	W
Tide Falling	▼	B	○	W
			●	G
Low Water	▰	Bu	●●	G

Depth Above Datum Shown by 3 Hoists in Parallel
(from l to rt)

KEY:

B ▼ or ● G Lt	B ■ or ● R Lt	B ● or ○ W Lt
per 0m 2	*per 1m 0*	*per 5m 0*

EXAMPLES

DAY (shapes)		DAY or NIGHT (Lts)	
▼■ ▼■●		●G ●R ●G ●R ○W	
▼		●R ●R	
▼		●R	
▼			
1m 8 (6 ft)	6m2	2m2	8m4

Special Signals Some of the major commercial ports also use supplementary signals to indicate movements by very large ships, those with special cargoes or ferries. If in doubt keep out of the way. It is always best to enter or leave a busy port under power – many insist that you should do so. On arrival at any major port get a copy of the local by-laws. Otherwise keep in mind Rule 9(b) of the International Regulations for Preventing Collisions at sea:

> A vessel of under 20m in length or a sailing vessel shall not impede the passage of a vessel which can safely navigate only within a narrow channel or fairway.

Weather Forecasts In addition to the BBC shipping forecasts put out at 0033, 0555, 1355, 1750 daily, on British time Radio 4 200kHz or 1500m, there are numerous local forecasts, applicable mainly to the English coast. BBC's long wave can be ready easily throughout the area covered by this book.

The French reporting areas from Dunkerque to Brest (with equivalent British areas):

No. 9	Sandettie	(Dover area)
No. 10	Manche Est	(Wight)
No. 11	Manche Ouest	(Portland and Plymouth)
No. 12	Ouest Bretagne	(N Biscay)

These areas are all covered on Radio France Allouis long-wave transmissions in French on 164kHz (1820m) at 0725 and 1850 GMT. Also Radio France on 1071kHz (170m) in West Brittany. In summer there are special small craft forecasts as well. There are eight local VHF forecasts within the area covered by the book. They are noted in the text for the ports concerned. Boulogne and Brest mention wave forecasts on 1771 and 1673kHz at 0703 and 1733.

Marinecall forecasts through UK telephone service cover French coastal waters as follows:

0898–500 456 Le Havre – Calais
0898–500 457 Channel Isles and Cherbourg
0898–500 458 N Brittany

VHF Frequencies

The universal calling and safety frequency is Channel 16 (156.800MHz calling) which must never be cluttered by routine traffic. Most merchantmen and all warships and coastal stations keep a listening watch on it, so it is permissible to call a ship on sighting, but be ready to switch to a working frequency. Here is a list of VHF channels and frequencies used as working frequencies by shore stations:

Ch 1	160.650MHz	Calais
2	160.700	Dieppe St Malo
3	160.750	Port-en-Bessin
9	156.450	Generally used by French yacht harbours
10	156.500	
11	156.500	Honfleur
12	156.600	Widely used for port control
13	156.650	
14	156.700	
23	156.150	Boulogne Le Havre
24	161.800	Dunkerque Dieppe Ushant
25	161.850	Boulogne
26	161.900	Brest/Le Conquet
27	161.950	Cherbourg
28	162.000	Le Havre Brest/Le Conquet
37	157.850	(Marina band)
61	160.675	Dunkerque
67	156.375	(UK Coastguards)
68	156.425	Ouistreham
70	156.525	Distress & safety exclusive
82	161.725	Le Havre Ushant
83	156.175	Plougasnou (Morlaix Bay)
84	161.825	Paimpol
87	161.975	Calais
88	162.025	Calais VHF Rdo Lt.Ho.

Radio (R/T or Rdo D/F)

Morse Code and Phonetic Alphabet

A	.–	Alfa
B	–...	Bravo
C	–.–.	Charlie
D	–..	Delta
E	.	Echo
F	..–.	Foxtrot
G	––.	Golf
H	....	Hotel
I	..	India
J	.–––	Juliet
K	–.–	Kilo
L	.–..	Lima
M	––	Mike
N	–.	November
O	–––	Oscar
P	.––.	Papa
Q	––.–	Quebec
R	.–.	Romeo
S	...	Sierra
T	–	Tango
U	..–	Uniform
V	...–	Victor
W	.––	Whisky
X	–..–	X-Ray
Y	–.––	Yankee
Z	––..	Zulu
é	..–..	

DEPTH CONVERSION SCALE.   Fathoms & Feet ——— Metres & Decimetres

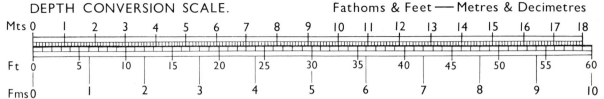

Conversion Factors (one place of decimals)

n.m.	Km	n.m.	Km
1	1.9	8	14.8
2	3.7	9	16.7
3	5.6	10	18.5
4	7.4	20	37.0
5	9.3	30	55.6
6	11.1	40	74.1
7	13.0	50	92.6

metres	ft/ins.	metres	ft/ins.
0.1	4"	0.8	2'7"
0.2	8"	0.9	2'11"
0.3	1'0"	1.0	3'3"
0.4	1'4"	1.2	3'11"
0.5	1'8"	1.4	4'7"
0.6	2'0"	1.6	5'3"
0.7	2'4"	1.8	5'11"

Planning for a Cruise to France   There is an admirable booklet, *RYA Cruising* C1/87 Vol. 1, which gives plain guidance so as not to be caught with your documents down on cruising to France. It is available from: Royal Yachting Association, Victoria Way, Woking, Surrey, GU21 1EQ (tel. 04862–5022). The French Government Tourist Office at 178 Piccadilly, London W1V 0AL (tel. 01–491 7622) is also worth contacting, preferably by a personal visit.

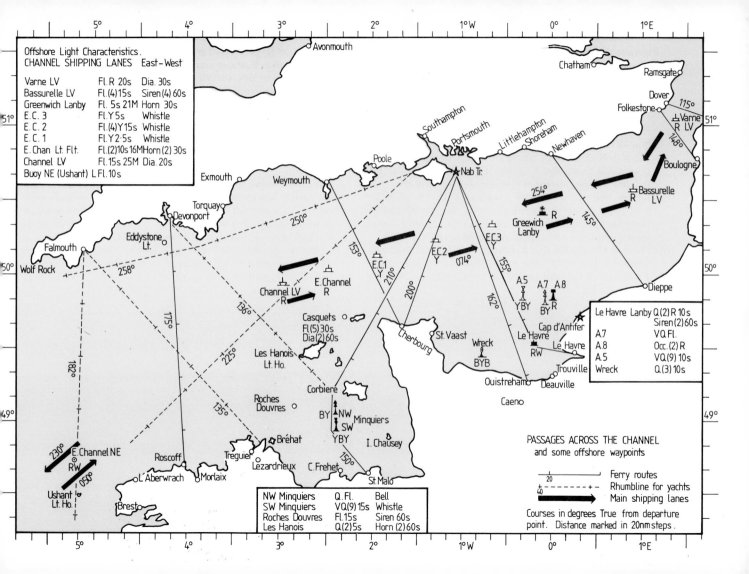

Offshore Light Characteristics.
CHANNEL SHIPPING LANES East–West

Varne LV	Fl. R 20s	Dia. 30s
Bassurelle LV	Fl.(4)15s	Siren (4) 60s
Greenwich Lanby	Fl. 5s 21M	Horn 30s
E.C. 3	Fl.Y 5s	Whistle
E.C. 2	Fl.(4)Y 15s	Whistle
E.C. 1	Fl.Y 2·5s	Whistle
E.Chan Lt.Flt.	Fl.(2)10s 16M	Horn (2) 30s
Channel LV	Fl.15s 25M	Dia. 20s
Buoy NE (Ushant)	L Fl.10s	

Le Havre Lanby Q(2) R 10s
	Siren (2) 60s
A.7	VQ. Fl.
A.8	Occ.(2) R
A.5	VQ(9) 10s
Wreck	Q.(3) 10s

NW Minquiers	Q. Fl.	Bell
SW Minquiers	VQ(9) 15s	Whistle
Roches Douvres	Fl.15s	Siren 60s
Les Hanois	Q.(2) 5s	Horn (2) 60s

PASSAGES ACROSS THE CHANNEL
and some offshore waypoints

Ferry routes
Rhumbline for yachts
Main shipping lanes

Courses in degrees True from departure
point. Distance marked in 20nm steps.

Signposts There are many unexpected aids to navigation to help you find your way across the Channel and make a safe landfall. Some of them are on the general chart on page 21.

Before departure

(a) Check crews each have *passports* – they may never be called for unless any of them visits a casino, wants to use a Eurocheque card at a bank or return to UK independently. Non-EEC citizens need French visas.

(b) *Clear UK customs* by filling in Part 1 of Form C 1328, obtainable from any Customs House and at most UK marinas. Keep the rest of the form for your return.

(c) Unless you are an officially registered British ship and hold *ship's papers* in a hardback cover, you can always put your boat on the Small Ships' Register. It only costs a tenner and can be obtained quickly through the RYA.

(d) Have a British ensign, a French flag for the starboard yardarm, and a 'Q' flag to be shown until cleared by French customs and police (immigration). In practice, even at large ports of entry like Cherbourg, let alone small ones like Barfleur, you may have difficulty in finding anyone to pay the slightest attention to your arrival – except the man collecting harbour/berthing dues and possibly the agent for duty free stores.

Cautionary Notes Many harbours listed in the remainder of the book have restricted access due to tide or weather. They are prefixed by an asterisk both in the Contents and on the chapter heading. The text following will make the dangers apparent.

Times quoted for opening and shutting of lock-gates may vary according to the tidal range (or 'coefficient', as the French say). If in doubt call the local harbour master on the telephone number listed. You will seldom be wrong if you show up at the lock-gates half an hour before local HW.

Above all, don't bring back a pet or stray animal from France, unless you are prepared to face the stiff quarantine regulations governing their entry.

PART TWO

PAS DE CALAIS – SOMME

Dunkerque – St Valéry-sur-Somme

including the main ferry ports for day-trippers, retreating armies
and invasion forces who hesitate too long while weighing up
the odds of making it to Kent

Soundings and heights in metres
Bearings and courses in degrees true
Distances at sea in nautical miles or cables

Safe navigable distances from breakwater to breakwater or fairway buoys
(in nautical miles)

RAMSGATE	RAMSGATE					
DUNKERQUE	39	**DUNKERQUE**				
CALAIS	27	**20**	CALAIS			
BOULOGNE	37	**41**	20	**BOULOGNE**		
LE TOUQUET/ÉTAPLES	48	**51**	32	**12**	LE TOUQUET/ÉTAPLES	
ST VALÉRY/LE CROTOY	66	**69**	50	**30**	19	**ST VALÉRY/LE CROTOY**
BRIGHTON	81	**96**	78	**65**	97	**71** BRIGHTON

1 DUNKERQUE

Charts: BA 1350 Fr 6500 Im C30 (CG 1010 Stan 1)

High Water *+00h. 50m. Dover   SP Dunkerque*
Heights above Datum *MHWS 5m8. MLWS 0m6.
MHWN 4m8. MLWN 1m5.*

DUNKERQUE is remembered by my generation for the miraculous deliverance in May 1940 of 340,000 troops, one-third of them across open beaches to the E of the town. It was not the first time the port had had an army waiting to be taken off. In 1588 the Duke of Medina Sidonia's fleet was caught off Calais because, with their deep draught, his ships were unable to navigate through the shoals to their rendezvous with the Duke of Parma's invasion army in Dunkerque.

Pictures taken in 1940 and the town's earlier fame as the home port of the famous corsair Jean-Bart in Louis XIV's day do not prepare one for the shock of first sailing into the harbour today. It is now France's third port, handling ships up to 300,000 tons on its 12 miles of quaysides. It has a vast industrial complex spewing smoke over the western side of the town, and a major shipyard to the E.

All this and most of today's city of 85,000 inhabitants and its economy have been restored since the war. Hence the inevitable name of the massive locks leading from the Avant-Port to the endless succession of commercial docks – Charles de Gaulle.

In the middle of it all, opposite the shipyard, and within walking distance of downtown Dunkerque, there are three local YCs each with its own pontoon berths, just 45 miles from Ramsgate, accessible at all states of the tides and perfectly sheltered.

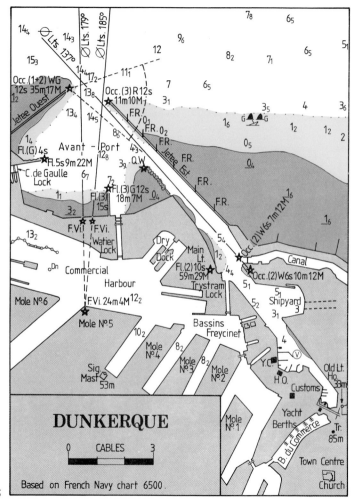

1.1 West jetty lighthouse with three conspicuous flanges

Approaches

From the West Pick up the Dunkerque Lanby Light buoy 4 miles N of the entrance to Calais. This is a 10m-high R tubular structure on a flat circular buoy with a 25M Fl 3 s. Lt and a continuous Rdo Bn, callsign 'DK' on 294.2kHz with a notional 10M range. Its fog signal is (3) 60 s. This buoy is $\frac{1}{2}$ mile ENE of the R. Dyck buoy – Fl R (2) 6 s.

Head 100° for $2\frac{1}{2}$ miles to pick up the first of fifteen pairs of Fl R and G buoys. R cans are even-numbered starting DW2 to port: G pillars, odd-numbered to starboard from DW1 to DW29 outside the entrance to Dunkerque harbour.

This channel (Passe de l'Ouest) is 15 miles long and in places only 3 cables wide. It has a least depth of 11.5m, but there are graveyard shoals on either side for most of the passage.

Between DW9 and 11 you pass 2 miles off Gravelines. Leaving DW15 to starboard you are right outside Dunkerque Ouest.

From the East Pass $3\frac{1}{2}$ miles off Nieuport towards the West Diep and the Passe de Zuydcoote and leave to port on SW'ly course the Nieuport Bank buoy (YBY pillar with W-cardinal topmark, (Q (9) 15 s.)); 4 miles farther on course 235° is the first of the E channel buoys (S-cardinal Q (6) 10 s.). It is No.E12. The six odd-numbered buoys to be left to port start with E11 8 cables S of E 12. Course 210° hits off the narrowest part of the channel, S of Banc Hills between E8 and E7. Note that E10 is the only one without a Lt.

Here course is altered to 260° (leaving all the R buoys to starboard) to pick up the G pillar E1 buoy with cone topmark and Lt Fl (2) G 6 s. The harbour entrance is $1\frac{1}{2}$ miles course 245° from here.

Harbour Entrance In following all the foregoing and especially when approaching the entrance to the Avant-Port, the tidal stream runs ENE across your course at up to $3\frac{1}{2}$ knots

26

1.2   East jetty showing red lights along breakwater and main town lighthouse on the right. Entrance for yachts is between these points

1.3   Another view of the lighthouse from the Yacht Club de la Mer du Nord pontoons opposite the shipyard

1.4   Visitors' berths at the Yacht Club on outboard end of pontoons

at Springs, starting $2\frac{1}{2}$h. before HW Dunkerque ($-$01h. 40m. on HW Dover). The WSW tide starts $3\frac{1}{2}$h. after local HW ($+$04h. 15m. Dover). Going through the entrance leave to starboard the W jetty Lt Ho 35m high (Oc (1 + 2) WG 12 s. with a range of 17M). The Tr stands 35m above the sea and looks like a pepper grinder fitted with three flat flanges just below the part carrying the Lt (pic 1.1). It is listed as a W Tr, but the stonework has aged and it looks more terra cotta. Its fog signal is (1 + 2) 60 s. Standard Lt traffic signals are shown here (see p. 17).

The E jetty-head (pic 1.2) is less impressive – just a W metal lattice tower with an R top, a mere 11m off the sea. Its Lt is Oc (3) R 12 s. and has a range of 10M. Foghorn (3) 30 s.

There is an unusual arrangement of F Vi Lts to help the big ships making the entrance on the correct course of 182°. They may be of help to check that the tide is being correctly offset. The rear Lt lines up with two forward ones having intensified transits on 185° and 179° respectively.

The most impressive and conspicuous landmark is the 59m high W Lt Ho 8 cables SE of the harbour entrance. Its Lt is Fl (2) 10 s. with a range of 29 miles. It lies on the W bank of the old port, the only one of interest to visiting yachtsmen. Directly opposite, on the E bank, is the entrance to the Wateringues Canal with leading Lts at its entrance, each Oc (2) 6 s. on W columns with R tops, lined up to 137°, the course a visitor should now be taking up-harbour.

1.5   The hospitable Yacht Club de la Mer du Nord

1.6   Old lighthouse beyond the Yacht Club with fishing club berths just around the corner to starboard

1.7   Sizeable keelboats in the Bassin du Commerce, only accessible through a lock and two swingbridges

VHF contact can be made on Ch 16, 12, or 73.

Berthing and Facilities   Just beyond the shipyard there is the first Yacht Hbr, which has 250 alongside berths. It is the property of the YC de la Mer du Nord, a hospitable little clubhouse on the W bank with a least depth at its berths of 3m85. Visitors should secure on the outside of the pontoon running parallel to the shore and farthest out (pics 1.3, 1.4 and 1.5).

FW, diesel and electricity all available. There are full repair and chandlery facilities. There is a gridiron and a 4½-ton crane.

Telephone number for the administration is (28) 66–79–90, while the clubhouse is on (28) 66–17–84. Weather forecasts on (28) 67–03–46.

The main Harbour Board offices are next door, and customs a block farther away: tel. (28) 66–96–64.

There are more pontoon berths farther upstream, but not of immediate use to visitors. The Fishing Club's berths are where the arm of the harbour ends with a causeway linking dockland with the centre of town (pic 1.6). There are yacht berths on pontoons in the Bassin du Commerce, but yachts can only get in or out through a succession of locks as part of the commercial docks area (pic. 1.7).

From the YC it is a quarter of a mile's walk to the heart of town, with all the amenities of a prosperous commercial and industrial city.

Communications   Unless you want to drive to Paris, in which case the start of the autoroute is only 10km S, travel is not easy. The E–W roads are hard work – the nearest ferries (to Dover or Ramsgate) are at Dunkerque Ouest, 5km away. There is no near-by airport.

Weather   On tape (28) 65–03–46 or on VHF Ch 61 at 0633 and 1133 (Area 9 Sandettie).

*2 GRAVELINES

Charts: BA 1350 CG 1010 Fr 650

High Water +ooh. 40m. Dover SP Dunkerque
Heights above Datum MHWS 5m9. MLWS 0m4.
MHWN 4m8. MLWN 1m7.

GRAVELINES is an unattractive suburb of Dunkerque over-shadowed by a massive nuclear power station on the beach immediately to its E. The harbour all but dries out at LW, but it nevertheless supports a moderate fishing fleet which takes its catches from around the rotting frames of the Spanish Armada, where they have lain outside the harbour since Drake put them there in 1588. I can think of no particular reason for going there unless you lock into the Bassin Vauban a mile inshore.

Approach and Berthing From the westward pick up the Dunkerque Lanby 4 miles N of Calais and follow the buoyed channel to No. DW5, then you will be 2 miles NW of the twin breakwaters and within the intensified 6° beam of the Oc W 4 s. Lt on the 30m Lt Ho at the root of the E mole. It is very conspicuous, with a B helical lollipop design on its W superstructure. By day bring it in transit on 142° with the conspicuous W water Tr inland, showing just open to the right of the church steeple in Petit Fort Philippe on the E side of the river.

From the E you sail past the 1940 evacuation beaches and the long industrialized coastline of Dunkerque until reaching the DW9 buoy. The course to be made good from that point is 139°, allowing for tides running parallel to the shore-line at up to 3½ knots at Springs. An onshore wind can make the

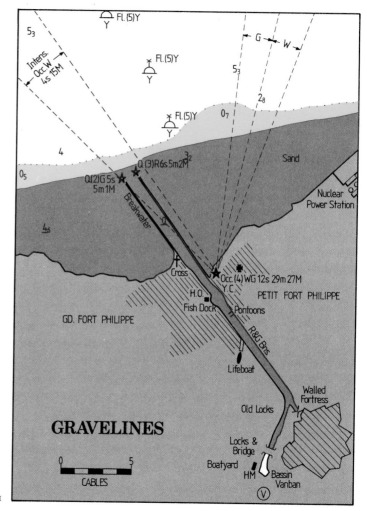

2.1 Lighthouse at Petite Fort Philippe on east bank at harbour mouth

harbour entrance hazardous. The Lts at the seaward ends of the breakwaters are Q (2) G 5 s. and Q (3) R 6 s.

Once inside the breakwaters the channel is clearly marked with R and G tripod Bns all the way to the lock-gates outside the Bassin Vauban. There is a waiting pontoon. The gates may open and the road-bridge be raised $1\frac{1}{2}$h. either side of HW.

Near the harbour entrance on the W bank at Grand Fort Philippe there is a commercial quay, not to be used by yachts. The handful of pontoon berths on the other side of the harbour are privately-owned by members of the local YC, whose premises are immediately in front of the spectacular Lt Ho.

Inside the Bassin Vauban there are a dozen pontoon berths, with shore power and water laid on, reserved for visiting yachts. There is also a major boatyard capable of any repairs. Draughts up to 2m0 can be accommodated.

The HM is on tel. (28) 23–13–42. Customs at (28) 23–08–52.

The YCs are the Gravelinois and the Centre Nautique de l'Aa (try pronouncing it).

Communications Sally Line ferries from the near-by Dunkerque West Gare Maritime to Ramsgate.

Weather See Dunkerque.

2.2   View from west bank showing numbered channel tripod beacons, old lifeboat station (right) and on far horizon prominent water-tower which forms daylight entry transit with the lighthouse

2.3   Waiting pontoon outside Bassin Vauban

3 CALAIS

Charts: BA 1352 Fr 6474 Im C30 (CG 1010 Stan 1)

High Water   +00h.25m. Dover   SP Calais
Heights above Datum   MHWS 6m8. MLWS 0m7.
MHWN 5m5. MLWN 2m0.

JUST 21 miles across the Straits of Dover Calais is the nearest French port to England. Indeed, for two centuries until 1558 it was part of England, which might justify a parallel claim to those demanding sovereignty over the Falklands or Gibraltar, unless the wishes of 80,000 inhabitants were held to be 'paramount'.

The links with England go beyond 140 daily ferry movements in the summer which handle over six million tourists. Here in 1588 Drake's fireships panicked the Spanish Armada into the wastes of the North Sea and oblivion. In the First World War it was uncomfortably close to the front line, but did not fall into German hands until the Second World War, in May 1940, after a stubborn, sacrificial rearguard action by the Green Jackets stopped the panzers from rushing Dunkerque from the W.

For nearly 200 years it has been the centre of the lace industry, brought to Calais from Nottingham.

Rodin's famous statue of the *Six Burghers of Calais*, who saved the population from being put to the sword by Edward III in 1347, is in the park in front of the colourful gingerbread baroque Town Hall, faintly reminiscent of St Pancras station.

Gales from the NW–NE across the sandbanks can make the entrance very uncomfortable, but, inside, the Bassin de l'Ouest has the whole of its right-hand quay over 600m long functioning as a secure Yacht Hbr.

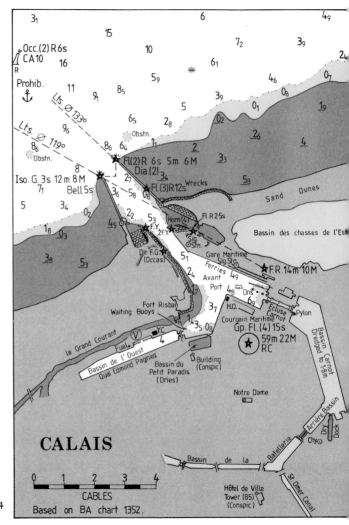

34

3.1   Entrance from seaward. Note new Harbour and Traffic Control Office (A).   Yacht harbour is off to right of picture

3.2   Ruins of Fort Risban on right, 1848 lighthouse on left. The yacht is about to pick up one of the waiting moorings outside the yacht harbour

3.3   View of yacht harbour in Bassin de l'Ouest from the swingbridge

For the best all-round view climb the 271 steps to the top of the old Lt Ho in the heart of town, midway between the ferry terminals and the marina.

Approaches   There is a bank (Ridens de la Rade) running parallel to the shore up to one mile off. Its least depth of 0m5 at LW Springs effectively discourages any direct inshore approach from the E, except on the top half of the tide and when it is not blowing from the NE–NW. Then it can be imprudent to enter at all.

The safest bet is to lay off a course to a point a mile W of the town and make your landfall on the R can bell buoy CA8 with a Q R light, leave it to port and head 095° for the entrance a mile away. A safe bearing of 110° on the town's most prominent light holds good all the way to the English coast

22 miles away. The light is Fl (4) 15 s. from an octagonal W Tr 51m high. It has a 20M Rdo Bn callsign 'CS' on 305.7kHz. As always in these parts the need to make full allowance for tidal currents in determining courses made good is paramount. Off the entrance the ENE stream starts $3\frac{1}{2}$h. before HW Dover, while it turns WSW 3h. after HW Dover. The maximum rate at Springs is nearly 3 knots.

The outer ends of the two breakwaters forming the entrance are marked as follows:

E head   W post 5m high. Lt Fl (2) R 6 s. 6M.
W head   W tower, G top 12m 8M. The Lt is Iso G 3 s.
          The fog signal is a bell ev 5 s.

By night a transit of the latter with the intensified F R 14M Lt at the Gare Maritime on 118° is a useful guide. By day it

36

3.4   Marina office with all club facilities

is better to come in on a 138° transit of the W jetty head with the Town's main Lt (see above).

It is obligatory to enter and leave under power and to keep out of the way of all commercial traffic (pic 3.1).

About 3 cables inside the entrance the fairway narrows. The ferries haul off to port to their RO/RO terminals. Yachts should alter slowly round the abandoned Fort Risban towards the lock-gates in front of the Bassin de l'Ouest (pic. 3.2).

Berthing and Facilities   The HM and port traffic control are now housed in a prominent, grey-slate three-storeyed building with one sloping side situated on the knuckle of the E bank of the narrowest part of the fairway. Lt signals in accordance with the Normal System govern traffic movement.

VHF on Ch 12.

There are 28 R mooring buoys laid right outside the lock and bridge, intended for yachts to await the rather infrequent opening times, which are for a few minutes 2h. and 1h. before HW and 1h. afterwards.

An Or light at the lock is a 10-min warning. G means go; R forbids all movements. The precise times are posted at the lock-keeper's office and in the Yacht Hbr clubhouse.

Inside the basin, where there is a least depth of 3m5, up to 120 visiting yachts can pick up any available berth on the right-hand side of the basin and then report to the office within the building, which has all the facilities of a YC, but is not so designated. The YC du Nord de la France has boat parking facilities in the old Fort, but not much else (pics 3.3 and 3.4).

The Yacht Hbr has FW, diesel, electricity and a crane for boat storage: tel. (21) 34–55–23. No restaurants of distinction.

The Customs are on: (21) 34–75–40.

Communications   Ferries to Dover and Folkestone. Hovercraft to Dover. SNCF to Paris.

Weather   Reports from Boulogne: tel. (21) 31–79–90, or VHF Ch 87 at 0633 and 1133. Area 9 Sandettie.

*4 BOULOGNE

Charts: BA 438   Fr 6436   Im C3   CG 1011   Stan 9
High Water   − *00h. 07m. Dover   SP Boulogne*
Heights above Datum   *MHWS 9m0.   MLWS 0m9.*
MHWN 7m0.   MLWN 2m7.

ALTHOUGH only 4 miles farther from Dover than Calais, Boulogne has surprisingly lagged behind as a tourist attraction, with 3,500,000 visitors a year. The thirteenth-century walled town dominating the city has as its centrepiece the Notre Dame Cathedral built in the mid-nineteenth century to replace one laid waste by the revolutionaries. It is on the site where a vision of Our Lady was claimed in the seventh century.

A

4.1   (A) Note north breakwater mostly submerged so as to reduce tidal current across entrance. Yachts follow the same route inward as car ferries

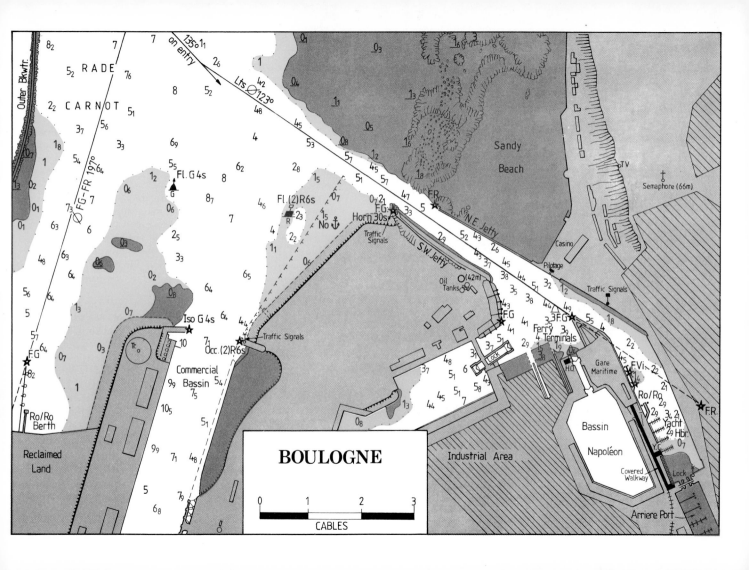

BOULOGNE

CABLES

0   1   2   3

RADE CARNOT

Outer Bkwtr.

Fl. G 4s

Fl. (2) R 6s

No ⚓

Horn 30s

Traffic Signals

S.W. Jetty

N.E. Jetty

Sandy Beach

Semaphore (66m)

Casino

Pilotage

Traffic Signals

Oil Tanks

F.G

3FG

Ferry Terminals

Gare Maritime

F Vi

Ro/Ro

Yacht Hbr.

F.R.

Bassin Napoléon

Covered Walkway

Lock

Arriere Port

Industrial Area

Iso G 4s

Occ.(2)R 6s

Traffic Signals

Commercial Bassin

FG

Ro/Ro Berth

Reclaimed Land

Tr.

on entry

Lts ⊘ 123°

FG - FR 197°

FR

4.2   *Head of south mole (Carnot)*

4.3   *Head of north mole*

It was the jumping-off point for two invasions of England, which never got beyond assembling all the troops in readiness, led by Julius Caesar and Napoleon Bonaparte – to name but two. Napoleon left a reminder in the shape of a Column 143m high on the skyline dedicated to his Grand Army.

Today it is France's most active fishing port.

The outer harbour (Rade Carnot) is over 4 square miles in area. For the most part it is dedicated to commercial traffic. The only home for yachts is in the Port de Marée just beyond the RO/RO ferry terminals and Gare Maritime, where there are pontoon berths for 90 boats.

Approaches   From the W there are virtually no off-lying dangers once across the NE-going main shipping lane. 8 miles to the N Cap Gris-Nez shows a 29-mile Lt Fl 5 s. from a W Lt Ho on the cliffs 72m above the sea. Its 30M Rdo Bn, callsign 'GN' is on 310.3kHz, the same frequency as the 20M Bn at Cap d'Alprech (callsign 'PH'). The latter is 2 miles S of Boulogne and has a 24M light Fl (3) 15 s. from a 15m W tower, B top 62m above sea level.

The N-going stream starts $2\frac{1}{2}$h. before HW Dover, turning to the southward 6h. later. It exceeds 3 knots at Springs.

The S-cardinal Boulogne Approach whistle buoy is 2 miles WNW of the entrance with a Lt VQ (6) + LFl 10 s., 7M. At first the entrance may be confusing, because most of the seaward half of the N breakwater is submerged, leaving only a rectangular box structure to carry the small Q R 7M Lt 10m above the water (pic 4.1). Opinions vary about the amount of water over the sunken breakwater, but most local powerboats and shoal-draught yachts go through the main entrance at all times, leaving the head of the Digue Carnot close to starboard.

This has a 22m W Tr G top showing a Fl (2 + 1) W Lt 15 s. with a range of 19 miles. The fog signal is a horn (2 + 1) 60 s. Resist the temptation to head straight for the entrance to the ferry port, because shoal water extends 7 cables from the

4.4   *Entrance to Port de Marée, shared by ferries and yacht harbour. Notre-Dame cathedral dominates skyline with Casino in foreground. Traffic signals on starboard hand*

beach on the NE and is uncomfortably close. So head off 2 points to starboard until the inner entrance is fully opened up on the leading Lts on 123°.

R and G Trs carry F R and F G Lts either side of the entrance. The harbour control tower is on the SW head and exhibits IALA Port Movement Lt signals with certain local variations:

G alongside centre Lt: no movements in or out except by ships authorized.

R or $\frac{R}{R}$ alongside normal Lts: no movements except by ships authorized to depart.

RR: Dredging taking place in main channel (pic 4.5).

These signals are repeated on the E bank facing down-harbour (pic 4.5).

The leading lights are:

Front (on the seaward corner of the Gare Maritime): 3 F

41

4.5   *Traffic signals, facing to seaward. The old harbour control structure is on the left, while the dredger is usually there*

4.6   *Small yacht harbour on west bank*

4.7   Secondary yacht harbour above Pont Marguet

G on an inverted triangle frame above a W column with R bands.
Rear: F G on a 43m Grey tower R top located on the Quai Gambetta which forms the NE (left) bank of the harbour. It is reserved for fishing boats.

Berthing and Facilities   Alongside the Gare Maritime are two RO/RO ferry terminals in tandem. Immediately upstream of them is the 85-berth Yacht Hbr with a little hut at the inshore end which does duty as the Bureau du Port (tel. (21) 31.70.01). Visiting boats should secure to the inshore end of the pontoon parallel to the wall. The clubhouse (tel. (21) 31–80–67) is a mile away, near the casino.

HM on Ch 12 and 16.

Customs tel. (21) 30–14–24.

Next there is the Pont Marguet carrying very heavy traffic from downtown Boulogne, which is at its NE end. It has a sluice and a lock-gate under it, which is just as well otherwise the 180 boats on four pontoons in the Arrière-Port would stay there for ever. The lock opens infrequently and only when the tide level in the harbour permits. It is no place for visitors (pic 4.7)

Although limited in scope, the marina has no depth problems, is well sheltered from any direction and is only a few minutes walk from the centre of town.

Communications   The best of any Channel port, with fast trains to Paris (2h.), ferries to Dover and Folkestone, flights from nearby Le Touquet.

Weather   Taped on (21) 31–79–90, or on VHF Ch 23 at 0703 and 1733. Area 9 Sandettie.

Charts: (BA 2451 Fr 6745 CG 1011 Im C31 Stan 9)

High Water   −00h. 10m. Dover   +00h. 12m. SP Dieppe
Heights above Datum   *MHWS 9m0. MLWS 1m0.*
MHWN 7m2. MLWN 2m7.

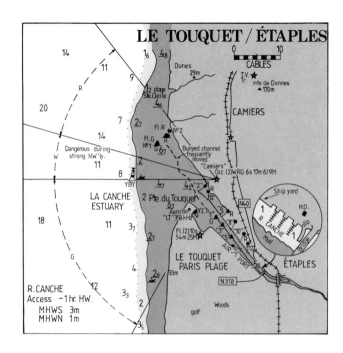

IN SPITE of its full name, LE TOUQUET-PARIS-PLAGE, it is as much a playground for big-spending Brits as the Parisians who own most of the lovely holiday homes set among the pines and silver birches. It is 175 miles from Paris but only 20 miles from Boulogne and the ferry from England. Those who want to play golf on its two magnificent courses, go to the casino, play tennis, go pony-trekking or take part in the endless leisure events organized by an enterprising local tourist office can also fly into the airport, which features arguably the best restaurant in town.

Not unnaturally yachtsmen who have seen the R. Canche at HW are tempted to think of sailing over the 50 miles from Ramsgate or 65 from the Brighton Marina.

Before doing so, have a look at the accompanying pictures (5.1, 5.2 and 5.3) showing what it is like anywhere near LW. It dries out to a trickle for 2 miles offshore. It is also a horrible entrance to make in strong winds from any direction, particularly so from any W'ly sector. However, 2 miles upstream at Étaples, right off the end of the airport runway, there is an 80-berth yacht marina, which could tempt the owner of a shoal-draught boat who finds conditions to his liking at the lower part of the estuary.

Generally the river channel will have 3m least depth all the way to Étaples within 1h. of HW Springs (1m2 at Neaps).

Entry should not be attempted earlier than 2 hours before HW.

Approach   Off the estuary the tide runs northward up to $3\frac{1}{4}$ knots at Springs from $2\frac{1}{2}$h. before HW Dover until it turns $3\frac{1}{2}$h. after HW Dover.

5.1   *The Canche estuary at low water. Bright building on the right bank (middle distance) is Le Touquet Airport*

The most prominent landmark is the 56m Or octagonal Lt Ho situated at the northern end of Le Touquet less than 1 mile S of the entrance to the R. Canche. Its Lt is Fl (2) 10 s. with a range of 25M. Near by is the Aero Bn callsign 'LT' on 358 kHz. Its range is 20M.

On the other bank just 1½ miles N of Le Touquet Lt is the R lattice-work 11m Lt-Tr at Camiers. Not so powerful with only 9M range in its W sector is Camiers Lt Oc (2) WRG 6 s. Its W sector between 090° and 105° will bring you to the W-cardinal pillar buoy with a whistle 1½ miles WNW of Pointe du Touquet.

In the R sector (105–141°) and quite close to the N shore will be found the buoys marking the start of the tortuous, shifting, not to say treacherous, channel to the Cercle Nautique du Touquet (CNT). No. 1 is a G con bell buoy with X topmark; its pair, No. 2, is an R can whistle buoy with a can topmark.

From here inward the channel is well marked by G and R buoys usually relocated in time to keep pace with the uncertain meanderings of the channel. Follow a local fishing boat in, with one eye on the echo sounder.

From the YC upstream is straightforward, with the channel

5.2   *Le Touquet Yacht Club at half tide*

5.3   *Off the yacht club at low water. Channel marked by red pillar and green buoys*

46

5.4   Marina at Étaples facing downstream. Fish-quay and boatyard on the left, Harbour Office out of picture right

clearly marked by R box-topped Bns to port and G triangle-topped Bns to starboard. Just don't cut any corners as there are sunken training walls on both sides.

Berthing and Facilities   A temporary mud berth can be obtained off the CNT where there is a slip and dinghy park (pics 5.2 and 5.3) but, from every point of view, it is better to go on to Étaples.

On the left bank you first come to the shipyard with its 120-ton lifting capacity for fishing boats and ability to build or repair yachts up to any size which will float on the river.

The town quay immediately upstream from the boatyard gives priority to the local fishing fleet, but yachts may seek permission to secure outboard of them, so long as they are prepared to take the ground.

Between the end of the quay and the bridge carrying the RN39 from Le Touquet to the E there are five sets of new pontoons accommodating 75 boats of under 10m LOA which are prepared to take the ground at LWS if they draw over 1mo. There is also a new hard for launching boats into the river from trailers (pic 5.4).

Enquiries for a berth or for weather forecasts can be made through the YC at Le Touquet (tel. (21) 05–12–77) or by calling the Centre Nautique Canche (CNC) on the waterfront at Étaples (tel. (21) 94–74–26). Area 9 Sandettie.

Customs are at Le Touquet airport.

FW, fuel and shore power are available.

There is the Syndicat d'Initiative on the quayside or, a block farther into the town, the Mairie will be found to be helpful.

Good shops and bistros are available within walking distance.

*6   ST VALÉRY-SUR-SOMME/LE CROTOY

Charts: *Fr 3800 CG 1011 (BA 2612 Im C31)*

High Water   − 00h. 20m. Dover   + 00h. 35m. SP Dieppe
Heights above Datum *MHWS 10m0. MLWS 0m7.*
MHWN 8m0. MLWN 2m5.

THESE two little villages on either bank near the mouth of the Somme estuary are both worth a visit – but only in settled weather, good visibility, and bearing in mind that the whole estuary dries out to a distance of 4 miles off Pointe le Hourdel, the little fishing village on the S bank near the open sea. Le Hourdel rarely has room for visitors and offers few amenities to be worth risking the tricky channel into it.

William the Conqueror embarked at St Valéry for his invasion of England. Joan of Arc was brought there by her English captors from Le Crotoy in 1430. The Somme was the scene of one of the bloodiest battles in the First World War and was no picnic in the Second World War. During the holiday season a narrow-gauge railway links the two little ports through 14km of lovely countryside.

Approach   The critical mark to identify is the N-cardinal BY buoy 4 miles WNW of Pointe le Hourdel marked 'AT-SO' (short for 'Atterisage–Somme'). Its Lt is VQ and it lies in the R sector of the 15M light at Ault (Oc (3) 12 s.), 8 miles SSW of Le Hourdel. Here the NNE-going current starts 4 hours before HW Dover, turning SSW 2h. after HW. The spring rate is $2\frac{3}{4}$ knots.

Le Hourdel Lt Ho is a prominent landmark by day – a W Tr G top, 18m high, standing up from a small cluster of houses close to the left-hand edge of the low-lying countryside

of dunes and marshes. Its Lt is Oc (3) WG 12 s. The AT-SO buoy lies in its W sector, range 12M (pic 6.3).

Some $2\frac{1}{2}$ miles SW of Le Hourdel is another W Lt Ho G top Fl R 5 s. 22M at an elevation of 32m. It is listed as the Cayeux light, but it is in fact in the village of Brighton.

About 11 miles NNE is the impressive Berck Lt Ho at the Pointe du Haut Blanc. On a featureless, flat coastline its 44m Tr with four broad R bands on a W background stands out well. The Lt is Fl 5 s. out to a range of 23M.

Even by the standards of Exmouth or Christchurch, the navigable channel into the Somme is a movable feature, but the G and R channel buoys are repositioned each time the sandbanks move. The total distance to thread one's way to St Valéry is a little over 9 miles, so a good time to depart from AT-SO buoy is 2h. before HW. When asked for a chart of the channel, the HO at Le Crotoy, which administers both ports, said 'N'existe pas'.

In 1987 the first pair of channel buoys were about 1 mile due E of the AT-SO buoy, but they have been 2 miles farther to the SE. Thereafter the channel meanders all over the place, well marked by sizeable buoys, mostly unlit.

About $\frac{1}{2}$ mile to the E of Pointe le Hourdel there is a RW striped buoy marking the point where the channel splits: *due E* for 1 mile to Le Crotoy along a channel with all its buoys marked 'C'; *to the SE* towards the wooded area on the right bank where the town of St Valéry-sur-Somme lies.

The last $1\frac{1}{2}$ miles of the approach is plainly marked by G Bns to starboard along a mole. At its seaward end there is a Lt Q (3) G 6 s. on a BW chequered Bn whence the course is 140° for 9 cables. Three of the last seven G Bns carry Fl (2) G 5 s. Lts, including the one where the mole joins the land. The lovely tree-lined embankment leading to the harbour and the entrance of the Somme Canal has a 6m W hut G top at its western end with a 9M light Iso G 4 s. (pic 6.6).

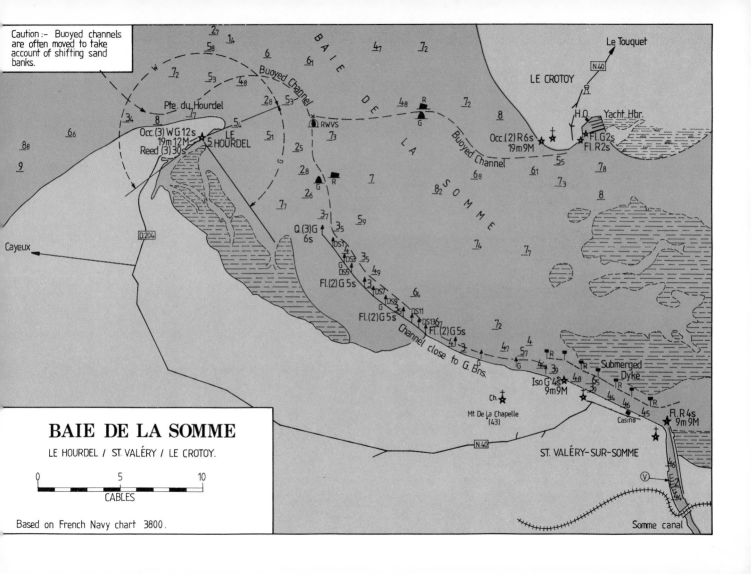

Caution :– Buoyed channels
are often moved to take
account of shifting sand
banks.

BAIE

DE

LA

SOMME

Le Touquet

N.40

LE CROTOY

7_2

2_7

1_4

5_8

6

4_7

7_2

6_1

W

3_4

7_2

5_3

4_8

Buoyed Channel

Pte. du Hourdel

2_8

5_3

RWVS

4_8

R

G

7_2

8

H.Q.

Yacht. Hbr.

8

7_7

5_4

LE
HOURDEL

5_1

7_3

Occ.(2) R6s
19m 9M

Fl. G2s

Occ.(3) W G 12s
19m 12M
Reed (3) 30s

2_5

6_1

5_5

Fl. R2s

7_8

6_6

2_8

G

R

7

6_8

7_3

8_8

2_6

G

8_2

8

9

7_7

Cayeux

3_7

5_9

7_4

7_7

D.204

Q.(3)G
6s

3_5

DS1

3_5

G
DS3

4_9

Fl.(2) G 5s

DS5

4_3

DS7

6_4

Fl.(2) G 5s

G
DS9

DS11

7_2

Fl.(2) G 5s

DS13

4_7

Channel close to G. Bns.

4_3

4_7

5_7

R

4

R

Submerged
Dyke

7_8

1G

R

Iso G 4s
9m9M

4_8

R

2_9

Ch.

R

4_4

4_6

4_5

Fl. R 4s
9m 9M

Mt. De La Chapelle
(43)

Casino

N.40

ST. VALÉRY-SUR-SOMME

BAIE DE LA SOMME

LE HOURDEL / ST. VALÉRY / LE CROTOY.

V

0   5   10

CABLES

Somme canal

Based on French Navy chart 3800.

6.1   *The channel into Le Crotoy with new marina at A*

6.2   *The seaward end of the Somme estuary with Le Hourdel in the foreground and St Valéry at B*

From here the port hand is marked by a succession of Bns with R can topmarks until reaching the mole parallel to the quayside which forms the harbour. Its extremity is marked by a W lattice Lt Tr Fl R 4 s. 9m 9M.

Berthing   The harbour is the last ½ mile of the approach to the 14km canal to Abbeville. To enter it, steer between the tree-lined mole forming its eastern side and the buildings along the quay forming the right bank (pic 6.7).

6.3   *Le Hourdel lighthouse*

6.4   *No room for visitors at Le Hourdel at low water*

Berths for yachts can be found on pontoons built out from the town quay beyond the coasters and fishing boats (pic 6.8). At the outboard end of the pontoons there is 2m depth at LW. They are pefectly sheltered in all weathers. Of the 290 berths 30 are reserved for visitors.

Facilities   The clubhouse of the Sport Nautique Valericain (SNV) is near the marina. Fuel and FW available and there is a 6-ton crane: a boat repair yard is on the dockside. The HO is nearer the harbour entrance on the Quai de Pilotes (tel. (22) 27–52–57), but overall administration is concentrated in Le Crotoy. Ch 9 is manned 2h. either side of HW.

St Valéry has a number of hostelries catering mainly for summer visitors, but the locals' own haunts are appetizing. There are complete shopping facilities, including an excellent chandlery.

Weather   Forecasts are posted locally near the Yacht Hbr. Area 9 Sandettie. On tape at (21) 05–13–55.

LE CROTOY   Only $1\frac{1}{2}$ miles N. across the Somme estuary is the little fishing village and holiday resort of Le Crotoy (pop. 2,500). Its attractions include a beautiful bathing beach when the tide permits, a modern casino and the famous turn-of-the-century Hôtel de la Baie on the water's edge in which the octogenarian patronne still personally acts as chef. Joan of Arc's statue is right outside.

Approach   From the buoy E of Pointe le Hourdel where the fairway splits (see above) follow the R and G buoyed channel towards the 11m high W lattice Tr alongside the Casino with its Oc (2) R 6 s. Lt.

Access can safely be made $1\frac{1}{2}$h. ± HW. The channel swings round the point on which the town is built to enter the little harbour on a N'ly course.

The port-hand jetty at the entrance has a 4m metal R post with a Fl R 2 s Lt. A G post on the other breakwater has a Lt Fl G 2 s. (pic. 6.10).

6.5   *Final approach to St Valéry with channel clearly limited by a mole and training wall*

6.6   *Seaward end of the esplanade*

6.7   *Harbour is entered by leaving tree-lined mole to port and houses to starboard*

6.8   *St Valéry seen looking downstream from Somme Canal locks*

6.9   *Entrance to Le Crotoy Marina just beyond pier, with red beacon (left). Sluice-gates (right) are not relevant*

6.10   *Starboard side of entrance at half tide. Swing hard to starboard to stay afloat*

6.11 *Fishermen's berths on port side. Dries out two hours before low water*

Berthing and Facilities   The harbour has been dredged to a least depth of 1m at the new pontoons, so it may be necessary to take the mud in a keelboat and time one's visit before Springs to avoid being neaped. Fishing boats secure alongside the western quay, where a visiting yacht could secure long enough to contact the local HO, which is block farther into the town (tel. (22) 27–81–44).

The nearby Club Nautique de la Baie de Somme (CNBS) keeps the pontoons mostly for its members. In all there are shoal-draught berths for 280 boats. Visitors will be allocated berths on the S side of the pontoons. The CNBS normally only functions in July and August, but has basic facilities.

Facilities ashore are in character with any small fishing port.

PART THREE

NORMANDY

Le Tréport – Cherbourg

The home of nuclear power stations, black slate roofs on
half-timbered buildings, the D-Day beaches, poteen-like
Calvados, cider with no resemblance to scrumpy,
incomparable Camembert and big tides.

Soundings and heights in metres
Bearings and courses in degrees true
Distances at sea in nautical miles or cables

NORMANDIE, CALVADOS, CONTENTIN

Safe navigable distances from breakwater to breakwater (in nautical miles)

	LE TRÉPORT	DIEPPE	ST VALÉRY-EN-CAUX	FÉCAMP	LE HAVRE	HONFLEUR	DEAUVILLE/TROUVILLE	OUISTREHAM	COURSEULLES	PORT-EN-BESSIN	ST VAAST	CHERBOURG (W)
LE TRÉPORT												
DIEPPE	13											
ST VALÉRY-EN-CAUX	28	15										
FÉCAMP	43	30	15									
LE HAVRE	66	63	38	23								
HONFLEUR	74	61	45	30	11							
DEAUVILLE/TROUVILLE	72	59	44	29	6	9						
OUISTREHAM	81	68	53	37	18	21	14					
COURSEULLES	83	75	55	40	23	28	21	11				
PORT-EN-BESSIN	92	80	64	49	34	40	33	23	12			
ST VAAST	104	95	78	63	53	69	53	46	35	24		
CHERBOURG (W)	118	108	82	77	70	77	72	58	54	45	26	

*7 LE TRÉPORT

Charts: BA 1352 Fr 5928 CG 1011 Im C31

High Water −00h. 30m. Dover −01h. 10m. SP Dunkerque
Heights above Datum MHWS 9m4. MLWS 0m7. MHWN 7m4. MLWN 2m4.

A SMALL fishing port at the mouth of the R. Bresle about half-way between Dieppe and the Somme estuary at Pointe le Hourdel. Local industry is supplied by coastal vessels drawing up to 15ft, in spite of the outer harbour's drying out to over a cable to seaward of the breakwaters. The shingly beach on the eastern side of the town (Mers-les-Bain) is for some reason popular with holidaymakers camping in the district. But the whole scene is discouraging to visiting yachtsmen, especially as they are obliged to berth nearly ½ mile away from the civilized part of the town. The aerial picture (7.1) 2h. after LW, taken during August, shows how few yachts have gone through the lock to their assigned berths top right of the Bassin à Flot. The remainder are on mud berths either side of the channel leading to the lock.

About 4km inland, perhaps the best reason for a yachtsman to visit Le Tréport, is the ancient town of Eu, with its twelfth-century abbey curiously dedicated jointly to Notre Dame and St Laurent O'Toole, primate of Ireland.

Approach From a distance Le Tréport appears as a break in the W cliffs, like so many other small ports on this coast. On wooded high ground inland of the port is a prominent water Tr, while the square Tr of the church of St Jacques in the middle of the town is equally prominent.

7.1 *(A) Few yachts in the Bassin à Flot. (B) Lock-gates shut. (C) Mud berths on port hand assigned to local yacht club*

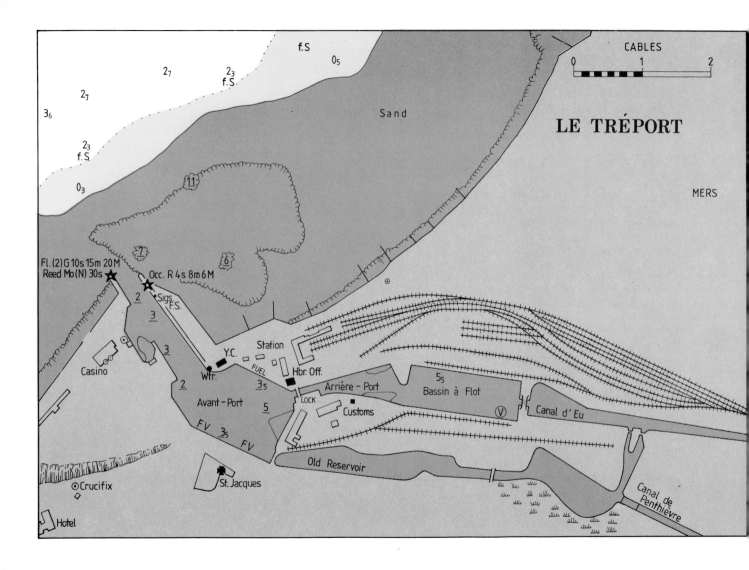

CABLES

0   1   2

LE TRÉPORT

f.S

0_5

2_7

2_3

f.S.

Sand

2_7

3_6

2_3

f.S

0_3

MERS

11

7

6

Fl.(2)G 10s 15m 20M
Reed Mo(N) 30s

Occ. R 4s 8m 6M

2

Sigs.
F.S.

3

3

Station

Y.C.

Wtr.

FUEL

Hbr. Off.

Casino

2

3_5

Arrière - Port

5_5

Bassin à Flot

5

Avant - Port

LOCK

Customs

V

Canal d' Eu

FV

3_5

FV

St. Jacques

Old Reservoir

Crucifix

Canal de Penthièvre

Hotel

7.2   Modest yacht club on the east side, facing to seaward

At night the W sector of the 19M Lt at Ault – 3½ miles NE of Le Tréport (Oc (3) WR 12 s. 95m high) – may be picked up together with the 20M Lt at the end of the W breakwater at the harbour entrance (Fl (2) G 10 s. 15m high). It is a W Tr G top. It sounds a reed every 30 s. in fog – morse 'N'.

Approaching on a SE'ly course, the E jetty Lt is on a 7m W column with an R top and base. Its Lt is Oc R 4 s. Beside it stand the Lt signals controlling harbour traffic (pic 7.1), using the Simplified Code.

The tidal stream runs across your approach course up to 2 knots at Springs.

Two miles E of the town at Eu airfield there is a 20M Aero-Bn on 330kHz callsign 'EU'.

Arrival should be timed to coincide with the opening of the lock into the Bassin à Flot, which is 1½h. before HW.

In NW'ly winds entry is not recommended. The Avant-Port is not at all comfortable and no place to hang about.

VHF Ch 16 and 12 – 2½h. HW + 1h.

Berthing   Once inside the Avant-Port it may be possible in settled weather to secure alongside the Quai François Ier on the SW side of the heart of the town, although it is usually reserved for fishing boats. The Quai Bellot on the opposite side is shared by the pilot boat and club moorings assigned by the YCB (Yacht Club de Bresle), a modest building at the inshore end of the E jetty (pic 7.2).

When the lock-gate is open, if need be sound three blasts

7.3   *Club moorings seen from clubhouse towards locks*

7.4   *View to seaward from lock-gates at half tide, Harbour Office (right)*

to get the bridge open as well. Then proceed straight through the Arrière-Port to the Bassin à Flot. Yachts may not berth in the former. Some charts still show a lock between these two basins, but it has been demolished (pic 7.1).

Facilities   FW can be obtained on the dockside. Fuel is just outside the lock-gate, right by the Bureau du Port (tel. (35) 86–17–91) on the E side.

There is a fully-equipped boatyard immediately outside the seaward end of the Eu canal.

There is a casino facing the western beach with the local Office of Tourism in it. Adequate shopping and bistros.

Weather   On tape: (22) 25–47–33.

*8   DIEPPE

Charts: BA 2147 Im C31 Fr 5927 (Fr 934 CG 1012 Stan 1)

High Water   −00h.30m. Dover   SP Dieppe
Heights above Datum   MHWS 9m3. MLWS 0m7.
MHWN 7m2. MLWN 2m5.

DIEPPE is a greatly underrated town and resort. Our grand-fathers swore by it – indeed many of them lived there, along-side Aubrey Beardsley, Sickert, Whistler and Oscar Wilde, to write, paint or keep a low profile towards their creditors. It has all the facilities Deauville has to offer, except polo and the jet-setters. The casino, gourmet restaurants and high quality hotels abound in the old town facing the beach. Day-trippers from Newhaven, 65 miles away, swarm to the hypermarket on the edge of town or blow their money in the open markets just a block away from the ferry landing. The surrounding countryside is not unlike Devon.

The beach is advertised as being the nearest to Paris (200km or 2h. by train). It is also a memorial to the famous Anglo-Canadian Raid in August 1942. The fact that the raiding forces were denied a covering barrage or a softening-up air bombardment preserved all the old buildings, at the expense of filling the war graves' plot on the road to the airport. As the official guide still says: '. . . their sacrifice hastened the day when the Nazi yoke was lifted from France'.

In days gone by it was the centre of the ivory trade. Until container ships took over a decade ago it was the principal port for bringing in bananas and other exotic vegetables. Now its principal trade is provided by the RO/RO ferries from Newhaven.

63

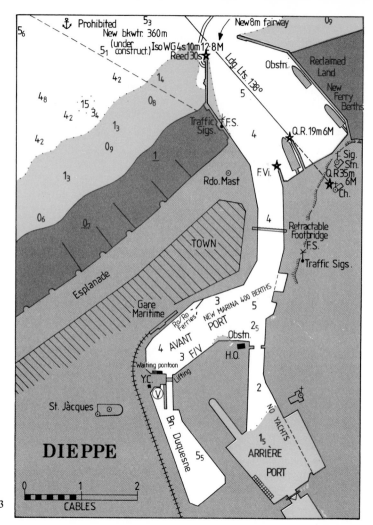

8.1 *(A) Bassin Duquesne with yacht berths. (B) Lock-gates. (C) Fishermen's berths. Yachts waiting can do so on pontoons to the right of lock-gates. (D) Land being reclaimed for new ferry terminal. (E) West breakwater being extended 360m to seaward*

8.2   Seaward end of west breakwater (Debbie Godfray)

Pêche, now the Bassin Duquesne. It is the old jetfoil terminal.

The Avant-Port is filthy dirty, with oil, flotsam and garbage piled into it by each nor'wester. However, many think these preliminaries are well worth surmounting. There is a plan to move the whole ferry terminal to the E side of the outer harbour where the land has been reclaimed. The entrance is being widened and deepened, with the outer end of the E jetty demolished. When that happens the Avant-Port will become a fully-furnished yacht harbour for 400 boats.

Approach The town is just 4 miles E of the imposing Pointe d'Ailly with its W square Tr G top Lt Ho 24m high, 98m above sea level. The Lt is Fl (3) 20 s. to a range of 34M. There is a reed (3) 60 s. in fog. On top of that it has a Rdo Bn on 310.3kHz, callsign 'AL' in the same group as the Royal Sovereign and also 50M range.

The town lies in a widish gap between white cliffs about 30m high. There is no less than 3m5 water all the way into the Avant-Port so, subject to the problem spelled out above, you can go in on any state of the tide. The belfry of Notre Dame de Bon-Secours on the skyline to the E of the town is conspicuous by day on making the correct course of 138°. The W signal station alongside the church is also prominent.

Call Dieppe Port VHF Ch 6, 12, 16. Yacht Hbr on Ch 09.

Make for the breakwater heads, allowing for a tide which can run up to 2 knots across the entrance, starting to the E at −05h. 30m. Dover, turning W at HW Dover. The W jetty head has a 7m W tower G top (Lt Iso WG 4 s. 12/8M). The W sector is about 3 points either side of the correct lead in.

The E jetty head has a W tower R top 8m high wth a Lt Oc (4) R 12 s.

The transit Lts are:

Front: on the old E jetty, a W metal frame R top 16m high Q R.

Rear: on clifftop 35m up a W hut R top and another Q R.

Unfortunately, of all the ways to get to Dieppe and enjoy its charms, going by yacht is not the easiest or necessarily the most pleasant. The harbour entrance funnels in a nasty swell when it blows from the NW. The outer harbour has a pontoon designated for yachts waiting to lock into the old Port de

8.3   Semaphore station and Notre-Dame de Bon-Secours on the eastern skyline, with traffic signals on the west side

8.4   Lifting bridge at lock-gates from Avant Port to yacht harbour with the old Seajet terminal on the right

8.5   Berths in the Bassin Duquesne seen on entry

At this point it is imperative to obey the local traffic signals. They are put out on VHF Ch 12. They are also displayed visually on the W jetty and at the corner of the harbour where one rounds up to get into Avant-Port. The full code is used (RWR = don't enter. GWG = don't sail. GWR = don't move).

There are additional signals used at the same time: for cross-channel ferries entering, by day Flag N (Bu and W chequers); at night, a G light; a ferry departing is notified by day by pendant 4 (W St George's Cross on R pendant). at night by a R light. The ferries always have priority.

Assuming one has timed one's arrival to go straight into the Bassin Duquesne (−2h. to +1h. on HW) the flag P will be flown to indicate that the lock is open. Two long blasts on the foghorn might activate the bridge operator (pic 8.4).

Berthing and Facilities   Immediately inside the lock there are a pontoon and some alongside berths on the western

8.6   The yacht club – Cercle de la Voile de Dieppe (CVD) – is the white, hutted building to the left of the lifting bridge. However, it is in the heart of town

quayside. Unfortunately there are only 80 berths available. The YC (Cercle de Voile de Dieppe – CVD) has a modest clubhouse just by the lock (tel. (35) 84–32–99). FW, fuel and some repair facilities are available on the spot. The shopping and eating out have no parallel – all within a few minutes' walk of the boat. Duty-free stores are available. Customs are on rue Descroisilles (tel. (35) 82–24–47). Ferries to Newhaven. Trains to Rouen and Paris. Some flights to Shoreham.

HO tel. (35) 84–10–55.

Weather   Forecasts on VHF Ch 2 at 0633 and 1133. They are also displayed at the clubhouse or can be obtained from Rouen by tel. (35) 80–11–44. Area 10 Manche est.

*9   ST VALÉRY-EN-CAUX

Charts: *CG 1012 (Fr 6794 Im C31 BA 2612)*

High Water   −ooh. 45m. *Dover*   −ooh. 17m. SP *Dieppe*
Heights above Datum   *MHWS 8m9. MLWS om9.
MHWN 7m1. MLWN 2m4.*

ST VALÉRY is built around a natural harbour situated in a valley between the W cliffs stretching from Dieppe to Fécamp. It is exactly half-way between the two. A former fishing port, it is now given over almost entirely to those using the 650-boat Yacht Hbr or the beach. Overlooking the harbour from the cliffs d'Amont is the memorial to the men of the 51st Highland Division who fought out their last battle here in 1940 before the panzers wiped them out and most of the town with them.

Approach   Since the Avant-Port dries out a cable to seaward of the breakwaters forming the entrance, no attempt should be made to enter before half-tide. There are drying-out berths alongside the quays and a few moorings on which to wait, but it is best to reach the lock when it opens ±2h. HW for boats drawing 1m50. Call VHF Ch 9.

Approach the harbour entrance on SSE'ly course. The more prominent Lt Ho is on the western breakwater, which protrudes farther to seaward. Its Lt is on a G Tr and shows Oc (2 + 1) G 12 s. 13m, 14M. At the seaward end of the eastern arm is a W frame Tr R top and a Lt Fl (2) R 6 s. 9m, 4M. Favour the E side of the fairway to the Avant-Port. The worst conditions for entering are in a NNE'ly wind.

Across the locks is a lifting bridge, which opens on the hour and half-hour whenever the lock-gates are open (pics 9.3 and 9.4).

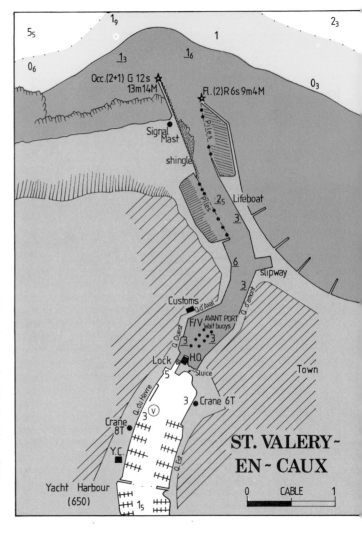

ST. VALERY-
EN-CAUX

9.1   *This half-tide shot shows how the entrance channel shoals on the west side*

9.2 *Perches marking the entrance channel. Note the swell running in on the starboard hand in light weather*

9.3 *Right ahead are the sluice-gates*

9.4 *Lifting bridge at the lock-gates*

9.5　*The Port de Plaisance. Note how the fairway is marked by heavy piles anchoring the pontoons from each bank*

Berthing　Visitors should make for the pontoons immediately inside the locks on the starboard hand (Quai du Havre). The HO is on the E. side of the bridge over the lock (tel. (35) 97–01–30). The water inside is maintained at 5m over datum. The aerial picture (9.1) shows that there are the supports of an old bridge beyond the fifth pontoon. The channel through them is clearly marked.

Facilities　There are two YCs of interest to visiting yachtsmen, both located on the western side of the inner harbour. The Club Nautique Valeriquais (CNV) is the newer of the two, the other being the Centre de Voile de St Valéry-en-Caux (CVSV). Their telephone numbers are: CNV (35) 97–10–88, CVSV (35) 97–04–22.

FW, fuel, repairs and chandlery are all readily available, as are the usual facilities of a holiday port. Caves du Port near HO recommended.

Customs at Fécamp, tel. (35) 28–19–40.

Weather　Forecasts posted at the Bureau du Port and at both YCs. Area 10 Manche est. Taped on (35) 80–11–44.

71

*10 FÉCAMP

Charts: BA 1352 FR 932 Im C31 CG 1012 (Stan 1)

High Water −01h. 00m. Dover −00h. 20m. SP Dieppe
Heights above Datum MHWS 7m9. MLWS 0m8.
MHWN 6m5. MLWN 2m5.

FÉCAMP lies 10 miles ENE of Cap d'Antifer (Fl 20 s. 128m, 30M) and 28 miles WSW of Dieppe. It is readily identifiable from seaward because the W cliffs rise steeply to the E from the harbour entrance to an elevation of 120m. The square Tr of Notre Dame du Salut dominates the skyline above Pte Fagnet, with a W signal Tr and TV mast near by.

The town has known better days as the main homeport for a fleet of deep-sea trawlers bringing back cod from as far afield as Greenland and the White Sea. It is still the base for a substantial fleet of coastal fishing boats and some commercial traffic in timber, liquid gas and minerals.

Approach Apart from the rocks extending $1\frac{1}{2}$ cables to seaward from Pte Fagnet there are no off-lying dangers. A boat drawing 1m50 can enter at any state of the tide, but a nasty swell runs through the narrow entrance when the wind is from the W–N sector. In such weather it is best not to enter until an hour before HW. Keep open the 065° transit of N pierhead and the semaphore on the clifftop above Pte Fagnet.

On rising ground to the SW there is a prominent water Tr. Just to the left are the church Trs of St Etienne and La Trinité. All three features are clearly shown in the aerial picture 10.1

The entrance, which is only 200ft wide, lies between the N breakwater with its Grey Tr R top (Fl (2) 10 s. 15m, 16M)

10.1 Note the line of moorings in the Arrière-Port (A), but visitors are encouraged to go to the pontoons by the yacht club (B). Berths in the Bassin Berigny (C) are quieter

72

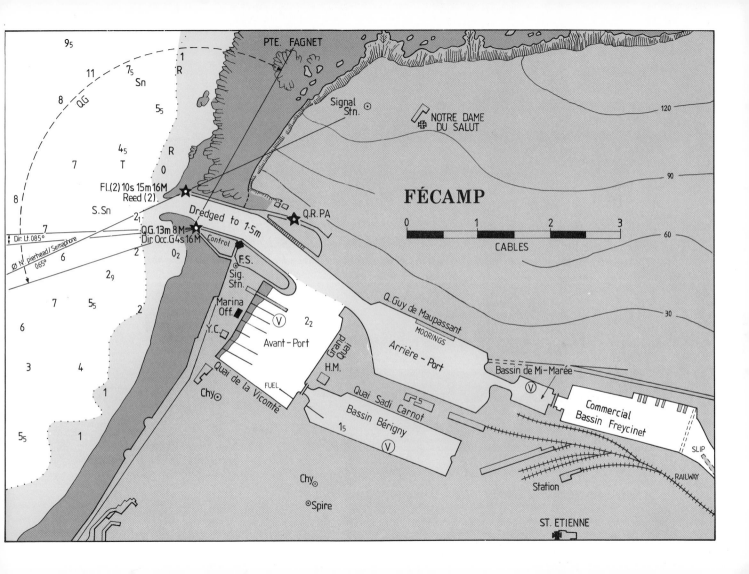

PTE. FAGNET

9₅

11

7₅

8   QG   Sn

5₅

R   5₅

7   4₅

T   R

Fl.(2) 10s 15m 16M   0
Reed (2).

8   S. Sn   2₁

7   QG.13m 8M
Dir Occ.G4s16M

Ø N° pierhead / Semaphore   6   2   0₂
065°

2₉

7   5₅   2

6

3   4   1

5₅   1

Signal
Stn. ⊙

NOTRE DAME
DU SALUT

FÉCAMP

Dredged to 1·5m

Control

Q.R. PA

F.S.

Sig.
Stn. ⊙

Marina
Off. ■

Y.C. □

Avant - Port

2₂

FUEL

Chy ⊙

Quai de la Vicomté

Grand Quai

H.M.

Quai Sadi Carnot

Bassin Bérigny

1₅

Ⓥ

Chy ⊙

⊙ Spire

Q. Guy de Maupassant

MOORINGS

Arrière - Port

Bassin de Mi-Marée

Ⓥ

Commercial
Bassin Freycinet

SLIP

RAILWAY

Station

ST. ETIENNE

0   1   2   3

CABLES

120

90

60

30

Dir. Lt. 085°

10.2   A nasty swell runs through the entrance. Minutes later this boat was under full sail and perfectly happy

10.3   Société des Régates de Fécamp (SRF) clubhouse and Bureau du Port

74

10.4   *Boats on the pontoon immediately outside locks, with the fuelling jetty just off the frame to the right*

10.5   *A boat emerging from the Bassin Berigny*

10.6   Ten miles WSW along the coast to the impressive Cap d'Antifer lighthouse

and the G tower (Q G 14m, 5M) at the end of the S breakwater, which also has an Oc G 4s. 16M directional light ± 1½° on 085° (see plan). The main Lt sounds a reed (2) 30s. in bad visibility within 2h. of HW.

There is also a Q R at the inshore end of the N breakwater.

Controls   There is a signal mast above a small office at the inshore end of the S breakwater, which controls traffic using the Simplified Code (see p. 17). A R flag or Lt indicates 'no entry'; G indicates departures forbidden, while R over G orders no movement in or out of the harbour.

The same mast flies code flag P (the Blue Peter) when the lock-gates are open, usually – 1½h. on HW until 30min. afterwards. VHF watch is kept on Ch 16, 12 and 9 for the Yacht Hbr.

Berthing   It is possible to go straight ahead through the Passe Botton into the Arrière-Port (pic 10.1) and pick up a mooring off the Quay Guy de Maupassant (he lived there), but there are eight runs of pontoons in the Avant-Port forming a 250-berth marina with all mod-cons. Visiting yachts should berth on the third or fourth pontoon after rounding to star-board to enter the marina area.

The berthing office is on Ch 9 and tel. (35) 28–13–58; it is situated in the YC house: Societé des Régates de Fécamp (SRF), tel. (35) 28–08–44.

For a more peaceful berth away from the scend, which rarely dies down, go through the lock to the Bassin Bérigny – upper right, pic 10.1. The Bureau du Port is just N (left) of the lock-gate. Here the depth is maintained at 5m. Outside in the Avant-Port it is shown as 1m50, but 2m is now claimed for most of the berths.

Facilities   FW on the pontoons. Fuel just to the right of the lock leading to Bassin Bérigny. The latter is for commercial traffic, but has a comprehensive boatyard there (C. Moré tel. (35) 28–28–15).

There is a slipway in the NW corner of the Avant-Port. Good restaurants and all provisioning needs can be met.

SNCF to Le Havre, Rouen and Paris.

Customs tel. (35) 28–19–40.

Weather   Reports posted at the YC or on tape from Le Havre on tel. (35) 42–12–19. Area 10 Manche est.

11 · LE HAVRE

Charts: *BA 2146 Fr 6683 Im C31 CG 1012 (Stan 1)*
Carte Guide de Navigation Fluviale: 'Paris à la mer par le canal de Tancarville'

High Water *— 01h. 18m. Dover   SP Le Havre*
Heights above Datum *MHWS 7m8. MLWS 1m1. MHWN 6m5. MLWN 2m8.*

LE HAVRE is a busy commercial centre of 250,000 inhabitants, almost completely rebuilt since 1945. It has successfully made the transition from being an international passenger terminal for great liners to being the third largest cargo port in Europe (container ships and tankers). It is also a popular RO/RO ferry terminal for traffic to Portsmouth.

For yachtsmen it is mainly of interest because its deepwater channels are unaffected by the state of the tide, there is a modern marina and it gives them access to the placid waters of the Tancarville Canal 25km along the 115km to Rouen or 360km to Paris, thus avoiding the somewhat exposed estuary seas in the lower reaches of the Seine.

Approach If coming from the Solent or farther west, touchdown should be near the Le Havre buoy which is described in the chapter on Deauville. From this point it is 10½ miles down a well-buoyed channel. Twin chimneys each 247m high are close to the leading line (pic 11.2), while the tower of St Joseph's church (105m) near the YC is also prominent, on the port bow.

11.1   Cap de la Hève lighthouse, white octagonal with red top, 32m high, 123m above sea-level, from which it is prominent by day. Note pylon with dish antenna to the right

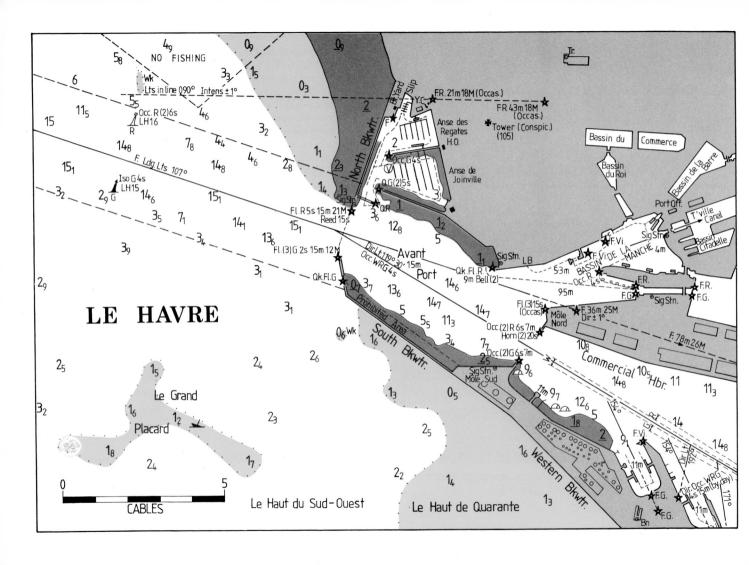

LE HAVRE

No Fishing

Wk

Lts in line 090° Intens ± 1°

Occ.R(2)6s
LH16
R

F. Ldg. Lts 107°

Iso G 4s
LH15

North Bkwtr

B. Yard
Slip
Y.C.
H.O.
Anse des
Regates
H.O.

Anse de
Joinville

Occ.G 4s

Q.G(2)5s

Sig Stn.
Q.R.

Fl.R 5s 15m 21M
Reed 15s

Fl.(3) G 2s 15m 12M

Qk.Fl.G.

Dir Lt 119° 30′. 15m
Occ.WRG 4s

Avant
Port

Prohibited Area

Wk

South Bkwtr

Le Grand

Placard

Qk.Fl.R.
9m Bell (2)

Occ.(2)R 6s 7m
Horn (2) 20s

Occ.(2)G 6s 7m

Sig Stn.
Môle Sud

Sig Stn. LB

Sig Stn.

Fl.(3)15s
(Occas)

Môle
Nord

F. 36m 25M
Dir ± 1°

F.V.

Tr.

FR. 21m18M (Occas.)

FR 43m 18M
(Occas.)

Tower (Conspic.)
(105)

Bassin du   Commerce

Bassin
du Roi

Port Off.

T'ville
Canal

Bassin
Citadelle

F.Vi.

Sig Stn.

BASSIN DE LA MANCHE 4m

Occ.R.

F.R.

F.G.

Sig Stn.

F.R.

F.G.

F. 78m 26M

Commercial   Hbr.

F.V.

Dir Lt
192°

Dir.Occ.WRG
4s 15m (by day)
171°

F.G.

F.G.

Bn.

CABLES

0   5

Le Haut du Sud-Ouest   Le Haut de Quarante   Western Bkwtr

11.2   Twin 247m chimneys conspicuous and close to 107° leading line on fairway. Yacht harbour is left of the north breakwater entrance and new short breakwater guarding its entrance

Although the two leading Lts are on tall Grey Trs (35m and 77m) they cannot be picked out by day. At night 27-mile fixed W Lts are intensified 1 degree either side of the 107° leading line.

Boats approaching from the NE can round the prominent Cap de la Hève close to and shape straight for the harbour entrance 2 miles distant. The lighthouse is a W octagonal tower 32m high with an R top, standing at 123m elevation above the sea. Its Lt is Fl W 5 s. with a range of 24M (pic 11.1).

The breakwaters at the entrance each have 15m W Tr structures at their ends. The northernmost one has an R top and a 21-mile Fl R 5 s. Lt. It also sounds a reed every 15 s. in poor visibility. The S one has a G top; its 12-mile Lt is VQ (3) G 2 s.

Give the end of the N breakwater a wide berth and swing to port to round the E extremity of the short new breakwater with Q R Lt. The entrance to the Yacht Hbr is between it and the end of the Digue Augustin Normand, which protects the berths from S–SW'ly blows. At its western extremity it has a weak Q (2) G 5 s. Lt on a G metal pole. There is an inner mole also with a Lt at its W end (Oc G 4s.)

Berthing The Anse de Joinville (least depth 3m0) between the two inner moles described above has 80 berths on the first of its pontoons for visitors. The other 950 berths include members-only pontoons in the Anse des Régates S of the imposing YC building, Société des Régates du Havre (SRH). Close to the NE corner of the inner harbour there is less water, down to 1m1, but mostly it has 2m0 minimum.

VHF traffic on Ch 12, 16, 20 and 22 are for controlling

11.3 New yacht harbour breakwater

11.4 Prominent St Joseph's Church overlooking Anse de Joinville now with pontoons all along the mole to the left

commercial shipping. Yachts should use Ch 9 or contact the HM on tel. (35) 21–74–00 or the HO on (35) 21–23–95.

Facilities FW and fuel can all be obtained in the Yacht Hbr.

Near the YC there is a slipway and a boatyard with cranes, also a chandler who is a main agent for French Navy charts and carries a selection of British ones (Heilmann).

The SRH (tel. (35) 41–42–21) is prestigious, well appointed, active in promoting international racing and has the best restaurant of any YC in the N of France (pic 11.5). It is open and well supported all the year round. Visiting yachtsmen who conform to local standards and don't stroll in wearing tee-shirts and frayed denim pants are welcome. It's worth the effort, since there are few other places to eat or drink within walking distance of Yacht Hbr. Le Havre's city centre is of little interest.

The Customs are at 201 Boulevard de Strasbourg, a taxi-ride up-town (tel. (35) 41–24–34).

Weather Forecasts can be obtained on (35) 21–16–11 or on VHF Ch 82 at 0633 and 1133. Area 10 Manche est.

11.5 Anse des Régates with clubhouse of Société des Régates du Havre – the best food of any yacht club in Northern France, but not served to visitors in T-shirts or frayed denims. Heilmann, the chart supplier, to right of clubhouse. By mid-1987 the whole basin will have pontoon berths, reserved for members

To Rouen via the Tancarville Canal

Access to the Canal involves going through five locks, starting with that leading into the Bassin de la Citadelle (see plan) which is 1 mile up-harbour at the far end of the Bassin de la Manche (Arrière-Port). Charts BA 2990 or Fr 6796 should then be consulted or, even better, the French guide from the sea to Paris quoted at the head of this chapter. Its text is in French, English and German. CG 1012 is perfectly adequate as far as Rouen. Best to consult the HO at Anse des Régates before setting out.

11.6 Harbour Control at north entrance to Bassin de la Manche leading to Tancarville Canal

*12 HONFLEUR

Charts: (BA 2146 Fr 4937, 6796 CG 526 Im C31 (Approach only))

High water −01h. 35m. Dover −00h. 25m. SP Le Havre
Heights above Datum MHWS 7m9. MLWS 1m3.
MHWN 6m6. MLWN 2m7.

HONFLEUR is a medieval port of refuge lying off the S bank of the Seine estuary, 7 miles up the deepwater channel towards Rouen and beyond. The old Bassin de l'Ouest in the heart of the city – now the Yacht Hbr – is surrounded by reminders of Honfleur's glorious years. Cartier and Champlain both sailed W from here, the latter founding Quebec in 1608.

Right alongside the lock into the Yacht Hbr is the seat of Governor in the sixteenth century, known as La Lieutenance, since he was the king's lieutenant. Today it houses the HO.

Also near by is the sixteenth-century Church of St Catherine, uniquely built by shipwrights entirely of wood. In the higher parts of the town, especially by the crucifix of Notre Dame de Grâce, there are wonderful views of the whole Seine estuary.

Approach Approximately $2\frac{1}{2}$ miles SW of the main entrance to Le Havre is the Rade de la Carosse where the Chenal de Rouen starts at the Priesland R buoy (No. 4) Oc (2) R. It lies in the W sector of the Falaise des Fonds Lt, a W square tower with a G top 15m high, situated $\frac{3}{4}$ mile W of the entrance to Honfleur. It is Fl (3) WRG 12 s. and has a range of 18M in the W sector. The G sector warns of the extensive Banc du Ratier.

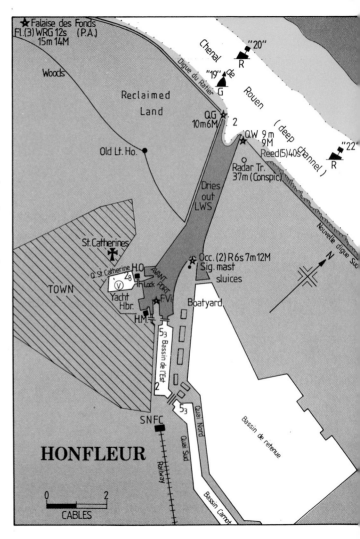

12.1 *Taken one hour before high water, so traffic is mostly moving inward. At low water it dries almost to the entrance. The yacht harbour is at (A)*

12.2　*The prominent control tower at the entrance directing traffic along the Seine estuary*

12.3　*Signal tower and lighthouse controlling entrance to Bassin de l'Est*

12.4　*Lock-gates to Bassin de l'Est. Not for yachts*

12.5   The old building (centre) is La Lieutenance where the Harbour Office is located. Sometimes visitors arriving by night secure alongside the small cut to the right, waiting for the lock-gates to open. But they are to the left

The channel itself is clearly marked by pairs of R and G buoys all the way to G buoy No. 19, right on the doorstep of Honfleur. This is dominated by the W 37m-high Traffic Control Tr with a prominent observation platform at its top immediately under the radars controlling steamer traffic.

The entrance is marked on its western head by a G frame Tr 10m high with Q G Lt. On the other side, by the control Tr, is a similar Y Tr, Q W Lt. In low visibility its reed sounds (5) 40 s.

At LW the approach dries almost out to the entrance, so it is as well to time one's arrival to about HW $-\frac{1}{2}$h. If early, one can get out of the fierce tidal current sweeping past the entrance at 5 knots or more by ducking inside the entrance and waiting there in mid channel. The flood runs only $4\frac{1}{2}$h., after which there is a 2h. stand.

There are three basins accessible through locks, but only the Bassin de l'Ouest is suitable for visiting yachts.

Protruding into the middle of the main fairway is a point

12.6   Lifting bridge and lock-gates to Bassin de l'Ouest

joined to the eastern shore by a sluice-gate. It has a tall signal mast with an enormous crossyard from which are displayed the shapes and Lts to control traffic and indicate depths for ships going into the commercial harbours (Bassin de l'Est). Alongside it is a prominent W lighthouse with a R top 12m high with a Lt Oc (2) R 6 s. (pic 12.3).

At this point you should sound one blast to denote your intention of entering the Yacht Hbr. You can also call on VHF Ch 11, 12 or 16.

Swinging to starboard you enter the Avant-Port, the bridge and lock-gate are both on the left of the prominent building La Lieutenance. The lock-gates carry the main road and only open intermittently during suitable tides at times displayed outside La Lieutenance. Fishing boats may be lying in the small cut on your starboard bow and alongside the town quay to port. You can secure briefly to the jetty on the NW side of the bridge, but it is not recommended to take the ground there.

Berthing   The Yacht Hbr has pontoon walkways round three sides of it. Secure bows to the pontoon and for choice pick up two stern buoys. There are some alongside berths immediately to port of the lock entrance and there is a slip by the HO. The depth is 2m8.

86

12.7 Boats berth bows-on to pontoons all round the yacht harbour, secured astern to small mooring-buoys. Well worth the effort of getting there

Yachts with their crews on board may stop for only a week.

Facilities Honfleur caters more for tourists and artists than yachtsmen. Nevertheless there is an excellent yacht yard by the eastern basin and mechanics are available. The old town has great charm; there are plenty of shops, restaurants, banks and hotels. The harbour is completely sheltered from all weathers. But there are no usual marina facilities and diesel fuel has to be carried from a local garage. Make your own arrangements for disposing of garbage.

The HO is on tel. (31) 89–20–02. The lock-keeper tel. (31) 89–22–57. The Customs are on tel. (31) 89–12–13. Traffic control is on VHF Ch 11 or 16.

There is an SNCF railway station and bus services to Le Havre (1h.) or Deauville ($\frac{3}{4}$ h.).

Weather Forecasts can be obtained by telephone to (31) 88–28–62. Area 10 Manche est.

*13 DEAUVILLE/TROUVILLE

Charts: BA 1349 FR 5530, 6928 Im C32 CG 526 (BA 2146 Stan 1)

High Water −01h. 30m. Dover −00h. 55m. Springs
SP Le Havre −00h. 10m. Neaps SP Le Havre
Heights above Datum MHWS 7m7. MLWS 1m1.
MHWN 6m5. MLWN 2m8.

THE TWIN towns of DEAUVILLE and TROUVILLE are separated by the R. Touques which all but dries on most tides. To the E the Trouville bank alongside the tree-lined Boulevard F. Moureaux is reserved for fishermen as far upstream as the bridge joining the two towns. It is one long open-air fish-market, with a wide choice of restaurants and shops on the other side of the road. Dominating the river entrance and the most conspicuous feature from seaward is the baroque casino with its thalassatherapy and cult movies.

To the W lies one of the favourite watering holes of the jet set – Deauville. If as a break from cruising you fancy a round of golf, a chukka of polo or losing your shirt among the Beautiful People either at the race track or on the tables, it's all here during August. You can walk 'les planches' along the edge of the beach and wave in fantasy to the whole cast, in what came to be known as the 21st Arrondissement of Paris, from Scott Fitzgerald to the Aly Khan, sipping Dom Perignon outside Ciro's modest little beach café. Today it's as likely to be Tory landowners, inside traders accoutred by Gucci or dishevelled pop stars with their expensive doxies.

The Trouville scene is not so glittering as Deauville, but it shows more life off-season and is generally less expensive.

There are only two choices open to visiting yachtsmen: the new marina (Port Deauville) inside a breakwater built out from the beach, or the two adjoining yacht basins of earlier vintage on the western side of the river. The inner one (Bassin Morny) is the home of the Deauville YC, where visiting British yachtsmen have been welcomed for generations.

Approach Arrival should be planned so as not to reach the entrance before half-tide. If there is a strong onshore wind and sea it is prudent to allow an extra hour's tide. In normal weather it is perfectly safe to enter by night. The point to make for is the unlit Trouville SWW-cardinal bell buoy (YBY) about 1 mile WNW of the harbour entrance.

On passage from the S Coast Leave the Le Havre outer fairway buoy to port, the buoy is R with a Rdo Bn callsign 'LH' on 291.9kHz, range 30 miles. The light is Fl (2) R 10 s. 10m, 10M. At this point it is 13 miles to the Trouville buoy, so the Bn can be useful as a back bearing.

Leave to starboard the Northgate N-cardinal buoy, Q Lt 3 miles to the WSW of the Le Havre buoy.

A course made good of 130° will cut through the R sector of the 7M Dives Lt (Oc (2 + 1) 12 s.) until picking up the W sector of the Trouville W breakwater (Fl 4 s.–B pylon on dolphin 16m high) at a range of 12M. The G sector says you're getting too far to the E. The W sector of the E breakwater Lt (Fl (4) WR 12 s. W metal tower R top 15m high) just open of the W jetty Lt will bring you on to the two leading Lts located near the right-hand edge of the casino on Pointe de la Cahotte. Both the breakwaters are submerged at HW, but are marked by Bns. The leadng Lts in transit on 150° are as follows:

Front – Oc R 4 s. 12M on a W tower with R top 11m high.
Rear – Oc R 4 s. 10M on a W metal Tower R top 17m high.

If approaching from the N or E (eg Le Havre or Honfleur) it is essential to keep clear of the shoal water – Banc du Ratier

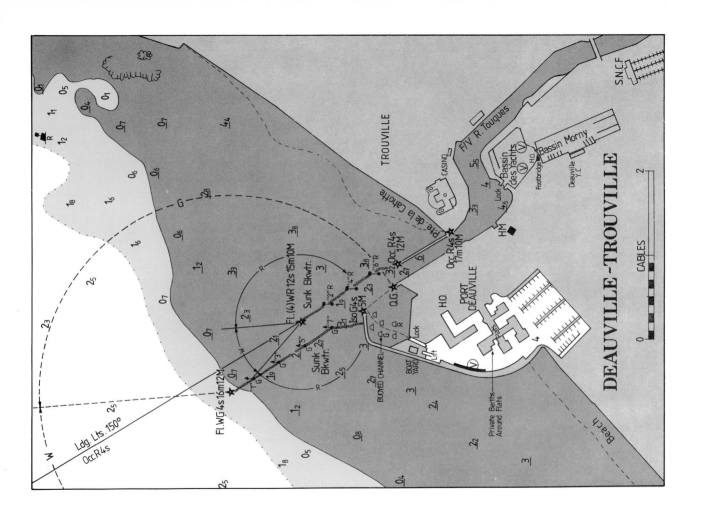

DEAUVILLE-TROUVILLE

TROUVILLE

F/V R. Touques

CASINO

Bassin des Yachts

Bassin Morny

Deauville Y.C.

Footbridge

H.Q.

Lock

HM

Occ.R4s 12M

Occ.R4s 17m10M

Pte. de la Cahotte

Fl.(4)WR12s15m10M

Sunk Bkwtr.

Sunk Bkwtr.

BUOYED CHANNEL

BOAT YARD

PORT DEAUVILLE

H.Q.

Lock

Lift

Private Berths Around Flats

Beach

Fl.WG.4s16m12M

QG5M

IsoG4s 5M

QG

Ldg. Lts.150°
Occ.R4s

CABLES

0   1   2

13.1   Near the top of the tide. Right fore is Port Deauville. The lock-gates into the old yacht harbour (A) are open and even the fishing vessels berthed along the left bank of the River Touques are afloat (B)

and Les Ratelets – which extend 7 miles due W of Honfleur and discourage any corner-cutting. The E-cardinal Semoy buoy (BYB) Q (3) 15 s. lies two miles NNW of Trouville and is within 3° of the leading transit described above. Leave it close to starboard as it marks wrecks close to seaward.

Waiting for the tide, it is recommended to anchor about 5 cables to seaward of the W-cardinal Trouville SW buoy in position 280° 1 mile from outer western breakwater.

Berthing and Facilities

Port Deauville   Turn to starboard around the Iso G 4 s. Lt

13.2   Looking to seaward at near low water, the west breakwater extension is nearly awash with the beacons all to be left to starboard before turning sharply into the channel for Port Deauville, or carrying straight on into the river

13.3   Lock-gates to Port Deauville

13.4   Inside Port Deauville

13.5 *Fishermen on the River Touques alongside Trouville boulevard*

13.6 *View from Bassin des Yachts through open lock-gates to seaward*

13.7 *Deauville Yacht Club inside Bassin Morny*

13.8   Footbridge separating Bassin des Yachts from Bassin Morny

on a G mast at the end of the mole, giving a wide berth to
port to the Q G Lt, then keep parallel to the mole (Digue
Brise-Lames) in a buoyed channel towards the lock-gates.
The lock-keeper can be contacted on Ch 9. R and G lights
control movements through the lock, which has a minimum
depth of 2m5 in it.

Inside the 900-berth marina, built in among a spectacular
property development of holiday apartments, boats up to 4m
draught can be accepted.

Up to 100 visiting yachts can berth on the pontoons inside
the mole on your starboard hand after clearing the locks. If
relying on walking to the facilities of Port Deauville you
should get as far inshore as possible. Otherwise negotiate a
vacant berth in the main part of the harbour – or use an
outboard to get to the shops and restaurants which are all at
the NE corner of the development in the Bassin Central.

Facilities in Port Deauville include travel-hoist and boatyard alongside the lock. Fuel, FW and electricity all available.

Bassin des Yachts and Bassin Morny   While it is possible
to dry out alongside the wall on the E of the river immediately

13.9   Bassin Morny. Some pontoon berths at inshore end. Trouville Casino in the background

S of Pointe de la Cahotte, it is best to await the signal on the mast and go straight into the first basin (± 2h. on HW approx). Visitors are expected to lie stern to the wall on the E side of the Bassin des Yachts, but space can sometimes be found on the pontoons there.

During the shoulder season or by pre-arrangement with the DYC, it is possible to pass through into the Bassin Morny and berth in a more convenient spot for getting to the town and enjoying the warm hospitality and excellent facilities of the clubhouse. The footbridge over the entrance will open on demand. Fuel and FW are available.

Contacts   The HO (on the W end of the footbridge) tel. (31) 88–28–71 or on VHF Ch 11.

Customs (near the SNCF station just by the bridge to Trouville), tel. (31) 88–63–49.

Port Deauville HO, tel. (31) 88–56–15.

DYC tel. (31) 88–38–19 or oo.

Communications   Turbo train to Paris 2h.

Bus to Le Havre $1\frac{3}{4}$h., thence ferry to Portsmouth 7h. Or ferry Ouistreham – Portsmouth $5\frac{1}{2}$h.

Weather   On demand by tel. (31) 88–84–22. Area 10 Manche est.

Charts: Fr 890 (BA 1821 CG 526)

High Water −02h. 30m. Dover 01h. 20m. SP Le Havre
Heights above Datum MHWS 7m4. MLWS 0m7.
MHWN 6m0. MLWN 2m3. CD is − 3m4.

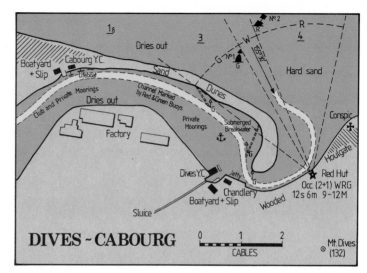

DIVES ~ CABOURG

PORTS used by William the Conqueror are as frequently claimed by local antiquarians as are beds where Elizabeth is reputed to have dished out her favours or where Lord Nelson slept on his way to joining HMS *Victory* for the last time. But the rapidly silting R. Dives estuary halfway between Deauville and Ouistreham can show provenance that it was the springboard from which 'Billy the Norman' set sail for England with 700 ships in company.

In the middle of the last century it was developed as a plush beach resort, with broad avenues all converging on its creamy Casino flanked by imposing holiday homes which would not look out of place in Belgravia. Marcel Proust spent his summers there. That it survives today is because the D-Day bombardments and landings spread westwards from a point only 5 miles along the coast. Since then industry and property developers have moved in, so that Cabourg's seafront next to the estuary is mostly high-bracket apartment buildings with boutiques and discos in their basements.

The estuary dries out completely at its entrance, but boats of 1m5 draught remain afloat in the channel farther upstream between the Dives and Cabourg YCs. A few commercial fishing-boats still operate, based on the quay on the Houlgate side of the river.

If the weather is settled it is worth a two-tide visit, if you have previously enjoyed sailing into Bembridge, Keyhaven, St Valery-sur-Somme or Le Touquet.

Approach It is dangerous to try and enter in fresh onshore winds or, without local knowledge, by night. The tidal currents across the entrance are negligible. The estuary dries one mile offshore, but rapidly deepens to seaward. Keep outside the 5m depth contour parallel with the shore until you spot the R and G buoys close inshore in the gap between Houlgate (wooded and hilly, with a prominent church on its seafront at the river entrance) and Cabourg, whose new apartment buildings end where the sand-dunes stretch half a mile to the W.

The two channel buoys are little more than a cable offshore. The approach course of 155° between them heads for a squat

14.1   Half-tide channel swinging clockwise from seaward in front of Houlgate Church and past green starboard beacon (left)

14.2   Dives Yacht Club and pontoon immediately upstream of fish quay on left bank

14.3   View downstream with Dives Yacht Club (right) and Houlgate beyond the sand-dunes (left). Channel between lines of moorings

R hut in the trees on the foreshore which is the Oc WR 4 s. 12M Lt, with R sectors either side of the 3°W Lt showing on the leading line. Access for 1m5 draught is normally possible 2h. either side of HW.

The channel then hugs the Houlgate side and goes briefly into the R sector all the way to the fishing quay. It then swings to starboard over towards the sand-dunes marked by G bns as far as Cabourg YC about one mile upstream.

Berthing   The HM is at the YC at Dives, tel. (31) 91–47–10.

If space permits, touch down at the fishquay at Dives or the pontoon in front of the local YC (SHRD) which is built out on stilts immediately upstream. They will then advise where to moor.

The HO for Cabourg is at the YC building. It is advisable to call before arrival ((31) 91–23–55) or, if departing from Deauville/Trouville, speak to the harbour authorities there.

As you approach Cabourg you find a row of pontoons on your starboard hand (see pic 14.4) and then a substantial and inviting jetty. It is strictly reserved for the lifeboat and the police. The next pontoon, just before the slipway and in front of the new YC is the place to secure and enquire of a vacant mooring. Shoal-draught boats will find room to take the mud off the fairway.

There is no VHF.

Facilities   Both YCs have boatyards and chandlers next to them. Fuel and water available. Simple fare available at either YC. One-design dinghy racing, sailboards, sea-angling and sailing schools are in full swing during the season.

Communications   Ouistreham 10 miles by road via the Pegasus Bridge, whence there is an excellent ferry service to Portsmouth in 5½h. SNCF and the main autoroute are 12 miles away at Caen.

Weather   Area 10 Manche est. Tel. (31) 74–74–74.

14.4   *Yacht Club pontoons on right bank*

14.5   *Cabourg Yacht Club with Harbour Office in same building*

*15 OUISTREHAM/CAEN

Charts: BA 1349, 1821 Fr 891 Im C32 CG 526 (Stan 1)

High Water −01h. 50m. Dover −00h. 25m. SP *Le Havre*
Heights above Datum *MHWS 7m5. MLWS 0m8. MHWN 6m2. MLWN 2m6.*

OUISTREHAM lies at the mouth of the 8-mile deepwater canal which runs parallel to the R. Orne from the cathedral city of Caen. It was the scene of the most bitter resistance put up by the Germans following the D-Day landings in 1944. The British airborne drop, which secured the beachhead by taking the vital bridge 4km upstream, is commemorated by being named Pegasus Bridge to this day. The Airborne Forces' D-Day Museum is next to the pub at the W end of the bridge.

Oceangoing ships up to 220m long can pass through the new western lock, with the approach channel dredged to 5m5 at LW. Yachts can get as far as the lock-gates in any state of the tide.

Approach Sailing across from England or from the general direction of Cap Barfleur, it is advisable to keep well offshore until you are sure that you are clear of the Plat du Calvados, rocky outcrops 5 miles either side of Courseulles, the next port, 9 miles WNW of Ouistreham. A sight of the Brittany Ferry on the Porsmouth-Ouistreham route is useful. Your first confirmed contact may well be the Pte de Ver Lt Ho, 2 miles W of Courseulles. Its Lt is Fl (3) W 15s. 42m 26M, one of the most powerful on the coast. It has its own 20-mile Rdo Bn (callsign 'ÉR' on 291.9kHz). The Lt Ho itself is not very conspicuous – a W tower with a Grey top only

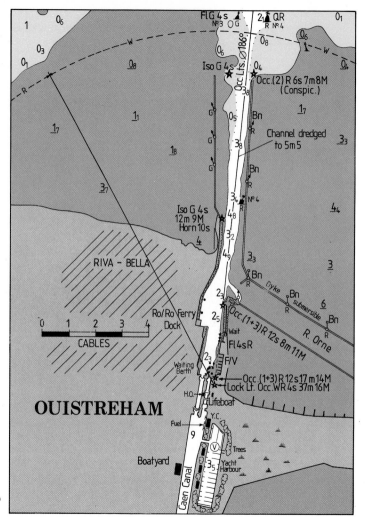

15.1   *Twin locks into Caen Canal. Yachts use the one on the left. New RO/RO terminal on right bank to seaward of locks on the Bella Riva side. Approach channel now dredged to 5m5*

15.2   RO/RO ferry berth on the west bank

16m high, partially hidden by surrounding trees. The shore has few distinctive features, an almost unbroken line of summer beach-houses. They all end abruptly at the E end of Riva-Bella, which is on the W bank of the entrance to Ouistreham and the Caen Canal. To the E the shore-line is flat and has no houses on it (R. Orne estuary) until the western outskirts of Cabourg. From a long way out a conspicuous feature is a square W building on the skyline SW of Riva-Bella, which looks like an office building but is in fact a silo.

Coming from the E you pass the entrance to R. Dives (see previous chapter), keeping 2 miles offshore until you have abeam the sandy stretch described above. The whole area is dominated by the imposing main lighthouse situated immediately to the E of both locks. It is 38m high, W with a R top. The Lt is Oc WR 4 s., the R sector covering shoals and rocks off Riva-Bella. Its range is 17 miles.

The main fairway should be picked up 2½ miles to seaward, where a RWVS whistle buoy marked 'OC' is the point at which large merchantmen may be at anchor for days or pick up pilots. The Lt characteristics are Iso 4 s. It is perfectly safe to approach at night, but there can be a big swell in the Channel in a northerly blow.

Course 186° for 1 mile passes between two spar buoys: No. 1 Fl G 4 s., while the R No. 2 is Fl R 4 s. By night this course is on a leading line with two R Oc (3 + 1) 12 s. Lts in line, with 11/14M range. Both are on lattice metal pylons wth R tops. The inshore one is twice as high at 17m. The channel is well buoyed. Both breakwaters are submerged at high tides from a point well inshore to 6 cables out. The port-hand sunk breakwater is marked by a R Tr Bn 16m tall (Oc (2) R 6s. 8M). This is Digue Est. It is paired off with an Iso G 4 s. Lt on the other side of the fairway 150m to the W.

15.3 *Yachts emerging from east lock. Control tower and signal lights on west side with main lighthouse, white tower with red top 38m high, on east side. Pylon is rear light of leading transit. Waiting berths for yachts on pontoons on east bank*

15.4 *Entrance to Ouistreham yacht harbour is a cut through east bank of canal just upstream of locks. Speed limit 2 knots. No fishing*

Half a mile farther on is the visible end of the W breakwater (pic 15.1) which is an equally imposing W structure G top on a dolphin. Its Lt is Iso G 4 s. It also has a foghorn 10 s. during the top half of the tide.

The entrance to the R. Orne is off to port, marked by R Bns from No. 4 buoy onward. Watch out for dredgers at work. The W bank has been excavated and a new RO/RO ferry terminal constructed. The 17,000-ton ferries turn off the R. Orne to dock stern-to. Keep well clear.

The Locks Pontoons for boats to lie alongside temporarily while waiting for the locks are on the E side to seaward of the fishing-boat berths.

The impressive new lock control building between the two locks is where the HO and the HM can be found. Contact on VHF Ch 16, 12 or 68. There are tide gauges and visual displays for depths above datum and controlling traffic in

accordance with French standard procedures (see p. 17).

Yachts always use the E lock.

By day and night there are light traffic signals for each lock:

R allows a designated ship to sail outward.

G for inward traffic.

W Lt under either of the others allows boats under 25m in length to enter or leave.

The locks normally operate ± 2h. of HW, except during July and August when they add at least another hour at either side of the tide.

Berthing

Yacht Harbour Just south of the locks in the Caen Canal there is a narrow cut through the eastern bank leading to a well-sheltered 650-berth marina surrounded by avenues of trees. The clubhouse of the Société des Régates de Caen-Ouistreham (SRCO) is at the NW end of the marina near a

15.5   Yacht harbour seen from yacht club slip at north-west corner

launching ramp. Visiting yachts should make for the pontoons on the eastern bank directly opposite the entrance and alongside the slipway.

Facilities   Around the Yacht Hbr there are boat agencies, chandlers and a boatyard which can handle most problems. Ouistreham village has little to offer. To get to the majority of shops and restaurants, it is necessary to walk across the lock-gates to Riva-Bella which is a fairly sophisticated resort.

There are FW and electricity at the pontoons, fuel on the canal side of the Yacht Hbr.

Telephone enquiries about the Yacht Hbr are on (31) 97–19–46. The HM, to whom a flight plan for going on up the canal to Caen should be submitted (to pre-arrange having the bridges open), can be contacted on (31) 97–14–43 or on Ch 68. The times of the first lock opening are displayed at each HO.

Customs are on the W bank (tel. (31) 97–18–62).

Weather   (31) 74–74–74 (Area 10 Manche est).

CAEN   This city of 125,000 inhabitants is redolent of history – much of it violent – from William the Conqueror and his Queen Matilda to some of the bloodiest battles of the Second World War. Three-quarters of the city was laid waste or put to the torch during June 1944, which proved literally to be the turning-point in the liberation of France. But, like

103

15.6   *Repair and chandlery facilities along west bank of yacht harbour*

St Malo, it has all been rebuilt in local stone, and the abbeys, churches and museums are open for business.

The passage from Ouistreham by the canal is child's play. No chart needed. The depth is 9m. It is a straightforward keep-in-the-middle passage; the bridges will open by pre-arrangement if one sticks to plan, not exceeding the 7-knot speed limit. Inward bound, contact Ouistreham locks on Ch 16, 68. If bound upstream, give way to vessels proceeding towards the sea. Allow 2h. all up.

The bridges are at the following distances upstream from the locks at Ouistreham:

Bénouville $2\frac{1}{2}$ miles,
Hérouville $5\frac{1}{4}$ miles,
Calix $6\frac{1}{2}$ miles.

Each bridge shows a G Lt when it is clear to pass through. If held up at Bénouville secure to the wall on the E bank and have a drink in the barge-restaurant, or cross the bridge to the Pegasus Inn.

Once inside the city limits, follow the canal to the swing bridge at La Fonderie, turning to starboard into the Bassin St Pierre where there are 125 pontoon alongside berths for yachts drawing up to 4m.

The HO is on the dockside above the first pontoon, where showers and WC are available (tel. (31) 93–74–47).

As a commercial port, the seat of the Prefecture of Calvados and a major tourist attraction, the town can offer all that a boat or her crew might need – sheltered alongside berths in the heart of a city full of top bistros and colour.

If a local shipping forecast should be needed before departure there is a continuous taped message (tel. (31) 71–74–74) or a report can be obtained on VHF Ch 12 or 68.

The local YC (Société Nautique de Caen et du Calvados – SNCC) is at 132 Rue Basse and the Calvados Motor YC is in the Hotel Malherbe near the race course.

Caen is served by express trains to Paris in 2h.

15.7   *Pegasus bridge at Bénouville, 2½ miles upstream. Wait alongside wall on east bank just out of picture (left)*

15.8   *The first house to be liberated in France (June 1944). Worth a visit if you have to wait for the bridge to open. Airborne Forces' museum next door to pub*

15.9   *Hérouville bridge, 5¼ miles from Ouistreham*

15.10   Autoroute viaduct on outskirts of Caen with Calix bridge beyond

15.11   La Fonderie swingbridge leading into Bassin St Pierre. Turn to starboard for yacht pontoons

15.12   Yacht harbour in the heart of Caen. Harbour Offices just beyond parked cars on the right

*16 COURSEULLES

Charts: *BA 1349, 1821 Fr 5598 Im C32 CG 527*

High Water *—02h. 20m. Dover —00h. 30m. SP Le Havre*
Heights above Datum *MHWS 7m0. MLWS 0m8. MHWN 5m6. MLWN 2m3.*

TWENTY miles W of Deauville and 9 miles beyond Ouistreham the river Seulles runs into the sea at the point where British forces landed on Juno Beach in June 1944. Nowadays its beaches are popular for other reasons, and it has developed as a holiday centre. There are two Yacht Hbrs: one in the middle of the town (Bassin à Flot) and one as an integral part of a property development (the Nouveau Bassin). The latter is a scaled-down version of the Deauville set-up.

Approach Outside the lock-gates the Avant-Port dries at

16.1 The new yacht harbour is to the right, alongside the River Seulles. Access is through a swingbridge (A). The main yacht harbour (Bassin à Flot) is right ahead through lock-gates

107

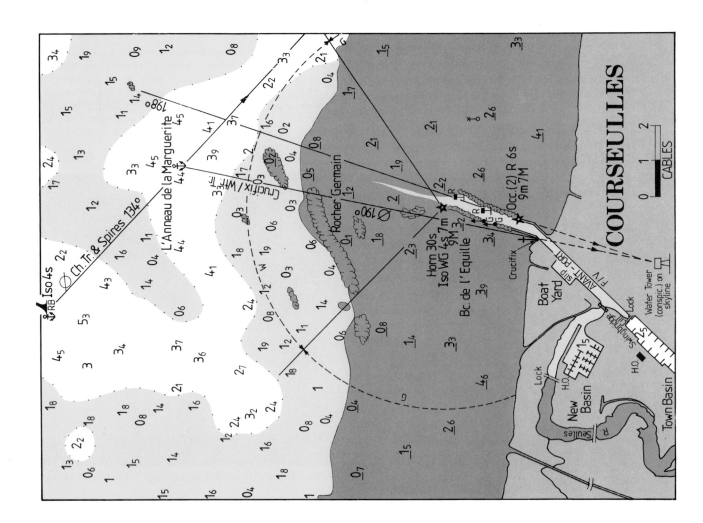

COURSEULLES

16.2   *Marks at the harbour entrance*

16.3   *Gate and lock control ahead. The swingbridge into the Nouveau Bassin can be seen to the right*

16.4   Nouveau Bassin within property development

LWS out to a distance of $\frac{1}{2}$ mile to seaward. The leading marks are the spires of the church la Déliverande $1\frac{1}{2}$ miles inshore on the hilltop in transit with the church at Bernières on the coast 1 mile east of Courseulles. A course of 134° takes the inward-bound yacht in deep water to the RBVS spar buoy (Iso 4 s.) just 1 mile NNW of the pierhead. There is good holding ground in its immediate vicinity, if waiting for the tide.

For longer-range identification there is the none too conspicuous Lt Ho in the trees at Ver, 2 miles W of Courseulles, a 16m W tower with Grey top at 42m elevation Fl (3) 15 s. with a range of 17 miles. It also has a 20-mile Rdo Bn on 219.9kHz (callsign 'ÉR' ·· − ·· · − ·).

From the fairway buoy leave the transit of churches and head 170° towards the dolphin with a G-topped wooden framework $1\frac{1}{2}$ cables to seaward of the western breakwater and separated from it by two G Bns in line. The Lt is Iso WG 4 s. to a range of 9 miles. The W sector shows between 135° and 235°, with G on either side covering the rocks. It sounds a horn ev 30 s. in fog.

At the root of the western breakwater there is a prominent crucifix which, brought into line with a conspicuous water Tr behind the town on 190°, provides an alternative approach within 2h. of HW.

The end of the E breakwater has a similar Lt structure with an R top. Its Lt is Oc (2) R 6 s. It also has two unlit Bns marking its seaward extension. This brought into transit with the Iso W, mentioned above, on course 187° can be used as a lead-in at night, always remembering the unlit Bns. The deepest part of the channel at entry is nearer the eastern side (pic 16.2).

16.5   Bassin à Flot above the locks. Bureau de Port and most facilities are on the right bank

Berthing   Once inside the Avant-Port there are drying berths alongside the eastern side. The opposite bank is mostly taken up by a long slipway in front of the boatyard. Just beyond this hard the R. Seulles runs into the Avant-Port under a swing-bridge which opens on demand up to ± 3h. on HW depending on tidal height.

The entrance to the New Harbour is over a sill on the S side of a mole down the middle of the river (3m3). Boats drawing 1m50 can lie alongside the pontoons there. This little marina has is own HO at the western end. Call VHF Ch 9.

The better bet, guaranteeing a least depth of 2m5, is through the lock-gates in the Bassin à Flot. The pontoons on the western side are most suitable for visitors, with the HO on the quayside. Some belong to the local YC – Société des Régates de Courseulles (SRC) whose clubhouse is on the eastern side of the basin (Quai Est) – tel. (31) 37–47–42.

Facilities   There is a yacht agency and chandlery, called Serra Marine, on the Quai Ouest, which can do all the servicing and afloat repairs.

FW at the pontoons. Fuel at the Quai Ouest.

For berthing reservations or enquiries about lock and swing-bridge opening call (31) 37–46–03, or check at the new lock control office on the western side of lock. Call VHF Ch 9.

The town has all the amenities one would expect of a somewhat up-market holiday resort, including one memorable fish restaurant and a number of hotels.

Weather is posted at the HO. Area 10 Manche est.

Charts: Fr 5515 BA 2073 Im C32 (CG 527)

High Water *−02h. 15m. Dover −00h. 45m. SP Le Havre*
Heights above Datum *MHWS 7m2. MLWS 1m1. MHWN 6m0. MLWN 2m6.*

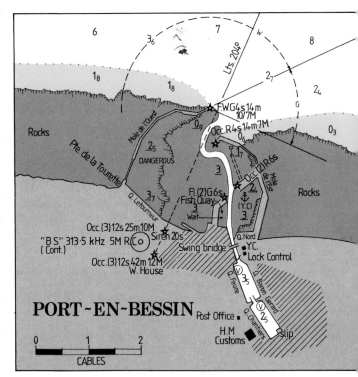

PORT-EN-BESSIN is an important fishing port and a harbour for coastal traffic. There are limited berths for visiting yachts who don't stay too long. It lies between the cliffs half-way from Courseulles to Grandcamp, 10kms west of Arromanches and the D-Day Gold Beach. One of its attractions is that it is the nearest Yacht Hbr to Bayeux. Its famous cathedral and museum with the anonymous cartoon-tapestry immortalizing the Norman invasion of Britain in 1066 is only 9km by road.

Approach Entry should not be attempted in heavy weather from the N or NE or before half-tide, even though there is over 2m0 right up to the outer breakwaters. The leading marks are a W house (42m) beyond a W tower on 204°. Both are Oc (3) 12 s. and the front one has a siren ev 20 s. On the western side of the town there is a Rdo Bn (continuous transmission on 313.5kHz, callsign 'BS' with a range of 5 miles).

After passing between the breakwaters (Oc R 4 s. on a R Tr to port and Fl WG 4 s. to starboard – the G sector covers the rocks close inshore) it is best to make for the inner harbour because the outer harbour dries out on its western side at LWS. Its pierheads have Lts Oc (2) R 6 s. and Fl (2) G 6 s. on either side. An R-topped unlit Bn marks the end of a submerged breakwater to port. Once inside, the moorings on

17.1 *High water view with (A) yacht club moorings – all dried out (B) lock-gates open (C) fish quay, where yachts can wait for lock to open, and (D) Harbour Office on west bank of yacht basin*

one's port hand are all privately owned by the local YC – Centre Nautique de Port-en-Bessin (CNPB) – which is located near the eastern side of the lock-gates leading to the inner basin.

The best place to wait is inside the seaward end of western inner quay, where a coastal vessel is seen in the accompanying

aerial picture (17.1). Here it also dries at LWS, but there is a minimum of 0m50 at LWN.

There is a swing-bridge across the outer end of the cut leading to the lock, which is supposed to open for 5 min on the hour and half hour during ±2h. of HW, which are the advertised times of lock opening. The bridge has R Lts to

17.2   Lock-gates open for entry

17.3   Fishing boats claim the best berths. Yachts proceed through the lock (now dismantled) to berth on west side beyond

show when it is shut. A prolonged hoot on a horn might also do the trick.

An R Lt or R flag indicates that ships may not enter the basin. G Lt or flag means no departure. R over G means no movement either way.

The lock control is on the eastern side (tel. (31) 21–71–77). VHF Ch 18 two h. either side of HW, when the lock may be opened.

Berthing and Facilities   In theory yachts may berth on either side just beyond the farthest piers inside the 500m length of the basins. The picture (17.1) shows yachts lying on the eastern side, while fishing boats tend to hog the other side,

which is the more attractive for being nearer the shops and bars. However it is always possible to talk an obliging fisherman into a berth outboard of his boat. The basins are maintained at 3m5 minimum depth at their N end and 2m5 at the other.

The YC is on the E side of the lock.

There is a slip and boatyard at the head of the basin.

The HO and Customs are at the town end of the fishmarket at the inshore end of the second basin on its W side. Tel. (31) 21–70–49 and (31) 21–71–09.

Weather is taped on (31) 74–74–74 or may be obtained at 0633 and 1133 on VHF Ch 3. Area 10 Manche est.

Charts: Fr 847 BA 2073 Im C32 (CG 527)

High Water −02h. 20m. Dover −01h. HW −00h. 30m. LW SP Le Havre
Heights above Datum MHWS 7m8. MLWS 1m1. MHWN 6m5. MLWN 2m8.

GRANDCAMP is a fishing port of little charm 4 miles W of Omaha Beach, which has recently developed successfully into being a Yacht Hbr and holiday centre with some elegant apartments built around the western half of the harbour. The eastern and southern quays are reserved for the considerable fishing fleet. A large modern fishmarket is located at the SW corner of the harbour.

Approach A rocky outcrop extends for a mile offshore, but it can safely be negotiated on the leading line at any time the lock-gates are open (normally ±2½h. on HW). The timing of the opening of the lock-gates is governed by the tides at Dunkerque (open at LW and shut at HW!).

The best approach is from a point midway between the two westernmost unlit N-cardinal buoys, 1½ miles offshore and to seaward of the rocks (Nos. 3 and 5). The course is 146° right for the pierheads. Off the end of the eastern jetty there is a W column with R top (Oc (2) R 6s. 10m 9M – Siren Mo (N) 30s.); the other pierhead has a W column with a G top (Fl G 4s. 9m 6M). The leading lights are both Q W, visible 10° either side of the 146° course. They are located at the SE corner of the harbour, each on 8m Grey posts.

It is not feasible to anchor short of the lock or to enter in a northerly blow.

18.1 Top part of tide with lock-gates open. Visitors' berths on outer end of main east-west pontoons. Harbour Office next to fish market at top righthand corner of harbour

18.2   Through this lock and alter 90° to starboard for visitors' berths

18.3   Visitors' berth at seaward end of either of these pontoons

18.4   North side of harbour, mainly for shoal-draft boats. Harbour entrance in middle background

Berthing There are 300 pontoon berths all with shore power and water with a least depth of 2m50; 20 are reserved for visiting yachts at the end of the first E–W pontoon after turning to starboard through the locks. The HO (tel. (31) 22–62–16) is at the SW corner of the harbour, next to the fishmarket. Contact on Ch 9 VHF.

Facilities There is a YC-Cercle Nautique de Grand-camp-les-Bains (CNG) – on the Quai Crampon (NE corner of harbour) open only in the season and weekends. Bathroom facilities at the HO.

FW and electricity on the pontoons. Fuel at the eastern fishquay (Henri Chéron).

There is a boatyard where all repairs can be made.

Provisioning is adequate. Bistros not too plentiful or classy. Yacht chandlery near the HO.

Weather Posted at the lock and the Bureau du Port. Area 10 Manche est, or by tel. (31) 74–48–11.

Charts: CG 527 Im C32 BA 2073 Fr 847

High Water +01h. *(approx) Cherbourg*
Heights above Datum *MHWS 7m30. MLWS zero.*
MHWN 6m00. MLWN zero.

ISIGNY lies 5 miles to the E of Carentan and has a much shorter and deeper channel to the open sea. But it is of interest only to boats prepared to dry out alongside the town quay. There is no lock and the navigable part of the river ends at the bridge in the centre of town (pic 19.2). See chart for Carentan.

Approach As for Carentan, except that the course from the E Cardonnet buoy is 235° to pick up the whistling RWVS pillar bell buoy 'IS' 1½ miles offshore and inside the 2m depth contour. If coming from the E it is necessary to keep to seaward of the three N-cardinal buoys marking the shoal water and rocks off Grandcamp. In a heavy blow from the NW access is not recommended.

There is a buoyed channel taking one on course 200° until picking up the leading marks on 173° to pass between a G-topped Bn to starboard and an R Bn to port, both unlit. The latter marks the eastern side of the straight channel 1½ miles long to the river junction.

At this point the 7m W Bn which carries the front leading light (Oc (1 + 2) 12 s.) is conspicuous. It should be left to starboard as course is altered to port to 125° to enter the last short reach to the town. The rear Lt on a 23m W metal framework with a B top has the same light characteristics and range (18M). The leading Lts are intensified in the section 171°–175°.

19.1 A few alongside berths on the west bank. Even the pontoon is aground

19.2   End of navigable water at bridge in mid-town

Berthing   The scene is not unlike Sandwich. The best berth is on the pontoons on the W side (pic·19.2) but it is also possible to dry out on the quay on the opposite bank nearer the bridge. FW and fuel are available. It is sheltered from all weathers.

The local harbour authority is at 5 Rue Hogues (tel. (31) 22–03–11), where the weather is posted. Area 10 Manche est.

Facilities   There is a local boatbuilder and a garage with yacht mechanics. Good shopping, hotels and restaurants.

*20 CARENTAN

Charts: Im C32 CG 527 BA 2073 Fr 847

High Water +01h. (approx) Cherbourg
Heights above Datum MHWS 4m10. MLWS 2m10.
MLWN as datum.

CARENTAN is a market town 4½ miles inland from the head of
the Baie du Grand Vey, which lies at the western end of the
D-Day beaches.

An imposing church (mostly twelfth century) dominates
the scene. It also features a fifteenth-century covered market
with Gothic archways. For yachtsmen there is perfect shelter
provided by the newly furnished marina. It is a good jumping-
off point to cruise to the Îles St Marcouf, which are only 8
miles distant from the seaward end of the Carentan Canal.
Grandcamp, St Vaast and Port-en-Bessin are within easy
reach, while Honfleur is only 55 miles to the E. Like Morlaix
it is a good place to leave one's boat between cruises.

Approach Do not attempt entry by night. Some 5 miles
S of Îles St Marcouf or the same distance from the E-cardinal
buoy marking the eastern extremity of the Cardonnet Bank
(BYB Q Fl (3) 5 s.) on a course of 255° find the RWVS spar
buoy with an R disc topmark marked 'CA'. It lies 3 miles to
seaward of the canal entrance. It is a whistle buoy but unlit.

The inward channel is well buoyed, with 10 unlit G buoys
to starboard and 9 R buoys to port. As the local chart warns, this
channel may vary according to shifting sand banks and may
wander off the leading Lts on 210°. The front Lt is Oc (3) R
12 s. with high intensity in the arc 209°–211° out to a range of
17 miles. Its structure is a 6m W post with a R top.

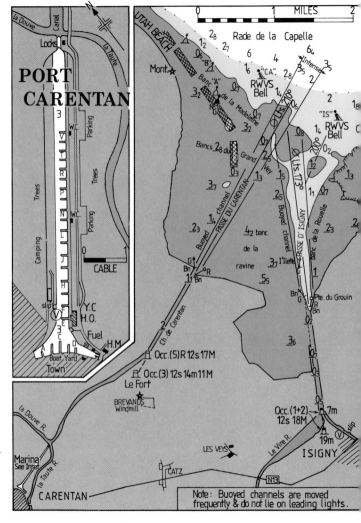

20.1   Lock-gates leading into Port of Carentan

The synchronized rear Lt is on a 15m W column with a G top. Its light is Oc (3) W 12 s. with a range of 11 miles showing over a 245° arc covering the whole bay. Both Lts lie on the E bank of the canal, the front one being 1½ miles from the canal entrance.

On passing between buoys Nos 9 and 10 alter to 245° to head for the canal entrance between G and R top-marked Bns; thereafter the course is 210°.

Depths   At LWS the whole approach route dries out to within half a mile of the Carentan buoys. The shallowest point is in the canal entrance where it dries 2m2, so care must be taken during Neaps when access may be restricted to boats drawing less than 1m50. Ideally one should leave the CA buoy inward-bound 1½h. before HW.

Two miles beyond the front leading Lt one reaches the confluence of the rivers Taute and Douve which encircle the town.

Entrance   The lock-gates are right ahead. Notionally they open 2h. either side of HW, but it as well to check with the HO on Ch 9 or tel. (33) 42-24-44. Off-season they sometimes do not open during the night. You can write to PO Box 450, Bureau du Port, 50500 Carentan, Normandie, for a complete schedule of times of opening and shutting for the whole year, including graphs to show hours of access for boats up to 3m50 draught.

Berthing   The locks keep a level of 5m inside the last ¾ mile of the canal, which has now been furnished as a 550-berth marina. Since there are towpaths on each side by the magnificent elm trees there is a lot of room for increasing the capacity (rather like Vannes). At present there are eighteen pontoons anchored to the E bank and another four across the head of the canal. Visitors should berth near the HO and YC (CN Carentais) located at pontoon E, the last one on the port hand after entry. Tel. (33) 42-04-11.

20.2   Pontoon berths downstream from the yacht club

20.3   Berths nearest the town at the head of the harbour

Facilities   Water and electricity are available on the pontoons. Fuel is just around the head of the harbour to port, near the boatyard. All repairs can be carried out. There are a 15-ton lift and two slipways.

Excellent hotels and restaurants. Good for shopping, including chandlery.

SNCF train to Paris St Lazare in $2\frac{1}{2}$h.

Weather   Posted at HO. Area 10 Manche est. Tel. (33) 44–45–00.

*21 ST VAAST-LA-HOUGUE

Charts: BA 1349 Fr 5522 CG 527/8 Im C32 (BA 2073)

High Water − 02h. 20m. Dover   + 01h. 00m. SP Cherbourg
Heights above Datum MHWS 6m5. MLWS 0m9.
MHWN 5m3. MLWN 2m3.

St Vaast has become one of the most popular destinations for S Coast yachtsmen since its harbour has been dredged, lock-gates installed and a 730-berth marina completed with a least depth 2m3. The old town forms one side of the Yacht Hbr and has a succession of attractive little stores and bistros, many of them featuring the local oysters for which St Vaast is famous. My favourite is the Café du Port. It is also an excellent place to stock up with wines from its extensive caves. The tiny Chapelle des Marins overlooks the harbour entrance. Inside are memorials to many local sailors lost in recent times.

Approach *From the N* Clear Cap Barfleur on a SSE'ly course parallel to the shore and about 1½ miles off (to avoid the worst of the lobster-pots and a few unmarked rocks SE of the town of Barfleur). Six miles on from Cap Barfleur you should have Pte de Saire abeam – a W Tr 10m high with an Oc (2 + 1) W 12 s. Lt. When it bears 295° it will be in transit by day with the prominent steeple of Reville church. Then alter to 200° until clear to the SE of Tatihou Island, when you round Le Gavendest S-cardinal buoy and head to leave another S-cardinal buoy (La Dent) to starboard on course about 260°.

From the E The left-hand edge of Fort de la Hougue is brought in transit with the W octagonal Lt Ho 90m above sea level and 1.7 miles beyond it at Morsalines on course 267°. The front Lt is Oc W 4 s; the Morsalines light is Oc (3 + 1) WRG 12 s. but only the W sector will be seen on the correct approach. This will bring you 2 cables S of La Dent, after which alter slowly to starboard and join the approach transit from the SSE as described below. The Fort de la Hougue/Morsalines transit is impossible to pick up against a setting sun, so just clear the two S-cardinal buoys.

From the SSE St Vaast is protected from the NE by the Île de Tatihou lying ½ mile off the entrance with a prominent seventeenth-century round Tr (with a small lookout Tr on its left-hand side). There is a similar tower at Fort de la Hougue, the isthmus S of the village. The fairway lies between these two on a course of 349°, with the left-hand edge of Tatihou in transit with the steeple of Réville village church.

On this course the two S-cardinal buoys 6 cables SE of Tatihou marking La Dent and Le Gavendest rocks are left to starboard, while on the port hand the E-cardinal buoys Le Manquet (½ mile to seaward and due E of the tip of Fort de la Hougue) and Le Bout du Roc are left to port. Also left to port is the Bn on Le Creux de Bas rocks. All these marks are unlit.

The outer end of the breakwater has an Oc (2) WR 6 s. on a W Tr with an R top 11m high. It has a siren (N 30 s.). Rounding the breakwater shape 270° for the entrance proper, with a W pedestal and a G top to starboard (Iso 6 4 s.) and a W hut with R roof to port (Oc 4 R 12 s.) The lock-gates are then immediately ahead. There is ample water to within ½ mile SSE of the breakwater. Thereafter it shoals rapidly and mostly dries out.

The lock-gates are open and shut at half-tide with some local variations. A straightforward R or G traffic Lt at the lock entrance controls entry or exit. The HO is on your starboard side alongside the gate. It can be contacted on Ch 9, or tel. (33) 54–43–61.

124

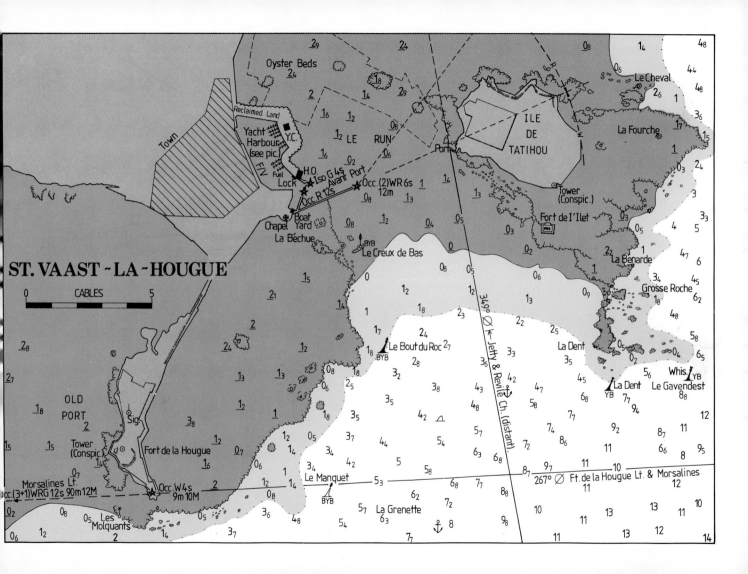

ST. VAAST ~ LA ~ HOUGUE

CABLES

0 _____ 5

Oyster Beds

Town

Reclaimed Land

Yacht Harbour (see pic.)   Y.C.

Fuel

Lock   H.O.

Iso G 4s   Occ. R 12s   Avant Port   Occ.(2)WR 6s 12m

Boat Yard

Chapel   La Béchue

LE   RUN

Port

Le Creux de Bas

BYB

ILE DE TATIHOU

Le Cheval

La Fourche

Tower (Conspic.)

Fort de l'Ilet

La Benarde

Grosse Roche

OLD PORT

Sig

Tower (Conspic.)

Fort de la Hougue

Morsalines Lt.

Occ.(3+1)WRG 12s 90m 12M

Occ. W 4s 9m 10M

Les Molquants

Le Manquet

BYB

La Grenette

Le Bout du Roc

BYB

349°

Jetty & Revile Ch. (distant)

La Dent

La Dent   YB

Le Gavendest   Whis.   YB

267°   Ft. de la Hougue Lt. & Morsalines

21.1   *St Vaast Marina with Tatihou Island in the background.   (A) Yacht club.   (B) Lock-gates, Harbour Office and fuel dock.*
Approach course indicated

21.2   Fort de la Hougue from the east

21.3   Réville Church spire in transit 349° with west end of Tatihou jetty

21.4   Rounding east end of St Vaast breakwater to enter open locks. Note the Chapelle des Marins at landward end of mole

21.5   Lock open. Bureau de Port on the right. Café du Port on fish quay beyond

21.6　Fishing boats use old quay on porthand inside lock-gates

21.7　Clubhouse of Cercle Nautique de la Hougue

Berthing (*1*) *Anchoring*: in settled weather a good anchorage can be found W of La Dent, for example, to wait for the tide. Although fishing-boats may be lying alongside the S breakwater, the small cut immediately inside the entrance is reserved for the lifeboat and the slipways of the yacht yard.

(*2*) *Inside the locks*: visiting yachts should swing to starboard and go alongside any of the first three pontoons (A, B or C). The first two are designed for larger boats, with 8m fingers and 3m3 depth of water. The town side of the marina is reserved for fishing-boats and other commercial craft.

Facilities　On the reclaimed land at the head of the pontoons there is the new clubhouse (Cercle Nautique de la Hougue) with ample car parking and winter berths ashore.

Its catering facilities are limited. There is a travel lift at the N end of the Yacht Hbr. FW and electricity are available at every berth. Fuel at a pontoon next to the HO. It can be ordered by tel: (33) 54–43–64 – usually only available forenoons.

The boatyard near the little church on the S side of the lock-gates seems to be efficiently run and has a well-stocked chandlery including charts.

The Customs are at the HO. Banks are shut on Thurs.

There is a good bus service to Valognes 17km away, which lies on the main railway line from Cherbourg to Paris.

Weather is posted at the Bureau du Port and at the YC. Area 10 Manche est. By tel. (33) 43–20–40.

*22 BARFLEUR

Charts: BA 1349, 2073 Fr 5618 Im C32 CG 528

High Water − 2h. 30m. Dover + 01h. 00m. SP Cherbourg
   Heights above Datum MHWS 6m5. MLWS 1m2. MHWN 5m3. MLWN 2m5.

A MOST attractive little fishing village situated 2 miles S of Cap Barfleur with its imposing Lt Ho alongside the remains of an earlier structure (pic 22.1). The harbour dries out completely, but along the quayside (Quai Henri Chardon) and anywhere in the NW half of the harbour the bottom is suitable for taking the ground. Its popularity with visiting British yachts has diminished since the new marina at near-by St Vaast-la-Hougue was completed. It is also exposed to E and NE'ly winds.

Approach From whatever direction one approaches give Cap Barfleur a wide berth and be sure to consult the tidal atlas. The currents run up to 4 knots and a race develops E of the Lt Ho especially when the N-going tide sweeping out of the Baie de la Seine from −03h. 20m. HW Dover meets the main E–W stream off the tip of the peninsula. I once kedged off Barfleur and took twenty-eight mackerel in as many minutes. The main 75m tall Grey B top Lt Ho shows Fl (2) 10 s. with a range of 27 miles. Its fog signal is a reed (2) 60 s. The Rdo Bn ('FG' callsign) on 291.9kHz has a 70-mile range and is the strongest of its group, which includes Cap d'Antifer, St Catherine's and Portland Bill.

Keep a mile offshore until the G unlit buoy with cone topmark to the E of La Grotte rocks is sighted. Come on to a SW'ly course so as to pass between another G buoy (Roches des Anglais) and an R one with can topmark to port, marking the offshore extremity of the rocks at Le Hintar. Course should now be 219° in transit with 2 square W Lt Trs. On the leading marks there is a least depth of 4m5 to within 1 cable of the entrance at LW. The forward one (7m high) is in a caravan park. The rear one is 13m high and has a G top on a square structure built above a prominent house at the head of the harbour (pic 22.2). Both are Oc (3) 12 s. 10M and are synchronized with one another. The harbour dries out to 2m4 above datum in the half suitable for taking the ground.

22.1 *Barfleur lighthouse with 75m grey tower, black top seen from the east just short of the overfalls*

130

ϕ 219°

22.2   *The port at* $1\frac{1}{2}$ *hours before high water. Transit* 219° *is shown. Harbour Office (A) will direct visitors to the drying-out alongside berth on quayside. It is easy to see the areas where it is not suitable to dry out – there are no boats there*

22.3   *Approach on 220°. Square tower of church is conspicuous by day*

22.4   *Front light of leading marks on transit 219° with rear light (pic 22.5) just open to the right*

Course 219° heads just to the left of the harbour entrance. La Vimberge rocks to starboard are marked by another G cone-topped buoy just 3 cables short of the harbour. At this point the bottom shoals rapidly and it is advisable to lie off or anchor until 2h. before HW, when it is possible to enter. There are some small moorings just off the fairway which are reserved for local fishing boats. The southern breakwater shows Oc R 4 s. at its extremity, just off the main approach transit. The inner breakwater (to starboard) has a Fl G 4 s. 7m.

Berthing   The best berths are alongside the quay on the starboard hand on entering, although the HM, whose office is next to the YC at the head of the slip inside the northern breakwater (tel. (33) 54–02–68) may direct visiting boats to lie up to four abreast farther inshore. All berths dry 2m. No VHF watch is kept.

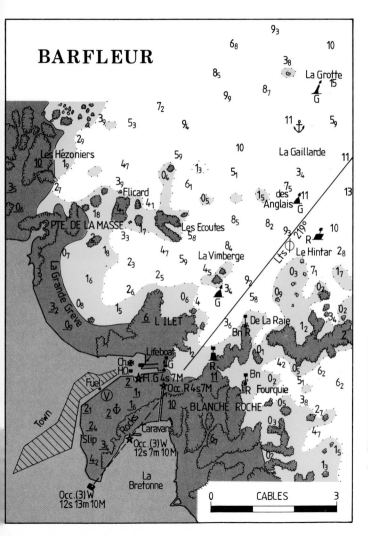

BARFLEUR

Les Hézoniers
Flicard
PTE DE LA MASSE
Les Ecoutes
La Vimberge
La Grande Grève
L'ILET
De La Raie
Bn R
Lifeboat
Ch
HO
G
Fuel
Fl.G.4s 7M
Occ.R 4s 7M
R
Bn
R Fourquie
BLANCHE ROCHE
Town
Rocks
Caravans
Slip
Occ.(3)W
12s 7m 10M
La Bretonne
Occ.(3) W
12s 13m 10M

La Grotte
G
La Gaillarde
des
Anglais
G
R
Le Hintar
G

CABLES
0   3

22.5   *Rear light of lead-in transit in south-west corner of the harbour*

22.6   On starboard hand entering. White hut in front of church is Harbour Office

22.7   Alongside berths at Quai Henri Chardon on north-west wall

Except for afloat berths at all states of the tide, Barfleur has most things a visiting yachtsman can wish for: water, fuel, good restaurants and bars, all kinds of shops and a garage with yacht mechanics. For the homesick, the main street is named after St Thomas à Becket (Archevèque de Canterbury). The pretty little church by the lifeboat station just N of the entrance has beyond it a delightful bathing beach. There are regular buses to Cherbourg. The nearest Customs are in St Vaast, 6 miles S.

Weather   Posted at the HO or taped on (33) 53–11–55. Area 10 Manche est.

23 CHERBOURG

Charts: BA 2602 Fr 5628 Im C32 CG 528 Stan 16

High Water *−03h. 20m. Dover SP Cherbourg*
Heights above Datum *MHWS 6m8. MLWS 0m5.*
MHWN 4m8. MLWN 2m8.

CHERBOURG lies in the middle of the shallow bay between Cap de la Hague in the W and Cap Barfleur to the E. The outer harbour (Grande Rade) which is inshore of the detached breakwater (Digue Centrale) and two moles (Digue de Querqueville and Digue de l'Est) is nearly as big as Portland and Plymouth Sound put together, being about 4 miles E–W and one mile N–S. The inner harbour (Petite Rade) is surrounded by the town of 90,000 inhabitants, which owes its existence to the massive artificial harbours dating back to Louis XVI's time, although not completed until Napoleon III in 1853 followed five years later by the opening of the naval dockyard.

The Petite Rade is divided into three zones, mutually exclusive to their users. The western end forms the naval base and dockyard, where nuclear submarines and frigates are built. The eastern part is the commercial port, with the faded glory of the old transatlantic passenger terminal (the first scheduled service to USA started in 1869) now used mainly by ferries from Portsmouth. On reclaimed land farther E massive offshore oil platforms were built and launched. The museum in Fort du Roule with its commanding view of the whole area from 112m up is worth a visit.

In between these two areas a 1,500-boat marina (Port de Plaisance Chantereyne) has been built with every conceivable facility on tap. It is now the only place where visiting yachts may lie. The old Yacht Hbr farther inshore is reserved for a few local boats, including fishermen. The old YC is shut and abandoned. Most of the traditional bars and restaurants are now a taxi-ride away.

Outside the Straits of Dover, Cherbourg is the closest

23.1 *Light at the east end of Digue Centrale with Fort Centrale to the right. The west entrance is 3.7km away at the far end of this massive breakwater*

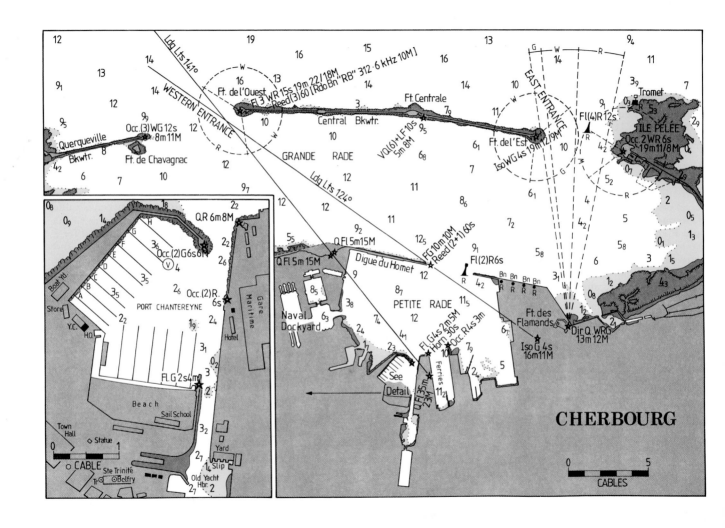

CHERBOURG

23.2   *Passing the east end of Digue du Homet – the whole area to the right of the beacon is forbidden. White buildings are part of the naval base and dockyard*

23.3   *Entrance to Chantereyne yacht harbour, with old transatlantic jetty to the left*

23.4   *Inside yacht harbour. Services yacht* Dasher *(Nicholson 55, dark hull) lying alongside visitors' berth on second pontoon from the entrance. Marina capacity now doubled (see chart)*

French port to the S Coast, only an overnight trip of 60 miles from the Needles, 84 miles from Torbay or 90 from Brighton. It is accessible at all states of the tide and affords excellent shelter from any direction.

It deserves to be even more popular than it seems to be for visiting British yachts, although it is often overcrowded. Those who race on the RORC circuit think of Cherbourg largely in terms of looking in thick fog and a 5-knot Spring tide for the CH1 buoy (Oc 4 s. RW stripes and a whistle which sounds more like a moan) 3½ miles NW of the harbour entrance. Many have spent hours kedged in its vicinity waiting for wind or tide. In the days before the Rdo Bn was established on the western fort, with a notional range of 20 miles, it could be an anxious landfall. Off-lying dangers exist only if one fetches up 5 miles to the eastward – not unheard of. Hence the comments attributed to Uffa Fox while navigating the schooner *Lumberjack* in thick fog. He was woken from a deep sleep to fix the boat's position. He took a sniff to weather and declared them to be just off Cherbourg. Later he attributed this uncanny accuracy to having smelled coal-dust and call-girls.

Another attraction of Cherbourg for British yachts is that it is an excellent, secure harbour in which to wait for the tide in either direction or for the weather to improve. It is also convenient and uncomplicated for storing ship for a cruise to W Cork or S Brittany. Crews joining from UK can use the ferries (4½h.)

Approaches From whichever direction Cherbourg is approached the tidal currents are likely to play a decisive part. If the wind has been blowing for any length of time from W or E it is advisable to put a bit extra in the bank by allowing stronger currents than those predicted. It is never safe to assume on a 12h.-passage from, say, Poole, that the tides will cancel each other out. If the visibility is not perfect, start checking by D/F bearings when you estimate to be 20 miles off-shore using:

Alderney AeroBn (callsign 'ALD') on 383kHz
Barfleur ('FG') on 219.9kHz
Cherbourg ('RB') on 312.6kHz

The last is relatively weak with a 20-mile range, so may not come up until late in the passage.

In extreme visibility by day Cherbourg will appear to lie in a dip in the skyline with Cap de la Hague forming a prominent right-hand edge of land. Near it is the massive nuclear reprocessing plant whose floodlights are especially prominent by night – rather more so than the loom of the city lights of Cherbourg.

Ferries to or from Portsmouth may use either entrance to the Grande Rade, but within those limits a chance sighting of one can be reassuring. The W entrance is the more popular, though there is plenty of room through either. The light on Fort de l'Ouest is the most powerful in the locality (Fl (3) 15 s.) with 22-miles range in its W sector and 18 in the R sector (covering NW–W–S) to prevent a boat coming from the W cutting it too fine off Pointe de Querqueville. There is ample water to within 60yds of the W breakwater where there is an R con buoy (Oc R 4 s.) immediately SW of the breakwater extremity to be left to port.

At the eastern entrance it also pays to shape close to the Fort de l'Est, coming in on the W sector of the Iso WG 4 s. with its 12-mile range. Here the rocky sub-structure of the breakwater extends 100yds to seaward and is unmarked. Approaching from Barfleur/Cap Lévy it is important to give a wide berth to the Île Pelée, the rocky outcrop on which the fort marking the NW extremity of the eastern mole is built. Give a wide berth to the unlit R Bn with can topmark (Tromet) and the R spar buoy (Fl (4) R 12 s.) marking La Truite and the port hand of the deep channel at the entrance.

23.5   Yacht club building at the town end of the breakwater

Once inside the Grande Rade through either entrance, head straight for the eastern end of the Digue du Homet, the western breakwater guarding the Petite Rade. Its fixed G Lt 10m high forms a transit with an Iso G Lt 4 s. 16m high on the reclaimed land at the eastern end of the Petite Rade. This transit on 124° brings an inbound ship straight from the western entrance to the Petite Rade. A safe course to pass through the eastern entrance is to stay in the W sector of the Q on the Fort des Flamands at the eastern end of the Petite Rade. Once inside, a course of 220° for 1 mile takes you to the entrance of Petite Rade, leaving to port an R spar buoy with topmark (Fl (2) R 6 s) off the end of the eastern arm of the breakwater – the Jetée des Flamands.

The twin arms of the old tranatlantic jetties with the RO/RO ferry berth at its head are then seen fine on the port bow. Course 200° for 6 cables will bring one to the narrow gap between the seaward end of the breakwater protecting the new Chantereyne marina (Oc (2) G 6 s.) and the western end of the arm on which the conspicuous Gare Maritime is situated, marked by a Q R.

Berthing   Swing to starboard round the end of the inner breakwater and head for the visitors' berths on pontoon G – the second one in from the entrance. There is a minimum of 4m water in the vicinity of the pontoons. It may be permitted to anchor briefly there while getting sorted out; to all intents and purposes neither berthing nor anchoring is allowed

23.6   *The old Avant Port, Cherbourg's first marina. Old yacht club boarded up. Berths reserved for locals. Fort du Roule on hilltop is where the last Germans held out in 1944 – now a D-Day museum*

anywhere else in Cherbourg. The marina is being extended by filling the southern half of the Yacht Hbr with pontoons.

Port Operation   The Marina Office (tel. (33) 53–75–16) is situated in the same bulding as the Cherbourg YC (YCC) near the travel-hoist, boatyard, chandlers and ship's stores. It should be contacted on Ch 9 or immediately after berthing. The Customs offices there (tel. (33) 53–79–65) are not manned all the time and it is not necessary to contact them as long as one's ships papers (Certificate of Registration) are in order. It is advisable to have valid passports including French visas for non-EEC crew, especially if a visit to the casino is contemplated, and a UK Customs Form C1328, completed before leaving UK.

Facilities   Information on every conceivable facility for sustaining a yacht or her crew can be obtained through the Yacht Club de Cherbourg (Ch 9 or tel. (33) 52–02–83).

Showers and heads are at the inshore end of pontoon C. Windsurfing, dinghy charters or instruction can be arranged through the Cercle Nautique Cherbourgais (CNC) within easy walk of the YCC. There are two other YCs (CNMC and CNEMC) near the magnificent sports complex immediately next to the Yacht Hbr, but they are reserved for French service personnel.

Local VHF contact for services outside those covered by the HO at the marina should initially be made on Ch 16 calling 'COM Cherbourg'.

Weather   Recorded forecasts are obtainable on tel. (33) 53–11–55 or from Radio Brest-Le Conquet (FFU). Cherbourg local weather is on Ch 27 VHF at 0633 and 1133. The port lies almost on the dividing line between area 11 (Manche ouest) and area 10 (Manche est).

PART FOUR

CHANNEL ISLANDS AND ADJACENT COAST OF FRANCE

Les Iles Anglo-Normandes et la Côte d'Emeraude
Omonville–Erquy

Soundings and heights in metres
Bearings and courses in degrees true
Distances at sea in nautical miles or cables

Tidal charts covering the area,
related to HW Dover

DISTANCES AROUND THE CHANNEL ISLANDS

Distances shown are safe navigable routes between breakwaters and/or estuary entrances (in nautical miles)

CHERBOURG	CHERBOURG						
ALDERNEY	21	**ALDERNEY**					
ST PETER PORT	41	**23**	ST PETER PORT				
ST HELIER	57	**40**	26	**ST HELIER**			
CHAUSEY [S]	77	**60**	48	**24**	CHAUSEY [S]		
GRANVILLE	83	**66**	53	**29**	9	**GRANVILLE**	
ST MALO	83	**66**	52	**30**	15	**21**	ST MALO
LÉZARDRIEUX	81	**65**	41	**41**	47	**56**	37	**LÉZARDRIEUX**

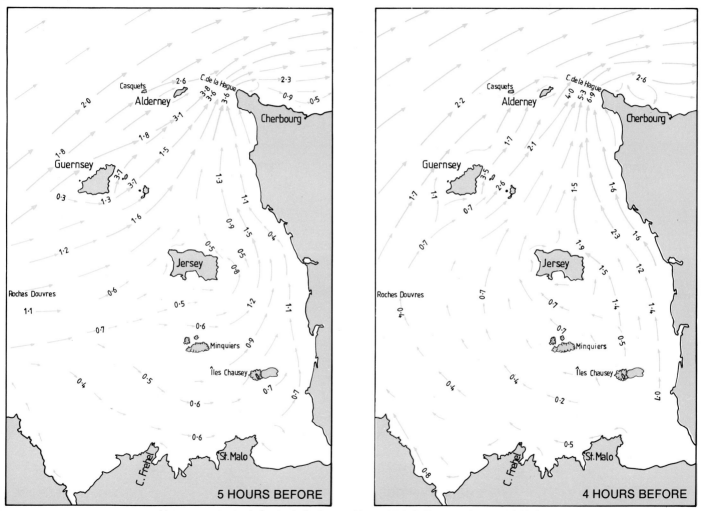

Mean current rates in knots. At Springs, add one-third. At Neaps, subtract one-third.

5 HOURS BEFORE

4 HOURS BEFORE

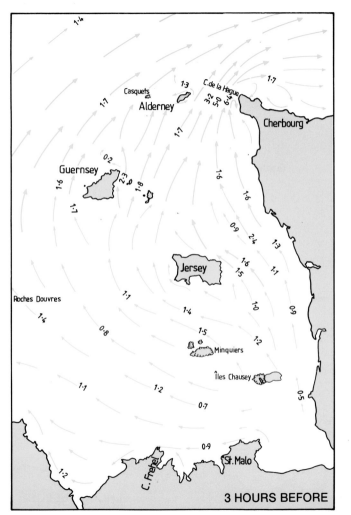

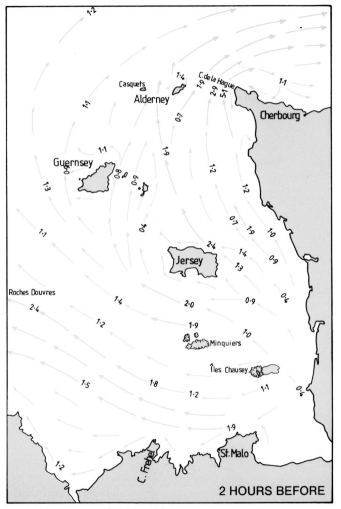

Mean current rate in knots. At Springs, add one-third. At Neaps, subtract one-third.

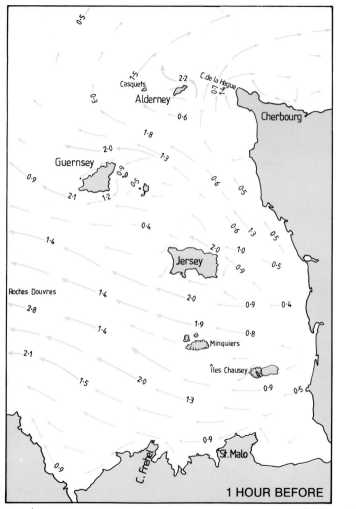

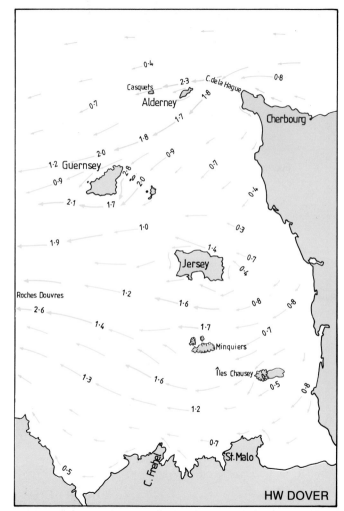

1 HOUR BEFORE

HW DOVER

Mean current rate in knots. At Springs, add one-third. At Neaps, subtract one-third.

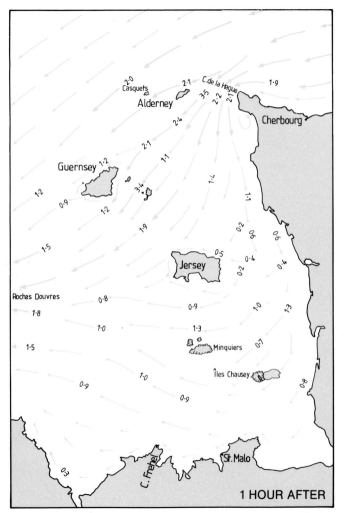

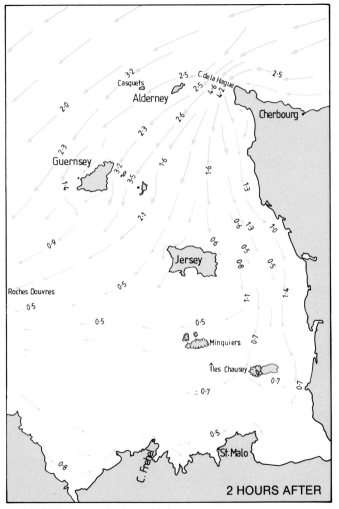

Mean current rate in knots. At Springs, add one-third. At Neaps, subtract one-third.

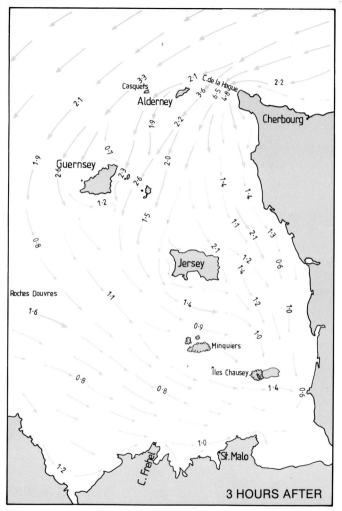

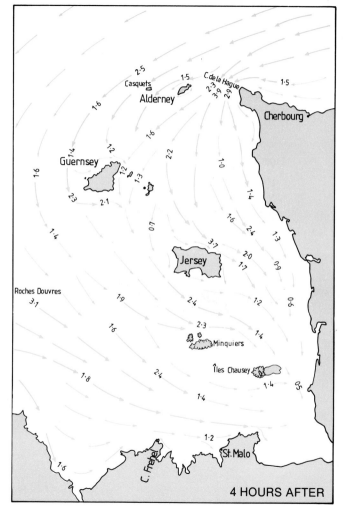

3 HOURS AFTER

4 HOURS AFTER

Mean current rate in knots. At Springs, add one-third. At Neaps, subtract one-third.

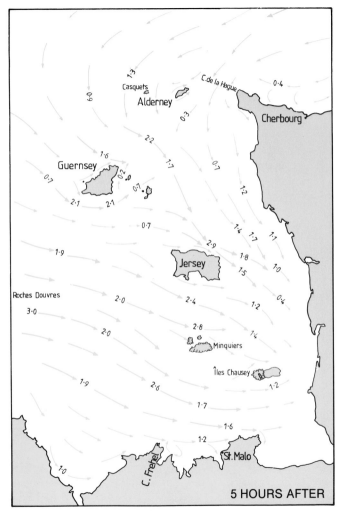

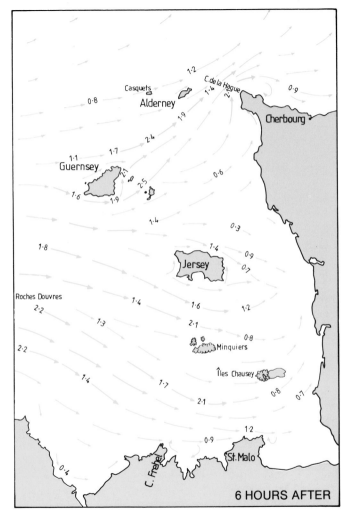

Mean current rate in knots. At Springs, add one-third. At Neaps, subtract one-third.

*24 OMONVILLE

Charts: Fr 5636 Im C33a (BA 1106 CG 528 Stan 16)

High Water *— 3h. 40m. Dover — 00h. 10m. SP Cherbourg*

Heights above Datum *MHWS 6m2. MLWS 1m1. MHWN 4m9. MLWN 1m1.*

THE MAIN attraction in this peaceful little fishing harbour lies in its being only 6 miles from Alderney Race and 8 miles west of Cherbourg, and thus a good place to wait for tides or weather to change. So long as the wind is settled between NNW and S it affords excellent shelter, but it is not a spot to be caught in if the wind should make up from an easterly quarter.

Approach From Cherbourg follow the coastline about a mile offshore until the village and breakwater lying on its N side appear. On rising ground above the waterfront cottages

24.1   *Omonville at half tide, showing why you should not attempt to lie alongside the seaward half of the breakwater. Front leading mark (A) Le Tunard beacon (B) Old Fort (C)*

24.2   Yacht giving Le Tunard beacon a wide berth. Landing steps on the half pier to the left

will be seen the little chapel of Omonville-la-Rogue with its distinctive steeple. A W lattice pylon with an R top sited on the foreshore in the SW corner of the port should be brought into line with the chapel on a course of 257° until bringing abeam to starboard the G Bn with triangular topmark on Le Tunard (or L'Etaunard) rocks about 1 cable ESE of the end of the breakwater. On the approach transit and to the west of Le Tunard Bn there is over 2m to within ¾ cable of the shore. At LW the rocks dry out.

By night the pylon shows an Iso WRG 4 s. Its 10° W sector has a range of 11 miles and brings the incoming yacht in along the approach described above. The R sector indicates being to the S of the correct approach. The G sector lies between N and 272° and says you are off course to starboard.

Coming from the N or W give a clear berth to the Basse Bréfort BY N-cardinal buoy lying 6 cables to the N of Pte de Jardeheu and its signal station. The buoy has a VQ 10M all-round Lt. Hold on until Le Tunard Bn bears 195° (and you are well within the G sector of the shore Lt).

The leading transit is Le Tunard Bn in line with the old fort forming the SE extremity of the harbour. It has a small apartment building on it. A jink to port will be necessary to clear Le Tunard before swinging to starboard on to the approach transit from the E, as already described.

Berthing   The harbour dries out along the breakwater and to a distance of ½ cable elsewhere. There are several permanent French Navy mooring buoys and 80 for yachts. Further information from the near-by village of Beaumont-Hague on tel. (33) 52–72–82.

Local fishermen use most of the inshore end of the alongside berths at the inshore end of the breakwater (dries 1m), which is only part suitable for drying out alongside, or pick up a vacant mooring W of Le Tunard Bn and go ashore at the slip or steps at the little pier. Pic 24.1 shows how crowded it can be in summer. It also shows the extent of the rocky outcrop at the head of the harbour and alongside the outer half of the breakwater.

Facilities   Omonville's famous old cottage-restaurant is no more, but there are shops and a new bar-restaurant at the pierhead which has been well reported. FW available on the quay and the local garage will supply fuel. Beaumont-Hague 5km inland has a regular bus service to Cherbourg.

Weather   See Cherbourg.

*25 ALDERNEY

Charts: *BA 60, 2845 Im C 33a Fr 6934 (Stan 16)*

High Water *−04h. 10m. Dover* *+00h. 45m. SP St Helier*
Heights above Datum *MHWS 6m3. MLWS 0m8. MHWN 4m7. MLWN 2m6*

ALDERNEY is only 60 miles from the Needles and no more than an overnight sail from any point of departure from Chichester or the West Country.

The island is less than 6 sq miles, with a winter population of 2,000. Although only 8 miles due W of Cap de la Hague at the NW tip of the Cherbourg peninsula, it has owed allegiance to the English crown for over 900 years. The locals are friendly and easy-going, largely dependent on tourism and fishing for their livelihood. As with all the Channel Islands, taxes on booze and cigarettes are modest and the licensing hours

25.1 *Cap de la Hague from the north, a 51m grey tower well clear of the land. It marks the eastern side of the Race*

25.2 *Alderney lighthouse at western side of the Race seen from north*

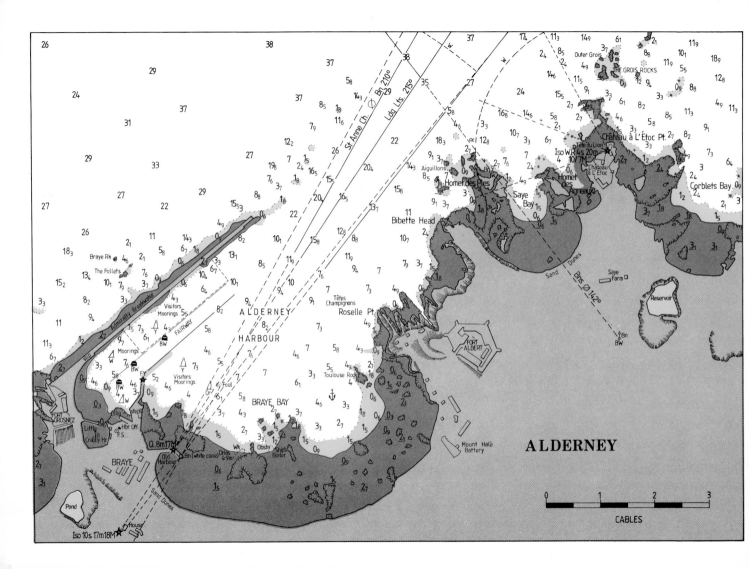

ALDERNEY

25.3   *Braye Harbour with 250 visitors' moorings either side of fairway leading to jetty. (A) Château à l'Étoc Point.*
(B) Fort Albert. (C) Old breakwater light (inconspicuous by day).   St Anne town on hill beyond

25.4 *Leading marks by day on 210°. (A) St Anne's Church in line with (B) white daymark at end of old breakwater (obscured by yacht) and (C) a water tower which looks like a church and is sometimes confused with (A)*

dangerously flexible. There is no VAT. Also, there is no hurry.

Its attraction for visiting yachts has been greatly enhanced by the number of new Y mooring-buoys for visitors having been increased to 250, a reliable and fast water-taxi service (so that it is no longer necessary to put one's dinghy over the side and worry about its floating off the slip or having its motor stolen during dinner), a supermarket and top-class restaurant all within two minutes' walk of landing.

Approach to landfall The only harbour is Braye at the NE end of the island, situated at the bottom of a steep hill $\frac{1}{2}$ mile from St Anne, the town. The harbour is open to NE'ly winds, when it is best avoided altogether.

The other factors which should be uppermost in one's mind when making a landfall:

(a) The Alderney Race runs up to 9 knots at Springs. Slack water $\frac{1}{2}$h. before HW Dover, after which it runs to the SW for

25.5 *New visitors' mooring on south-east side of harbour*

25.6 Entrance to Little Crabby Harbour. Fuel and chandlery hard to port through the pierheads

25.7 New white moorings for visitors hold fast during Hurricane Charlie (August 1986)

the next 5½h. It turns to the NE 6h. before HW Dover and starts to slack off 5h. later. Sailing from Cherbourg to Braye against a light westerly breeze in poor visibility I once held on to starboard tack for just a few minutes too long in a Class I ocean-racer and found myself shooting down the rapids in the direction of Quenard Pt. Even with a powerful motor, normally good for 7 knots, we were unable to make the last mile to Braye, so had to give up lunch at the Divers and go S of the island – next stop the Scillies.

(b) Coming from the NW, if you first sight the Casquets (looking like a laden merchantman), consult the tidal atlas and decide then and there whether the last 8 miles to Braye harbour are best negotiated by standing well to the N of Burhou, or if the extra 3½-mile passage S-about Alderney is not going to be quicker.

(c) Approaching from the S, if you look like missing the tide at the Race, you could catch the last of the flood by an early decision to head up for the Ortac channel between Burhou and the Casquets, or through the Swinge close W of the main

island. In poor visibility under these circumstances it is best to go outside the Casquets altogether.

Navigational Aids

Radio The AeroBn situated in the middle of Alderney, callsign 'ALD' on 383kHz, is continuous and has a range of 50 miles.

The Casquets Radio Bn, callsign 'QS' on 298.8kHz is also a 50-mile signal. It is grouped with Start Pt and Roches Douvres.

Cap Barfleur, callsign 'FG' on 291.9kHz, is 35 miles E of Alderney, but its 70-mile signal is useful for fixing with either of the two Bns mentioned above.

The Channel LV, callsign 'CR' on 287.3kHz, is a continuous Bn but has a range of only 10 miles. Situated 30 miles WNW of Alderney it is only of interest to boats making a passage from the West Country. Those coming from the Solent can get a position check on ECI buoy 20 miles NNE of Cap de la Hague (see chart on p. 21).

25.8   *Casquets lighthouse from the NNW. White tower 37m above sea. From a distance often confused as a merchant ship*

Lights   Cap de la Hague is Fl 5 s. from a 51m Grey Tr. Its range is 23 miles and has a foghorn ev 30 s. Before seeing the loom of Cherbourg or even Cap de la Hague, the lights of the nuclear processing plant on the 180m skyline 3 miles SE of the Lt Ho will appear, just as one sees the glow of the Fawley cracking-plant before sighting the Needles from the SW.

Alderney Lt Ho is 1 mile E of the entrance to the harbour. It is Fl (4) 15 s. with a range of 28 miles. The fog siren is (4) 60 s. The Lt is in a W round Tr 32m high with a B band 37m above sea level.

Château à L'Étoc Pt Lt is a W column ½ mile W of Alderney Lt Ho. It is Iso WR 4 s. Its W sector between 111° and 151° from seaward clears the end of the submerged breakwater. As it happens, the S edge of the W sector is in transit with Alderney Lt Ho on 111°.

The Casquets is Fl (5) 30 s. 37m above sea level with 28 miles range. The Tr is W, 23m high. There is a Dia fog signal (2) 60 s.

Harbour Approach   By day head for St Anne's church spire (not to be confused with a squat water tower to its right) on 210°, which should be in transit with a W cone Bn on the end of the little breakwater of the Old Harbour. In practice simply middle the harbour entrance, keeping well inside the shoal water which extends 3 cables NE of the seaward end of the Admiralty breakwater. It has a least depth of 1m2, but there can be overfalls in the vicinity.

By night bring into transit the Q W Lt 17M range with the Iso W 10 s. rear Lt, range 18M. These Lts show over 10° sectors either side of the 215° transit course.

Berthing   Yachts must either anchor where they can or pick up one of the 250 Y conical visitors' mooring-buoys close to the breakwater and SE of the fairway. Under no circumstances can boats go alongside the breakwater or jetty, which is reserved for commercial craft including the hydrofoil from Guernsey, or pick up W mooring buoys which are private.

Call water-taxi on Ch 12 – work on Ch 6.

VHF watch is maintained on Ch 16 and 12 from 0800 to 1800. The Harbour Officer, who doubles as Customs Officer, is to be found between these hours at the office at the inshore end of the jetty, tel. 048–182 2620.

Facilities FW, showers and heads available at the berthing quay near the HO.

Diesel and chandlery is available at Mainbrayce Ltd in the Inner Harbour (call Ch 37), petrol and Calor gas from Alderney Stores & Bunkering Co (the Sail Loft), Braye Street.

Alderney SC is next to the HO; welcomes yachtsmen, but not open all the time.

Showers, heads and laundromats on the Commercial Quay.

Boat repairs are available near the harbour.

Landing on the Admiralty Breakwater or slip is forbidden.

Land either at the steps at the inshore end of the jetty or at the Sapper slip just below the SC.

'First and Last' restaurant, three good pubs and a supermarket all at Braye harbour. There is a wider choice of shops and restaurants in St Anne, a mile up the hill.

Airline direct flights to the other Channel Islands, Southampton, Bournemouth and Cherbourg. Hydrofoil to Guernsey.

Weather Reports on BBC Radio 4 (200kHz) Area Portland. Also on Ch 25 or 82 from Jersey. Marinecall by tel. 0898–500457.

Charts: Fr 827 Im C33a (BA 3655 CG 1014 Stan 16)

High Water   −04h.33m. Dover   +0h.05m. SP St Helier
Heights above Datum   MHWS 11m2. MLWS 1m4.
MHWN 7m9. MLWN 4m0.

LYING 13 miles NE of Jersey and 22 miles S of Cap de la Hague, Carteret with Barneville, its twin town on the opposite side of the R. Gerfleur estuary, is more of interest for its beaches, excellent restaurants and hotels than as a port for visiting yachtsmen. However, it is recommended as a possible day excursion from Gorey on the E coast of Jersey in high-speed ferries whose timetables are dictated by the tides and need to be checked (for example, some of the departures are at 0500). For a boat prepared to take the ground and stop over through LW it is straightforward to enter or leave any time within an hour of HW. In settled conditions you can stretch that by an hour.

Approach   Cap de Carteret immediately N of the harbour entrance has a prominent Lt Ho with a Grey square Tr 15m high on top of the cliff. The light is 81m above sea level and shows a 26-mile range Fl (2 + 1) 15 s. and a horn (3) ev 60 s. Shoal water of less than 2m will be encountered 0.9 miles S of the harbour entrance at Springs. In violent W'ly winds there may be a big sea breaking over the bar ½ mile outside the entrance, which dries 3m3 at LWS. The precise depth and position of the bar tends to move, and there are no fairway buoys. The tidal currents running parallel to the coastline attain 4 knots at Springs, but are nearly slack during the last hour before local HW.

26.1   *Near high water Carteret looks attractive, with the channel clearly defined. (A) is the Gare Maritime (B) the main hotel and slipway (C) Port de Refuge, and (D) the 'Marina' soi-disant*

26.2   Gare Maritime with Jersey ferry alongside and south-bank mole exposed

26.3   View of harbour at low water, from public slip

26.4   *The 'Marina' at low water. Compare with picture 26.1*

The western breakwater 500m long lies N–S with an R-topped W Lt Bn at its extremity (Oc R 4 s. 6m 7-miles range). A mole on the eastern side of the entrance is considerably shorter than the breakwater. It is submerged at the upper end of each tide, but has a G Bn Fl (2) G 5 s. at its southern extremity, which always shows.

There is a prominent W hotel on the riverside. The G Bn should be brought into transit with the left-hand edge of the hotel on a course of 010°. Give the R-topped Lt Bn on the western breakwater a fair berth, as it has shoal water close alongside. Once inside, favour the left bank, keeping close to it all the way.

Berthing

1   The first and best berth alongside the wall is reserved for the ferries (pic 26.2 shows one dried out) alongside the pretentiously-named Gare Maritime, a wooden shack with Customs and the HO nearby. But there is sometimes room upstream of them.

2   If not fully occupied by fishing boats a drying berth alongside the quay S of the R Bn with can topmark may be sought, but between this Bn and the slip outside the two big hotels (Marine and Angleterre) there are stone groynes.

3   Immediately upstream of the hotels is a small cut (Port de Refuge) where one can dry out alongside.

Beyond that one comes to the 'marina', a collection of mud berths. But be warned, the stench of the mud and slime at LW is overpowering.

Facilities   Besides the hotels and excellent restaurants (one of which rates two crossed forks in the *Guide Michelin*) there are a yacht chandlery, garages with yacht mechanics, FW and provision stores. The small YC (CN Carteret-Barneville) has a sailing school.

The port authority's tel. is (33) 04–70–84.

Customs (33) 54–90–08.

Weather   Posted at the YC. Area 11 Manche ouest.

27 GUERNSEY

Charts: BA 807, 808, 3140 Fr 6903 Im C33a
Stan 16 (CG 1014)

High Water −04h. 50m. Dover +00h. 10m. SP St
Helier

Heights above Datum MHWS 9m0. MLWS 1m0.
MHWN 6m7. MLWN 3m5.

GUERNSEY, at 27 sq miles, is the second largest of the Channel
Islands, 9 miles long and just 4½ across at its widest point. It
is the seat of government of the ancient Bailiwick of Guernsey,
which includes Alderney, Sark, Herm and Jethou. Its resident
populaton of 55,000, to which each year are added 400,000
tourists attracted by tax-free shopping, superb sandy beaches
and a catering trade geared to the needs of visitors accustomed
to more restricted or expensive facilities.

Even before the opening of North Beach Marina and the
extensive dredging of the harbour in 1987 10,000 yachts
visited Guernsey each year, hence the edict that visiting boats
cannot stay beyond 14 days without special permission from
the HM. One of Guernsey's special attractions to visitors in
their own boats is the wide variety of day-trips which can be
made to quiet anchorages on the four smaller islands lying
within six miles of St Peter Port. Creux harbour on the E
coast of Sark is the most attractive and has 1m4 water at
LWN. Local ferries also ply between them and claim priority
alongside the available berths at Herm or Sark. It is thus
preferable to anchor off.

St Peter Port

The only town on Guernsey is also the one sheltered
harbour accessible at any state of the tide (pic 27.10). It is 65
miles from Weymouth, 82 from the Needles and 95 from
Plymouth. From a distance the island looks like a steep-to
plateau (90m maximum) which it is along the S coast. On a
sunny day the landfall may be announced by sun flashing off
the greenhouses (tomatoes and flowers) long before the low-
lying beaches of the NW coast are seen.

Approach There is an AeroBn emitting continuously on
361kHz callsign 'GUR' with a range of 30 miles, but it is
located near the SW extremity of the island. Call St Peter
Port Radio on Ch 16 (works on Ch 78 and will give linked
GPO calls on Ch 62).

From the Alderney Race The most direct route is through
the *Little Russel Channel* just 4 miles from St Peter Port, but
unmarked rocks lie in wait 2 miles NE of the entrance to the
channel. Whereas the tidal streams run along the grain of
the channel, up to 5 knots at Springs, it has marked E–W
components across one's track not very far to seaward. The
tide starts to ebb to the SW 1½h. before HW Dover and will
be flooding to the NE 6h. later, or 4½h. after HW Dover.

Assuming tide and visibility permit an approach through
the Little Russel, the first Lt to be picked up will be Platte
Fougère (Fl WR 10 s. 15m 16M). Its R sector 085°–155° covers
the unmarked Braye rocks which extend 1 mile to the NW.
Its R is W, with a B base and broad B band half-way up. It
has a Racon Bn, callsign 'P'.

The eastern side of the channel is first marked by the BW
Bn on Tautenay rocks, one mile due north of Herm. Its light
is Q (3) WR 6 s. 7m high and 7M range. The R sector (215°–
050°) warns of outlying dangers to the E and S.

Right in the middle of the channel is the BW chequered
stone Tr 8m high on Roustel shoal (pic 27.1). Its Q 7M Lt

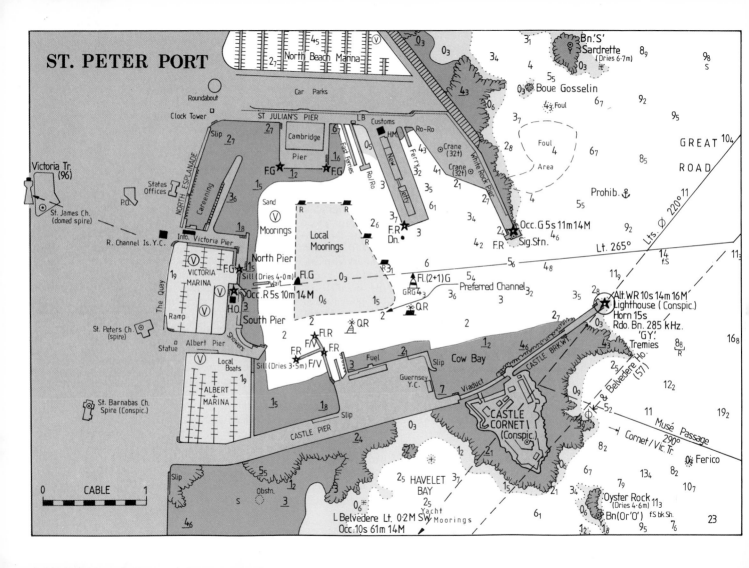

should be brought in line on course 198° with an Iso 4 s. Lt 9-miles range on top of the 19m high flat fort on Brehon tower (pic 27.2).

The alternative transit is 208° aligning Brehon with the 14M light on St Martin's Pt 2 miles S of St Peter Port. It is Fl (3) WR 10 s., a 9m flat building 15m above the sea. Its R sector only applies if cutting the corner too fine from the SW.

Brehon should be left to port. The harbour leading Lts on 220° bring into transit: St Peter Port Castle breakwater (Alt WR 10 s. 14m 16M) – pic 27.5 – and Belvedere (Oc 10 s. 61m 14M), a small W Tr with an Or stripe, perched on the cliff beyond Castle Cornet and also nearly in transit with twin radio masts, each with F R Lts.

Between Roustel and Brehon the Platte Lt is left to starboard. It should not be confused with Platte Fougère mentioned above. It is 7 cables ENE of the entrance to St Sampson. Its Lt is Fl WR 3 s. 6m and 5M. The structure is a G con stone Tr.

A local Rdo Bn at the end of the southern breakwater transmits continuously on 285kHz, callsign 'GY', but its range is only 10 miles. The foghorn ev 15 s. from the same point may be useful. It is synchronized with the Rdo Bn. It makes its callsign 'GY' four times and then emits a steady note for 27 s. The horn sounds off at the start of the steady radio transmission. The number of s. from the start of the dash until the horn is heard times 1.8 is the distance off in cables.

The breakwater head to starboard – White Rock Pier – has a 14M Oc G 5 s. Lt on the signal station 11m above the water.

A F R Lt at the pierheads prohibits entry or exit, except for small boats under power who must keep well clear of big ship movements.

The Big Russel Channel between Herm and Sark is much easier if there are doubts about tides or visibility. It is 3 miles wide with some off-lying dangers stretching 1 mile SSW of

27.1   *Roustel beacon on porthand near entrance of Little Russel*

27.2   *Brehon tower one mile south-west of Roustel beacon*

27.3   *Petite Canupe Beacon outside Beaucette Marina (Vale)*

27.4   *Entrance to St Sampson*

27.5 *Entrance only 18m wide. Leading marks: orange board above tide-gauge and windsock on flagpole at right-hand edge of clubhouse*

Jethou. Sark has a new Fl (4) 15 s. Lt at its N extremity (Courbet du Nez). Keep it wide to port and favour the W side of the channel, passing close to seaward of another two new Lts marking dangers to the E of Jethou: the Noire Pte Lt Fl (2) WR 15 s. 8m 6M and, 1.5 miles farther SW, the N-cardinal buoy at Fourquies Rock (Q W). Then head SW to leave the Lower Heads S-cardinal buoy to starboard. Its Lt is Q (6)+LFl 10 s. From there to the harbour entrance is a little over 2 miles on course made good of 305°. From Alderney it is only 2 miles farther than going through the Little Russel.

There are various short cuts, of which the Musé Passage is the simplest: by day this lines up the right-hand edge of Castle Cornet with the castellated Victoria Tr (96m) on 291°.

From St Malo or Jersey the approach is simple. Just head for St Martin's Pt (see above) and leave it to port.

From the N or W it is easiest to approach St Peter Port S-about the island, giving the awesome Les Hanois Lt Ho a wide berth, because unmarked rocks extend some distance to seaward. This is particularly so if coming down from the Casquets (as in the RORC race from Cowes) where dangers lurk 2 miles off the NW shore of Guernsey. The Lt Ho is Grey with a helipad on its top 36m high. Its Lt is Q (2) 5 s. with a range of 23 miles. It has a horn (2) 60 s. The AeroBn 'GUY' is 2 miles due E of Les Hanois. The tide off the corner turns about the same time as in the Little Russel. Close along the S coast it runs mostly E–W.

Berthing in St Peter Port St Peter Port radio keeps watch on Ch 16 VHF with Ch 78 and 12 (Port Control) as working frequencies. Ch 62 for linked calls. R fixed Lts on White Rock and New Jetty pierheads indicate ferries are moving in either direction.

At the harbour entrance the Port Control boat will direct

165

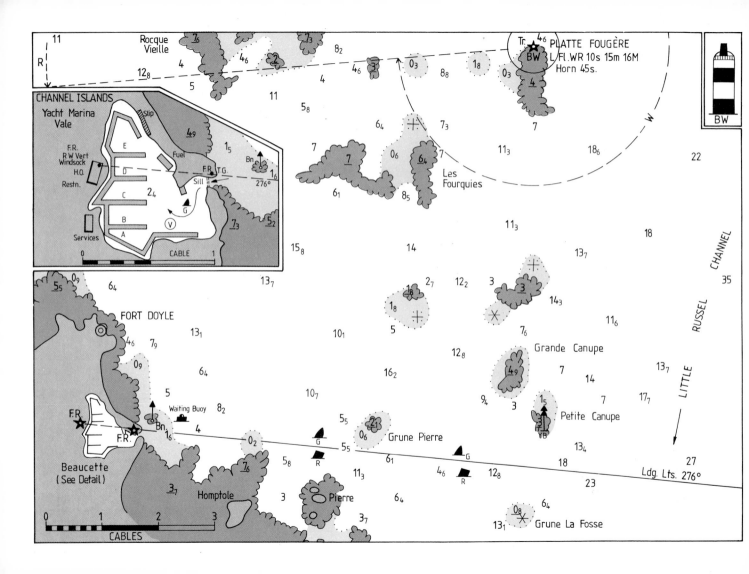

27.6   Entrance to Victoria Marina for visitors, at low water, with sill showing. Note two yachts on waiting pontoon

visiting yachts to their berths. That may be on the buoys W of Victoria Pier or on pontoons on the Victoria Marina, tel. 0481–25987 (pic 27.6). The 2m dredged fairway splits 2 cables inside the harbour entrance at a GRG con buoy with G triangular topmark (Gp Fl (2 + 1) G). The preferred arm of the fairway goes close past the fuel pontoon and Guernsey YC, then swings clockwise past the end of the new fishquays towards the waiting pontoon outside Victoria Marina, whose 265 pontoon berths are now solely for visitors. The other arm sweeps NW anti-clockwise off the end of Cambridge Pier and through the visitors' moorings to the waiting area. The water between these two fairways is reserved for swinging moorings belonging to locals. Big yachts may be directed either into the Albert Marina or the North Beach Marina, both of which are otherwise reserved for local boats.

Entrance to the marina is only possible 3h. either side of HW. There is a depth of 1m9 maintained in Victoria Marina. Tide gauges indicate the water over the sill. There is a waiting pontoon outside the sill if the tide is not suitable, but it dries at LW.

A Customs/Immigration form must be completed within 2h. of arrival. The HO and Customs Office are both on the jetty of St Julian's Pier, which protects the harbour from the N Tel. 0481–20229 for HM and 26911 for Customs.

There is a speed limit of 4 knots in the harbour, which also applies to yacht tenders. Batteries may not be charged after noon.

North Beach Marina (pics 27.10, 11, 12)
This 950-berth new Yacht Hbr completed in 1987 has depths from 4m5 to 2m7 inside a sill at its N corner. It is approached on a 270° fairway from a Q G buoy established on Reffée rock just half a mile N of the end of Castle breakwater. There is an Oc RWG Lt inshore with 4° sectors from 264° to 276° (W ± 2° on 270°) leading to the E arm of the entrance with a Fl R Lt at its end. There a tight turn to port leads into the harbour. Entry is at half tide.

Channel Islands Yacht Marina, Vale (pic 27.9).
This is better known as Beaucette. On the NE extremity of Guernsey there used to be a flooded quarry of that name. They dynamited a cut, thus letting in the sea creating a 200-berth marina in perfect shelter. The approach channel is from the Little Russel, about half-way between Platte Fougère and Roustel Bns. The entrance is not easy to spot even from a mile off. So look for Fort Doyle on the right-hand edge of land. The marina is 2 cables S of that point.

Some 7 cables due E of the entrance is the unlit S-cardinal YB Bn marking the Petite Canupe rocks, with the letters PC on it (pic 27.3). Leaving it close to starboard, head inshore on course 277°. In the summer the channel is marked by two

27.7 *Looking towards the harbour entrance from inside Victoria Marina*

27.8 *The careening harbour north of Victoria Marina. Castle Cornet in middle distance with Guernsey Yacht Club on its right*

27.9   Beaucette (Vale) Marina. (A) Visitors' berths. (B) Clubhouse and Harbour Office. (C) New services. (D) Fuel pontoon

pairs of small R and G fairway buoys.

The leading marks are: Front – A wide Vert R line and pole over a W background on the N head of the entrance; Rear – a mast on the W clubhouse building has a W board with an R Vert stripe on it. There is also a windsock on the same mast. (In pic 27.5 this board is temporarily down for repainting.) There are F R Lts on both leading marks.

To avoid hitting the N side of the entrance or the rock with a Bn just outside, it is necessary to make a late jink to port to pass through the entrance and leave to starboard the 'breakwater' made of old tractor tyres. Pic 27.5 shows the very prominent tide gauge giving the level over the sill. It has 2m7 over it at half-tide and there's 18m0 in the basin at all times. Entry can always be made ± 3h. on HW, sometimes for longer. There is negligible cross-current just off the entrance.

Listening watch is kept on VHF Ch 16 and 37.

Visitors' berths are just inside the entrance on the S side. Fuel, FW, provisions and chandlery are all available.

The HO is on the top deck above the restaurant, which is excellent. Telephone numbers: Harbour Administration 0481–45000 and 47071; restaurant 47066.

The only snag about this marina is that it is a long taxi-ride to St Peter Port and even farther to the airport, but, as mentioned above, there is no need to leave the marina area at all during a short visit. L'Ancresse Bay is generally reckoned to be the finest bathing beach on the island. It is within walking distance.

St Sampson

Between Beaucette and St Peter Port is the harbour of St Sampson, which dries out beyond its entrance. It has a dock-yard and too many other manifestations of its commercial character to be of interest to visiting yachtsmen, but some boats have winter berths there, and it is the only place where major repairs can be carried out. The HM keeps watch on Ch 16.

27.10   St Peter Port with North Beach Marina under construction.   (A) Guernsey Yacht Club.   (B) Victoria and Albert Marinas.   (C) Harbour Office.   (D) New lock-gates

From a point equidistant between Platte and Brehon Lts, the leading marks on course 286° are: the post on the S pierhead (Lt F R 3m 5M) in line with the 12m-high clocktower F G Lt on the S side, close to the entrance of the inner harbour.

Guernsey Facilities   St Peter Port has everything to be expected in a thriving tourist resort and financial community. The R. Channel Islands YC is on the front right opposite the NW corner of Victoria Marina. Guernsey YC is half-way along Castle Pier. It conducts most of the racing.

There is an efficient information office on Victoria Pier.

Communications   By air and/or sea to the other Channel Islands, St Malo, Cherbourg, Weymouth, Portsmouth, London and many provincial airports.

Weather   BBC 200kHz. Area Portland. Marinecall 0898–500457. VHF from Jersey Ch 25 or 82.

170

27.11   *North Beach Marina. View from lock-gates*

27.12   *North Beach Marina. View of open lock-gates from inside*

27.13   *Les Hanois lighthouse, 36m grey tower with helipad. View from WSW with Fort Saumerez beyond (left). The area is notorious for extent of offlying dangers to seaward of the lighthouse*

27.14   *St Martin's Point from south-west. The lighthouse is the small building at extreme right only 15m above sea-level – not conspicuous by day*

28 JERSEY

Charts: BA 1137, 3728 Im C33b Stan 16 Fr 5232 (CG 1014)

High Water −04h. 33m. Dover +00h. 05m. SP St Helier
Heights above Datum *MHWS 11m1. MLWS 1m3. MHWN 8m1. MLWN 4m1.*

JERSEY is the largest and most prosperous of all the Channel Islands. It is 10 miles E–W and only $5\frac{1}{2}$ miles across at its widest point. There are 80,000 inhabitants, swollen by about 800,000 visitors a year. Besides servicing the tourists, the principal industry on the island is making money. The *Financial Times* seems to be required breakfast-time reading. A stroll downtown brings one face-to-face with many familiar brass plates found also outside offices in the City of London, but it is also redolent of history from William the Conqueror's day to the Nazi occupation in 1940–5.

This is the nearest British territory to France, just 12 miles W of the Cherbourg peninsula, 22 from the Île de Chausey and 36 from St Malo.

With its huge rise and fall of tide, nearly 10m at Springs, it was never a popular place for visiting English yachts, unless

28.1   La Corbière lighthouse off south-west corner of the island seen from the north. Note causeway linking the shore

ST. HELIER

From BA chart 3278.

CABLES

28.2   Noirmont Point from the west

they were prepared to dry out, row miles ashore in a dinghy or suffer my experience alongside in St Helier. We went ashore for dinner leaving our bulwarks level with the quayside. Returning three hours later we had to get back on board by way of the upper spreaders. Now it's all changed, with a magnificent 450-berth marina in the heart of town and even bigger ones planned, either by locking in the Old Harbour or as entirely new ventures (next to the new RO/RO ferry harbour, or along Havre de Pas, SE of the power station).

Approach to St Helier Although entry over the sill to the new marina is ± 3h. on HW and sometimes better, access to La Collette Yacht Basin immediately outside the main harbour entrance is at all states of the tide; there is a waiting pontoon for boats who have time to kill. On passage to St Helier from any direction it is therefore easier if the ETA can be adjusted to the top half of the tide.

On passage from the N. Around La Corbière Lt at the SW corner of the island (pic 28.1) the tide turns S'ly 3h. after HW Dover ($-4\frac{1}{2}$h. on HW St Helier) and runs strongly to the E along the S coast until 5h. before HW Dover (or HW St Helier). That suits very well, since one could make the 35 miles from Alderney Race or any intermediate point on the same tide. Like Les Hanois, La Corbière Lt Ho has shoal

28.3   La Grève d'Azette light on waterfront one mile south-east of St Helier. Vertical orange board on pylon. By day it is rear mark for 082° transit with Dog's Nest beacon. By night it is front light for same transit with Mount Ubé light one mile ENE

water with breaking seas up to 7 cables to WNW over Green Rock. But it is an 18-mile Lt Iso WR 10 s. from a 19m W stone Tr 36m above sea level (pic 28.1). Its foghorn sounds C ev 60 s. Its R sectors warn those who are either cutting it a bit fine around Grosnez Point or taking a chance to the SE of

28.4   *St Helier.   (A) Platte Rock beacon to be left to port on dredged deep channel to new RO/RO terminals at (G).   (B) Tanker harbour.   (C) La Colette yacht harbour.   (D) Jersey Marina.   (E) Old harbour.   (F) Land being reclaimed*

28.5   New RO/RO terminals under construction (1987) outside existing harbour. Seen at low water

the buoyed channel past St Brelade's Bay. It has a Rdo Bn callsign 'CB' on 305.7kHz with a 20-mile range.

A safe check on one's approach course from the N is the W-cardinal buoy (Q (9) 15 s.) marking the Banc Desormes 4 miles NW of Grosnez. There is plenty of water to pass either side of it, provided that by day you keep La Corbière open of the right-hand edge of Jersey on 177°; or by night you stay in the W sector of Grosnez light (Fl (2) WR 15 s. 50m 19M). There is also a continuous AeroBn at the end of the runway over St Ouen Bay: callsign 'JW' on 329kHz.

Past Corbière you run parallel to the shore about $\frac{1}{2}$ mile offshore for 3 miles so as to pass close to seaward of the BW hooped Tr on Noirmont Point 18m above the water (pic 28.2).

It is a 13-mile Lt Fl (4) 12 s. The Western Passage for deep-draught ships passes between Noirmont and an N-cardinal buoy with Q G Lt 3 cables outside on course 082°.

By night this is easy, with two shore Lts in transit (Oc 5 s. 14M from La Grève d'Azette on the beach SE of St Helier and Alt WR 14M from Mt. Ubé 1m farther inland). By day on 082° 1½ miles after Noirmont it may be easier to pick up the W pillar-and-globe Bn on the Dog's Nest rocks in transit with the R Vert board on the 20m W Tr of La Grève d'Azette 1.3 miles beyond it. 2 cables short of it the Q G conical buoy marking East Rock is on the transit (pic 28.3).

Here you alter 60° to port on to the R and G passage (023°) for 7 cables to the harbour entrance – so called because the

28.6   *Entrance to Old harbour at high water*

28.7   *Old harbour at low water*

front leading light is Oc G 5 s. 8m 11M on a W daymark, while the rear Lt is Oc R 5 s. 20m 12M on an R structure (pic 28.4).

On the way in you leave close to port the Platte Rock R lattice Bn (Fl R 1.5 s). The approach channel has been widened by dredging up to the harbour entrance and blasting to a least depth of 2m5 all the way to the new RO/RO terminals.

From the SW-about the Minquiers You can head for Passage Rock N-cardinal buoy (VQ) off St Brelade's Bay 125° – 2 miles from Corbière Lt – and then follow the Western Passage as described above leaving to starboard the channel buoys heading for the Dog's Nest; or keeping 2 miles offshore, head towards the Demie de Pas Lt Tr 1½ miles SSE of St Helier (YB tower, Lt Mo (D) WR 12 s. 11m 14M with foghorn (3) 60 s.). About 1½ miles short you pick up the R and G passage described above and head for the harbour on 023°.

28.8   *Fuelling point at St Helier Yacht Club. Tide-gauge indicates bottom of low water Springs*

28.9   Sill and gate into Jersey Marina. Note traffic lights

From the E or E-about the Minquiers Aim to leave the Demie de Pas (see above) ½ mile to starboard and make good a course 341° along the S Passage, heading towards a BW mark bearing 341° on the shore of St Aubin's Bay, being sure to leave the R can Hinguette buoy to port (Fl (4) R 15 s.). Just short of the E Rock buoy, alter to 023° on the R and G Passage described above.

It is all straightforward provided you remember that the tidal currents run EW up to 3½ knots at Springs and 1½ knots at Neaps.

Berthing in St Helier Traffic is controlled from the signal Tr at the head of Victoria pier. The fact that you pass two other harbour entrances on your starboard hand before you get there should not disturb you. The first is the tanker berth; the second is the entrance to La Collette 130-berth Yacht Basin, which is shared by the fishing fleet who have their own quay on its S side.

Traffic control Listen on VHF Ch 14. The Lt signals are simple:

G   vessels may enter, but not leave

R   cleared to leave but not enter

R and G   no movement permitted. An exception to this is a Q Amber Lt which allows boats of less than 25m LOA to enter or leave under power against the signals above. In doing so, keep to starboard of the fairway.

The speed limit is 5 knots. No battery charging after noon.

Entrance to the marina is normally ± 3h. on HW. A tide gauge shows the water over the sill, and R or G lights control movement. If you draw over 1m8 you should inform Port Control so as to be allocated a suitable berth. Inside the marina visiting yachts normally go to F or G pontoons, the farthest from the entrance, although boats over 12.5m LOA or 2m draft may be accommodated on A pontoon. The HO is tel 0534-79549. Stays of more than two weeks' duration must be cleared with the HM tel. 0534-34451.

If you arrive before half-tide or want to be away from downtown St Helier you can go on to a holding berth in La Collette. Thanks to the new RO/RO harbour it is now well protected from the swell, but the facilities ashore are limited. There are Q R and G fairway buoys at the entrance. Be sure to leave the R can buoy to port on turning to starboard to

28.10   Gorey. Leading transit of 298° on seaward end of breakwater and church steeple (A)

enter. It looks all wrong, but there is a long list of groundings by yachts who have left it the wrong side. There is a waiting pontoon.

Fuel is available only outside the marina on the S pier by the St Helier YC opposite the harbour entrance. You need half-tide to go alongside. All other facilities are available on the dockside of the marina.

Other Harbours and their Approaches   The only other harbour which allows a boat to lie afloat at all states of the tide is *St Catherine* at the NE extremity of the island. It is a single breakwater, wide open between E and SSE and you have to anchor off. Once ashore there are only very sketchy amenities. However, it can be approached from the NW down Le Ruan Channel between Jersey or the Paternosters and Les

28.11 *Gorey Harbour with Mount Orgueil Castle (right)*

Écrehou. This channel is deep and 3 miles wide, but not recommended in poor visibility. There is no Lt of any significance until you pick up the Fl 1.5 s. at the end of the St Catherine breakwater. It has a range of 13M. Final approach should always be made from due E or somewhat N of it. Tuck close under the end of the breakwater and anchor in 3m5 about a cable offshore.

Farther S by 1½ miles from St Catherine is *Gorey*, the picture postcard little port under the lee of the floodlit Mont Orgueil Castle, with plenty to commend it ashore by way of hostelries and sight-seeing. It is the home port of the vedettes which ply between there and Carteret on a bizarre timetable dictated by the tides. If you fancy a day-trip with an 0500 departure, it's worth it. Customs can be cleared here.

The harbour all but dries out and is very crowded in the summer. The only afloat berths are those alongside the outer

28.12   St Aubin looks inviting at high water

28.13   St Aubin Castle at low tide

end of the pier, and they are usually taken up by ferries or fishing boats. There is a local HO to appeal to, but, unless you are prepared to dry out some distance up-harbour, it is not too attractive.

Approaching from any direction keep $\frac{1}{2}$ mile to seaward until the leading marks are picked up on 298°. They are: the Lt Tr at the end of Gorey pier in line with Gorey church steeple. There are Lts, but it would be lunacy for a visitor to attempt entry at night, not knowing whether there is even an anchor berth available.

Passage from S-about the island is by way of the Vi Channel, which is an A-level examination for coastal navigators. Provided you find the W-cardinal Canger Rock buoy (Q (9) 15 s.) 3 miles SSE of La Rocque Pt and leave it close to starboard on a course made good of 075° it is worth a go. If the visibility is less than 5 miles, forget it – unless you have a local pilot. There is an RWVS spar buoy Fl 10 s. 2 miles beyond Canger Rock buoy. Here course should be altered to port to put the unlit Bn on Petite Anquette 1 mile away broad on the star-

board bow. You must then pick up the 332° leading line of Verclut Pt (at the inshore end of St Catherine breakwater) and turret on Coupe Pt (right-hand edge of land) just $\frac{1}{2}$ mile beyond it. From this point it is a little over 3 miles to pick up the Gorey Harbour transit. First you should leave to port the unlit R can buoy marking Le Giffard Rock, 2 miles from the Vi Channel.

The other and even more attractive harbour is *St Aubin* just 2 miles W of St Helier across the bay. It is the home of the well-appointed and very hospitable R. Channel Islands YC (Jersey). But it dries out to a distance of $\frac{1}{2}$ mile from the entrance, well beyond the historic St Aubin Fort (pic 28.13) where some dinghy sailors keep their boats hauled out. The small harbour is packed out, so there is no point in going there except to anchor off for the top half of a tide or by prior arrangement.

If determined to do so, the safest course is to head inshore at Diamond Rock R can buoy (Fl (2) R 6 s.), a port-hand buoy on the Western Passage just under 1 mile E of Noirmont Point

28.14   Low water. South breakwater kept clear for crane operation

and a similar distance W of the Dog's Nest. Here you head for the Martello Tower on the shore NE of St Aubin Harbour on course 345°, leaving well open on your port bow the Grosse Rocks Bn and the Castle. As soon as you have a clear sight of the harbour entrance, head towards it on course 252°. The fairway is marked by small R and G buoys. If you must approach by night, the N pierhead has a 12m metal Lt Tr with a 10–mile Lt Iso R 4 s. There is also a WRG directional Lt with ± 1°W Lt on course, a 5° G sector if off course to starboard and a corresponding R sector 5° to south of the W sector.

There is no resident HM at St Aubin, so visiting yachts

28.15   Men in boat trying to disperse mud in harbour entrance with chemicals

must take pot luck in a free-for-all. Securing alongside the S breakwater is prohibited because it is where the crane operates. You might be lucky and find a drying berth on very soft mud against the E breakwater. There are no plans to lock the harbour in.

Facilities at Jersey The island has sub-tropical vegetation, many luxurious homes, several hotels of the very highest class, restaurants to satisfy the most fastidious, bars and bistros for all tastes and wonderful tax-free shopping.

It is also famous for its new all-purpose leisure and conference centre built within Fort Regent overlooking St Helier, with access by cable car. In the country there is the under-ground hospital just as the Nazis left it in 1945 and, near by, Gerald Durrell's world-famous zoo. La Moye golf course near the SW tip of the island is of international standard. There are surfing, board-sailing, horse racing and much pageantry and junketing.

Every kind of chandlery and yacht repair can be undertaken.

The Tourist Information Office is next to the HM's at the town end of the marina (if you survive crossing the road there). The HM is tel. 0534–34451.

28.16   Royal Channel Islands Yacht Club at St Aubin

St Helier is linked by sea to the other Channel Islands, to Carteret, Granville and St Malo on the French coast and to Weymouth and Portsmouth by regular ferry.

Occasional sea mist and crosswinds permitting, there are flights to Southampton, London, Paris, Guernsey, Cherbourg, and many provincial airports in Britain, while charter aircraft come in from all over Europe.

Weather   Posted at the HO. See also Guernsey.

29   ÎLES CHAUSEY

Charts: Fr 829, 830 CG 534 (BA 3659 Im C33b)

High Water   −05h. 00m. Dover   −00h. 15m. SP St Helier
Heights above Datum   MHWS 12m9. MLWS 1m9. MHWN 9m8. MLWN 4m9.

THE ÎLES CHAUSEY are a formidable collection of rocks and reefs spread over an area 6½ miles E–W and 2 miles across which emerge at LW after a fall of as much as 11m to look like the surface of the moon.

The only inhabited island is La Grande Île, where about 100 residents go fishing or make the most of the day-trippers who swarm over the place in the summer after making the 10-mile crossing from Granville or 15 miles from St Malo in vedettes. If you put your boat aground you are apt to suffer the indignity of having cows grazing round your keel at LW.

All the action – by which I mean a general store, a friendly bar-restaurant and the landing points – are at the SE end of Grande Île. Here also is the narrow deepwater channel where afloat berths or moorings can be found even at LW Springs.

All the charts make it look more difficult than it really is, if one does not get too ambitious in attempting any of the entrance channels except that close SE of the only Lt Ho (pic 29.2).

Approach   From anywhere but the N there is deep water up to the SE point of Grand Île, where the most prominent feature is the 19m Grey square Tr of the Lt Ho, standing 40m above sea level (pic 29.2). Its Lt is Fl 5 s. with a range of 23M. Hold off about ½ mile until the 3 E-cardinal Bns leading

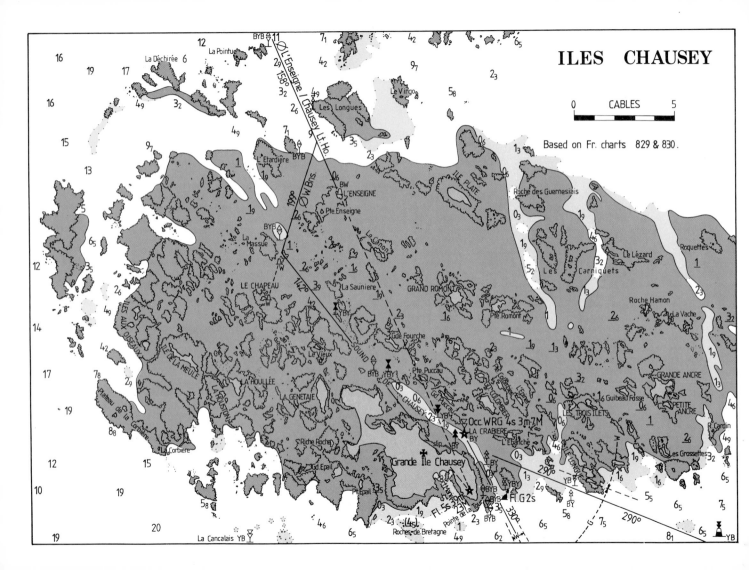

ILES CHAUSEY

CABLES
0   5

Based on Fr. charts 829 & 830.

29.1   *Chausey near high water.   (A) Lighthouse on Pointe de la Tour.   (B) The Sound anchorage in deep water opposite landing slip.   (C) Hotel restaurant*

29.2   Lighthouse on approach from south-east with line of E-cardinal beacons to be left to port

out from the pt can be left clear to port on the approach course of 332°. This will put ahead La Crabière Est, a conspicuous B tripod structure with Y top on a rock on the opposite side of the fairway from the slipway used as a landing point on the top half of the tide. It has an Oc WRG 4 s. Lt. Its W sector 3° either side of 332° in transit with an unlit W tower B top, L'Enseigne, 1¼ miles beyond Crabière tripod, but none the less easily picked out.

Of more immediate interest is the G con buoy marking Les Epiettes with a Lt Fl G 2 s. on it. Leaving this buoy to starboard it is prudent to 'borrow' a little to the E of the transit especially at LW where there is shoal water across the channel from the W. At the S-cardinal Bn, to be left to starboard, one is in the pool of relatively deep water which continues along the well-marked channel for a further ½ mile.

Approach from the North   Those with local knowledge find the dog-leg Grande Entrée approach from the NW along unlit transits through the rocks simple enough. But coming from St Helier it saves only 1½ miles against using the deep-water channel Entrée de la Deroute W-about Chausey. It is

recommended that this course should be adopted at least until one has had the experience of sailing out to sea through the Grande Entrée from Grande Île anchorage.

The rocks extend 2½ miles to the NW and W of Grande Île with only one Bn to mark their limit (La Concalaise in the WSW).

The Entrée de la Deroute channel is marked by the E-cardinal Les Ardentes pillar buoy (Q (3) 10 s.) 3.7 miles SE of the NE Minquiers buoy. After steering SW for 3½ miles from rounding Les Ardentes in the W sector of La Crabière Lt (see above), follow the line of the Chausey outcrops round to the S and SE until picking up the normal approach described above.

Tidal streams of up to 3½ knots run to the SW past the western side of Chausey from 2½ h. before HW Dover, turning northward 3½ h. after HW.

Close to the N or S of the islands the E-going stream starts 2½ h. after HW Dover. The tides run W from 2½ h. before HW Dover.

29.3   *Day beacon on porthand near lighthouse*

Inside the anchorage off Grande Île the tide is not so fierce, somewhat under 3 knots. It runs to the NW for 9h. from $5\frac{1}{2}$h. before HW St Helier (2h. after HW Dover). The reverse stream only runs for $3\frac{1}{2}$h. at most.

Departure through NW channel – Grande Entrée

Leaving the anchorage on 310° proceed to the pair of W- and E-cardinal Bns close off the northern tip of Grande Île. Through there on course 325° for 9 cables you should be heading for the E-cardinal Grunes de la Massue Bn with the W chimney Bn marking La Massue fine on the port bow.

Another W chimney Bn will be seen wide on the port beam (Le Chapeau). Coming up to Grunes de la Massue Bn, alter 5 points to starboard to 020° bringing the two W chimney Bns on to a stern transit. Half a mile on, this course will bring an

29.4   *Approaching La Crabière Est with ferry landing on left*

29.5 *Ferry landing near top half of tide. Steps to left lead to hotel*

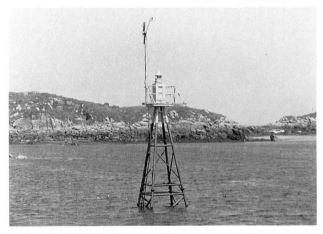

29.6 *La Crabière Est near the best spots to anchor*

29.7 *La Crabière de l'Ouest with local boats on moorings*

29.8 *Low-water scene with 52-foot yacht afloat near La Cra-bière de l'Ouest (Ambrose Greenway)*

E-cardinal Bn abeam and take you on to the reverse transit of L'Enseigne W tower (B top) with the main Grande Île Lt Ho on course 335° for the open sea. After taking this departure course for ½ mile there is an E-cardinal Bn to be left clear to port. At this point the echo sounder should give a sudden and clear indication that you have broken clear of the archipelago formed, it is said, by a cataclysmic event thirteen centuries ago.

There are several other well-attested channels through the rocks, some of them leading into the Sound, but these are outside the scope of this book.

Berthing and Facilities Finding a suitable spot to anchor in the Sound, especially during July and August, is a matter of luck. There are several mooring buoys which may be available. For example, the YC Granville have some of their own. So have the vedettes, which rarely stop overnight, so opening the possibility of picking one up. My solution is to ring the landlord at the Hôtel du Fort to book a table (tel. (33) 50–25–02), when he may have a constructive suggestion.

Whatever happens you will not be allowed to lie alongside either the jetty used by the vedettes at low tides or the slipway for HW use. Wherever you leave your dinghy, look ahead to the height the tide is likely to have reached when you return. Many have found their dinghy afloat but its painter secured out of reach underwater. At Springs the rise and fall is 11m (36ft).

Apart from the hospitality of the hotel, the local store offers limited provisioning.

There are no Customs or police at Chausey, so in theory you should have officially entered France first, but they are well accustomed to visiting yachts from St Helier.

Weather Area 11 Manche ouest.

*30 GRANVILLE

Charts: Fr 5897 Im C33b Stan 16 BA 3672

High Water −05h. 10m. Dover −00h. 15m SP St Helier
Heights above Datum MHWS 12m8. MLWS 1m4. MHWN 9m6. MLWN 4m6.

GRANVILLE is an old walled city of 16,000 inhabitants built on a high (50m) promontory jutting westward into the sea just N of the Bay of Mont St Michel. It is 20 miles E of St Malo and only 9 miles from the Îles Chausey, to which day-ferries run all through the season.

Although there are still some fishermen operating from the harbour, recently it has developed more as a resort, especially for yachtsmen, in the sheltered harbour on its southern side.

Approach If coming from Jersey or the N the right-hand edge of the town is the Pte du Roc, with its 16m Grey Lt Ho with R top at an elevation of 49m. The Lt is Fl (4) 15 s. Stand about 3 cables off it on a SE'ly course to pick up Le Loup Bn (BW bands with disc topmarks) 24m high lying 3 cables S of the breakwater protecting the Avant-Port. The aerial picture (30.1) taken near HW (both locks are open) has Pte du Roc just off frame, but shows Le Loup in the foreground. Its characteristics are Fl (2) 6 s. to a range of 11M. 2 cables NW of Pte du Roc is an unlit R Bn (Tr Fourchie) with a horn (4) 60 s.

Approaching from the W, head for the W-cardinal YBY whistle buoy marking an isolated rock at Le Videcoq. Its Lt is QV (9) 10 s. From this point head 090°. The port is 3½ miles ahead.

It is possible to enter the Avant-Port at half-tide in a boat drawing 1m50. The line of approach is to line up the seaward end of Hérel marina breakwater Lt (Fl R 4 s. 7M – a W tower with R top) with a small château on the hill surrounded by trees except for a conspic. lawn in front of it on 057° leaving Le Loup a cable to starboard. When the entrance to the Avant-Port is well open, alter to port and go for it between the breakwaters. The western arm has Iso R 4 s. 12m 7M on a W framework with R top. Its opposite number is Iso R 4 s. G and the W tower has a G top.

Berthing You can lie alongside the western breakwater but it dries out. The locks with the Bassin à Flot open ± 1h. on HW. This basin is primarily intended for commercial traffic, but, as the picture (30.1) shows, yachts can get permission from the HM (next to the lock on the E side) to go in, where there is a least depth of 4m, tel. (33) 50–12–45.

Access to the magnificent 850-berth Hérel Yacht Hbr, with 150 alongside berths reserved for visitors, is clearly shown by the electronic digital depth indicator situated near the end of the marina breakwater. When it reads 'O.O' the entrance is shut with a hinged gate keeping the water level inside at upwards of 1m7. When the tide has risen sufficiently to give 1m4 through the inner gate, the indicator clearly shows it and continues to act as a tide gauge. This arrangement is similar to that showing the water over the sill at St Servan.

The two poles marking the narrow entrance gate are 4m high and have Oc R 4 s. and Oc G 4 s. Lts respectively.

There is a large area S of the marina mole with sufficient water held in by a sill to enable the very active sailing school (CRNG) to function at all tides.

The marina office is in the splendid clubhouse of YC Granville. Contact on VHF Ch 9 or tel. (33) 50–20–06.

Visiting yachts should make for one of the two pontoons directly in front of the clubhouse: F or G.

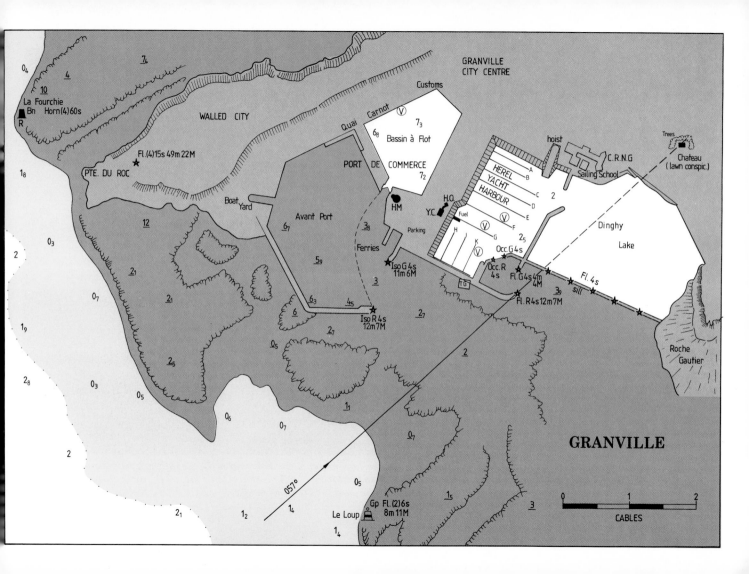

30.1   *The walled city of Granville near high water. In the foreground is the BW beacon Le Loup which must be left a cable to starboard on course for the new breakwater of Hérel yacht harbour.   (A) is the Avant Port.   (B) is the Bassin à Flot which still attracts visiting yachtsmen.   (C) is the boat repair yard.   (D) Marina office.   (E) Visitors' berths*

30.2   *Le Loup Beacon*

30.3   *Lock between Avant Port and Port du Commerce*

30.4   *Digital tide gauge on new breakwater*

30.5   *Day transit for entry. Beacon at end of Hérel breakwater in line with château between trees with conspicuous lawn on 057°*

30.6   Entrance to yacht harbour over the sill between piles in foreground

30.7   Inside yacht harbour with walled city on high ground

Facilities The clubhouse itself is sufficient for most crews' needs. There is a repair yard near by and a gridiron and travel-hoist at the NE corner of the marina. Excellent shops.

FW and electricity on all berths. Fuel at the inshore end of pontoon G.

Ferries for Jersey and Chausey berth just inside the Avant-Port, next to the marina car park.

Good hotels and restaurants. For an extra diversion there's always the casino – or the Aquarium.

Weather Taped forecasts on tel. (33) 50–10–00 and on display at the clubhouse. Area 11 Manche ouest.

196

Charts: CG 535 Fr 5644 (Im C33b BA 3659)

High Water −05h. 00m. Dover −00h. 15m. SP St Helier
Heights above Datum MHWS 13m3. MLWS 2m0. MHWN 10m3. MLWN 5m1.

THIS holiday resort and fishing port is much better known for its oysters than its suitability for visiting yachts. It is on the western edge of the Bay of Mont St Michel, just 4 miles SSW of La Pierre de Herpin Lt Ho a mile NE of the Pte de Grouin. Its W tower has a B top and bars and it is 24m above sea level. Characteristics: Oc (2) 6 s. 17M with a siren Mo (N) 60 s.

La Houle-sous-Cancale, the little anchorage behind the 200m long Môle de la Fenêtre dries out to 7m5 but it might be possible to lie alongside for a couple of hours near the top of the tide (pic 31.1) while the fishing fleet is at sea. There is a prominent disused Lt Tr at the inshore end, while a W metal pylon with G top marks its seaward end (Oc (3) G 12 s.).

Head S from the Pierre de Herpin Lt Ho for 3 miles when

31.1   *La Houle anchorage for oystermen with its 200m long Mole de la Fenêtre and temporary alongside berths on the top half of the tide*

31.2   *Classy shops and bistros beyond the public landing point (French Government Tourist Office)*

31.3   *Afloat moorings close north of the harbour*

the Île de Remains will be abeam. If the wind is settled in a W'ly sector a good anchorage and some buoys can be found $\frac{1}{2}$ mile farther S of the rocky islands les Roches de Cancale but it is still 1 mile SW to the harbour entrance and the tide runs at 3 knots. At Neaps one can safely anchor a lot closer.

Berthing and Facilities   Ashore the CNC (Club Nautique de Cancale) may offer a mud berth, but it will be very exposed to the SSE. HO tel. (99) 58–64–75. The Hotel Continental near the mole has its own moorings afloat at all tides just N of the town. Worth a visit for a meal anyway. Tel. (99) 89–60–16.

There are some excellent fish restaurants and all kinds of shopping, including oyster-stalls.

Weather   See St Malo.

Charts: BA 2700 Fr 5645 Im C33b CG 535 Stan 16

High Water − 05h. 15m. Dover − 00h. 20m. SP St Helier
Heights above Datum MHWS 12m1. MLWS 1m4. MHWN 9m1. MLWN 4m4.

THE BAY of St Malo lies 30 miles S of Jersey separated by the notorious 'Minkies' (Plateau des Minquiers). It is the mouth of Le Rance, which leads into the canal system emerging at the mouth of the R. Vilaine into the Bay of Biscay about midway between the Morbihan and St Nazaire.

Behind a protective chain of rocky outcrops up to 3 miles offshore, on either side of the river mouth are the towns of St Malo and Dinard. They could not possibly be more different.

Dinard is an Edwardian summer resort with shuttered, grand houses, sumptuous hotels set in tropical gardens and the sleepy elegance of another age. Right up to a generation ago it was the done thing to roll around at anchor in the Roads and row ashore to the slipway used by the vedettes plying to and from St Malo.

At that time the walled city of St Malo was being faithfully rebuilt in its original style (with indoor sanitation) after having been flattened in August 1944. Its inhabitants are fiercely proud of their history and traditions. They are 'Les Malouins' whose buccaneering explorers brought riches and glory home from the seven seas. In the New World they were the first to stake a claim on the islands now better known to Spanish-speakers as Las Malvinas – literally meaning the men of St Malo.

The restoration of the lock-gates in St Malo opened up a complex of deepwater basins, all named after those free-wheeling corsairs of the sixteenth and seventeenth centuries, and established St Malo as a major commercial and ferry port. Yachtsmen soon followed, and in due course the famous Cowes–Dinard Race had to change its name to incorporate St Malo. There was an embarrassing period in the 1970s when the prize-giving had to be duplicated by consecutive ceremonies on each side of the Rance.

Nowadays, with the addition of the huge marina in the sandy bay off St Servan, such moorings as Dinard has to offer to visiting yachtsmen are rarely taken up by British yachts.

Approaches from the West (a) *Chenal de la Petite Porte* – the main fairway. One look at a chart has made many a cruising yachtsman hesitate before visiting this most agreeable of all Brittany ports. In fact it is dead simple by day or night – except in thick fog – especially if one sticks to the main fairway from the NW.

A course made good of 147° from the W-cardinal SW Minquiers whistle buoy (Q (9) 15 s.) for 15 miles or 7½ miles due E from Cap Fréhel fetches up at the St Malo Petite Channel whistle buoy (RWVS with disc topmark and LF Lt). Two miles farther to seaward are the two buoys marking Le Vieux Banc: The W-Cardinal YBY one, Q (9) 10 s. and the N-cardinal BY bell buoy (QF). Here the tide starts running to the E + 02h. Dover (− 5½h. St Helier), turning W 6h. later. Maximum rate 2 knots.

At the St Malo buoy, sail 130° 2 miles to the prominent Lt Ho (le Grand Jardin) just to the W of the Île de Cezembre (33m high). The Lt Ho is a Grey Tr 38m high (Fl (2) R 10 s. 15M). The rear leading Lt, La Balue, is F G with a 25-mile range, but among all the city lights it is not easy to pick out, and it is 5 miles beyond le Grand Jardin. By day it is even more difficult.

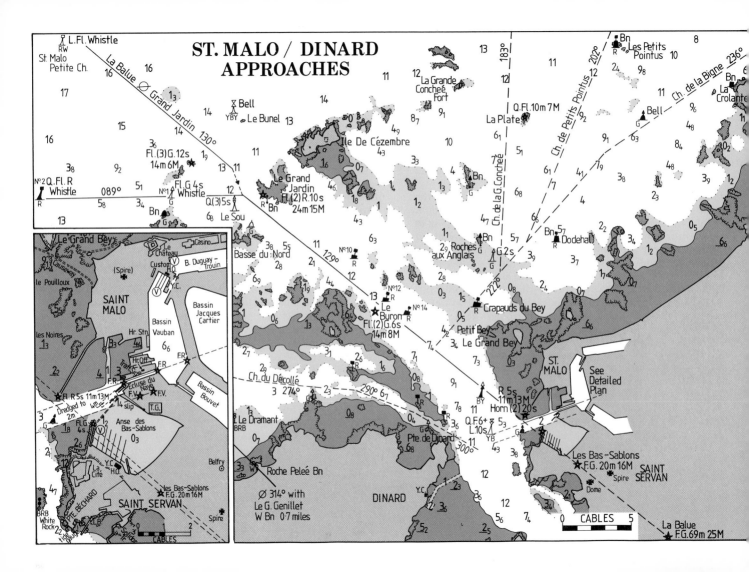

ST. MALO / DINARD APPROACHES

32.1 *Unusual aerial view from south-west. (A) Anse de Solidor on the Rance side of St Servan. (B) St Servan yacht harbour. (C) Les Bas Sablons from main channel leading light. (D) Lock-gates to St Malo. (E) Walled city of St Malo. (F) Bassin Vauban Marina*

32.2   Le Grand Jardin lighthouse with red beacon immediately inshore

32.3   Les Courtis green beacon half a mile north-west of Le Grand Jardin to be left to starboard, with red Pierres des Portes beacon beyond. It is a porthand mark on the Chenal de la Grande Port from the west

It is easier to hold a steady bearing on le Grand Jardin, keeping clear to the eastward of les Courtis, a 21m G Tr with a Lt Fl (3) G 12 s. It lies $\frac{1}{2}$ mile NW of le Grand Jardin. Leave it to starboard and, as you approach the main Lt Ho, make a 2-point alteration to starboard to clear the Lt Ho. It has an unlit R Bn close to the S. As soon as the lighthouse bears NE alter back to 130° so as to leave the unlit G channel buoy marking Basse du Nord well to starboard. The E-cardinal Le Sou pillar buoy – Q (3) 5 s. – is well clear to the W.

It is on record that le Grand Jardin has a Rdo Bn on 294.2kHz callsign 'GJ', but I have never heard it. Its claimed range is only 10 miles.

One mile beyond No. 5 buoy is the stubby G Tr 14m high called le Buron (pic 32.4). Its Lt is Fl (2) G 6 s. 8M. It is opposite the R unlit No. 12 buoy, with No. 14 just beyond it, both to be left to port. If entering at night one can now pay

32.4   Le Buron green tower half-way to harbour entrance

some attention to the leading Lts. Both are F G, the front one being a W square Tr with B top above the St Servan Y Hbr; the rear one is La Balue, a 37m Grey square Tr already described.

The only shoal water to be avoided is the Plateau de la Rance in the middle of the fairway. Its northern extremity is marked by a BY unlit N-cardinal buoy which must be left to starboard, unless you are making to anchor off Dinard. It may be easier to head straight for the 10m high W tower with R top marking the SW end of the Môle des Noires, the main St Malo breakwater (Fl R 5 s.) making sure the tide is not setting you on to the unlit N-cardinal buoy.

Round the end of the breakwater on to a course of 075°, at which point the decision has to be made whether to go on into the Bassin Vauban alongside the walled city or to berth in the St Servan marina, locally known as the Port de Plaisance des Sablons.

32.5   *Fort la Grande Conchée to be left to starboard at seaward end of Chenal de la Grande Conchée on course 182°*

32.6   *St Servan Marina with St Croix dome and front main channel leading light almost in line. Notice at end of breakwater reads 'Attention au seuil' ('Watch out for the sill')*

32.7   View of walled city from the yacht club across Bassin Vauban. Boats berth three abreast, bows south

(b)   *Inshore – le Chenal de la Grande Porte*   Pick up the R pillar whistle buoy Les Buharats (Q R) 1.7 miles due W of le Grand Jardin and head on 089° with the latter Lt in transit with the Dir F R 40m 25M Lt at Rochebonne 4¼ miles farther to the E on the mainland. Its Lt is intensified over 1½°. Leave the No. 1 G fairway buoy (Fl G 4 s.) off Basse à Colas close to starboard and alter a point to starboard to pass the new Le Sou E-cardinal buoy, thence to join the main fairway on 129°;

(c)   *Inshore – le Chenal du Décollé*   None of the leading marks is lit, so this channel is best confined to outward passages and the courses shown on my chart are thus marked. However, in good visibility from a point close W of Les Buharats buoy you might pick up the 134° transit of two W Bns: the first on the rock le Grand Genillet, the other 6 cables farther beyond it at Roche Pelée on the shoreline. Hold that course until the islet off Pte du Décollé comes abeam, then alter to 105° and follow the marked route all the way to Pte de Dinard 2½ miles to the ESE. It is marked with R and G pole Bns with topmarks.

32.8 Harbour Office in Bassin Vauban. Apply here for times of going up the Rance or for entering Bassin Duguay-Trouin

32.9 Bridge open to enter Bassin Duguay-Trouin

Approaches from the East   There are three suitable approaches from the E, either Granville or Chausey. While they save up to 3 miles against using the main channel described above, none is suitable except in good visibility by day and accepting that there is as little as 0m5 at LWS just before the junction of these NE approaches with the main fairway.

These channels are a lot simpler on departure, due to the distance to some of the unlit leading marks.

(a) *La Bigne Channel*   Start on the E-cardinal BYB buoy marking the Basse aux Chiens 1 mile NW of Pte du Meinga and ½ mile ESE of the YBY Rochefort Bn Tr. The course is 222° for $1\frac{1}{4}$ miles on a transit of La Crolante Tr (a clear right-hand edge of land off Pte de la Varde) with le Grand Bey (a rocky hump-shaped island just clear of the right-hand edge of the ramparts of St Malo). Half a mile short of La Crolante Tr, alter to 236°.

This brings into line Le Buron Tr (see above) and Villa Lonick 2 miles W of Dinard on Pte Bellefard which has a W stripe painted on its face. As it is over 5 miles away it is better to concentrate on picking up a G bell buoy 7 cables beyond La Crolante. This is left to starboard.

Then, 3 cables on, alter to 222°, shaping to pass midway between the R Bn in Grand Dodehal and the G buoy marking

32.10   Inside Bassin Duguay-Trouin there is always room. Harbour Office to left. Quic-en-Groigne Castle in background (right)

les Roches aux Anglais. Next leave the R can-topped buoy marking les Crapauds du Bey to port. This is the shallowest part of the approach. But 3 cables farther you hit the main channel about half-way between Le Buron and the break-water.

(b) *Petits Pointus Channel* Not so nail-biting in its early stages. About 1 mile W of the Rochefort Bn Tr come on to 202° to leave the unlit G bell buoy marking la St Servantine Rock to starboard. The transit is the right-hand edge of the fort on le Petit Bey in line with Pte de Dinard in the town itself.

Leave to port the R Bn marking les Petits Pointus rocks and straight on to join la Bigne channel at the R Bn marking Grand Dodehal rock. Both are unlit.

(c) *Chenal de la Grande Conchée* One mile ENE of the Île de Cézembre is the prominent little flat-topped fort la Grande Conchée (pic 32.5). Leave it 3 cables to starboard on course 183° and La Plate Lt Bn (Q 10m 7M) close port. At the G con buoy Fl G 2 s. marking les Roches aux Anglais you join the other two channels on 222°. This channel is often used by the hydrofoils from Jersey. It saves 2 miles.

32.11   Tidal gauge showing 0m38 over the sill to enter yacht harbour in Anse de Bas-Sablons (St Servan)

A large-scale chart shows several other rock-dodging channels, but the ones described above will cater for the average yachtsman. For peace of mind I should always enter by the main NW channel past the Grand Jardin, but, if heading to the E, take the Petits Pointus channel, providing there is sufficient water over the first ¾ mile.

Berthing and Facilities

(a)   *St Malo*   Yachts berth either at the N end of the Bassin Vauban or the W end of Bassin Duguay-Trouin. For either it is necessary to enter through the lock between the RO/RO ferry berth to starboard and the hydrofoil terminal to port. The HM is in a prominent control Tr on the left of the locks. He is on VHF Ch 12 and uses the following signals to govern traffic:

R flag or Lt   no entry
G flag or Lt   no exit
R and G flags or Lts   no movement
Flag P or W Lt to the left of the other   gates open
Flag V indicates the movement of ferries which, along with all other commercial traffic, including fishermen, take absolute priority over yachts. They are not supposed to enter the lock without first being hailed.

Entry is normally $-2\frac{1}{2}$ HW and $+1\frac{1}{2}$h. Waiting buoys can be picked up on the N side of the approach channel to the lock-gates. There is a least depth of 6m3 inside.

There are no visitors' berths as such, so it's a matter of finding a space on any of the three long pontoons running S from the HO. No. 1 pontoon on its town side is for boats under 7m long. Boats over 11m long should either berth alongside the ramparts beyond the ferries or alongside the yacht clubhouse on the mole beside the entrance to the basin beyond (Duguay-Trouin). The bridge will be lifted to enter the latter. The easiest summer month for finding berths is August, when all the locals are away cruising.

Boats should berth three abreast, bows-S. Then report to the HO (pic 32.8) – tel. (99) 56–51–91 – which is alongside the local Tourist Information Office.

The YC (SN Baie de St Malo) is hospitable and well accustomed to visitors from the UK. Its tel. (99) 40–84–42.

(b)   *St Servan*   If the new 720-berth marina at St Servan is preferred, just remember that there is a sill 2m above datum running from the little breakwater on your starboard hand across to a point near to RO/RO berth. The depth of water over it is indicated by digital electronic display across the bay from the marina. Visitors should berth on the first pontoon inside the mole, clearly marked as such. The least depth is 1m7.

32.12   St Malo inside Môle des Noires

32.13   Slipway and ferry landing at Dinard

32.14　View from vedette landing towards the Yacht Club de Dinard with its new pier for use of yachts in dredged mooring area

The HO is next to a little bar at the town end of the car- and boat-parking area near the travel-lift. The SNBSM has a clubhouse there (tel. (99) 81–78–01).

FW, fuel and electricity are available at both places. There are also chandlers and repair facilities near-by.

The taxi fares to St Malo can mount up, but St Servan has plenty to offer hungry, thirsty or sleepy sailors unless their tastes run to the more sophisticated amenities of the city or they can't stay away from the casino. The hassle and uncertainty of the lock-gate operation is avoided.

Customs at the Gare Maritime, tel. (99) 81–74–56.

(c) *Dinard*　There are no alongside berths at Dinard, but there is a 2m dredged area with moorings opposite the new quay (pic 32.14) clearly marked by perches with cardinal topmarks or buoys. The Dinard YC clubhouse is full of memories of the days when the big cutters used to race over from Cowes. (To this day the most sought-after trophy of the race is one given by Edward VII.) Tel. (99) 46–14–32.

The moorings are approached between three pairs of pillars leading in towards the White Ferries' landing ramp with a dredged depth of 1m.

FW and fuel can be obtained at the quay.

Communications　Besides ferries to the Channel Islands and Portsmouth there is an airport 3 miles SW of Dinard and SNCF from St Malo to Rennes and all points beyond.

Weather　Forecasts at the YC and HO, or tel. (99) 46–18–77. Also on VHF Ch 2. Area 11 Manche ouest.

*33   DINAN via The RANCE

Charts: CG Navigation Fluviale – Bretagne (Fr 4233)

THE COMPLETION of the massive hydro-electric barrage across the Rance $1\frac{1}{2}$ miles S of the entrance to St Malo opened up the first 3 miles as a peaceful cruising area with numerous attractive unspoilt villages to anchor off.

From the barrage to Port Dinan is 12 miles with one further lock to negotiate at Chatelier, only 3 miles short of your destination.

The medieval walled town of Dinan was saved in 1395 for its inhabitants by their champion Du Guesclin getting a points verdict in single combat against the Duke of Lancaster's man,

Canterbury. From the English Gardens inside its ramparts you look down 75m to its 'harbour' immediately downstream of the first bridge on the whole canal system, for which it is necessary to lower your mast to the statutory headroom (2m50) for the remainder of the voyage southward to the Bay of Biscay, 47 locks away.

Main Barrage and Locks   Without local knowledge it is necessary to check in with the HM at St Malo lock-gates or the HO in the yacht marina in Bassin Vauban or at St Servan. There you will be given all the information on times of opening of the barrage and the second lock at Chatelier. It is mandatory to carry on board the printed instructions issued by the barrage authorities. A shortened version in English is also available, but the excellent Carte Guide *Navigation Fluviale* gives it all in English as well. The electricity authority will give any further information required on (99) 46–21–87.

33.1   Heading upstream from Solidor Bay, St Servan. St Croix dome (right), Solidor tower (left)

33.2   Approaching barrage on each side buoyed areas to keep boats away from sluice-gate turbulence

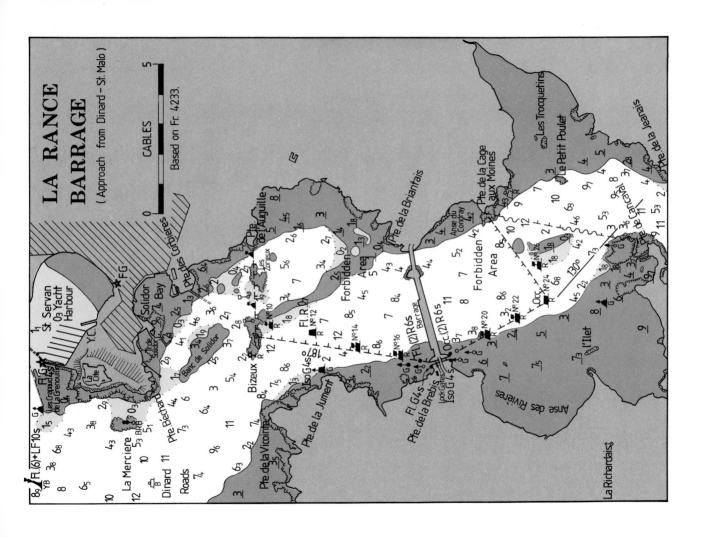

33.3   Buoyed channel leading to lock-gates at west end of barrage

*33.4   Yacht heading upstream. Lock signal (cone point down)
clears entry south-bound*

The French chart 4233 stops at Chatelier and is not helpful.

Briefly, the barrage locks can open whenever the level is 4m above datum, with a minimum of 2mo in the lock. The back of the printed instructions gives the precise times of the opening there and at Chatelier. Or the lock-keeper can be called on tel. (96) 46–21–87.

Normally the lock opens on the hour every hour when there is 4mo in the Rance basin at St Suliac (3 miles upstream). The lifting bridge which carries all the road traffic between St Malo and Dinard will be opened any time during the first 15min after each hour.

After 2000 and before dawn it is normally necessary to give 2h. advance warning by telephone or to pull the bellrope at the lock entrance, which will respond with an illuminated panel 'Appel reçu'.

It is advisable to reach one of the waiting berths on the dolphins or lie in sight of the gates 20min before intended

33.5 *Approaching St Suliac, 3 miles from barrage. Note pagoda on headland*

33.6 *Slipway at St Suliac. Restaurant is first building on right at the end. 2m0 depth off end of slip*

33.7   Bridge at Port St Hubert (23m clearance)

33.8   Château Chêne Vert opposite Mordreuc, 1¼ miles upstream from St Hubert. Here the river narrows

entry (pic 33.3). By night the NE dolphin has a Lt Fl (2) R 6 s. while the SE dolphin (upstream) is Oc (2) R 6 s. The NW side of the entrance has Fl G 4 s.

Approach   Leaving St Malo, make for the W side of the river and pick up the R Bn on Bizeux, a rocky islet ½ mile S of the landing point in Solidor bay on the S side of St Servan. Hereafter follow the channel leaving the R buoys close to port until reaching No. 16 just short of the lock-gates. La Jument, a G tower on the W bank, is Iso G 4 s. 6m high.

By day the locks will open when a B cone point downwards is displayed, or a G Lt by night. Coming downstream, a B ball or an R Lt is displayed. Outward-bound craft take priority.

33.9 *View from Mordreuc showing afloat moorings*

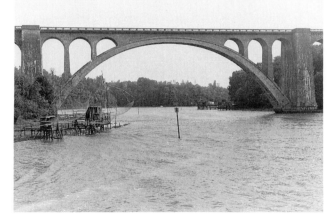

33.10 *De Lessard railway viaduct one mile beyond Mordreuc (19m clearance). Note fishing nets either side of well-marked channel*

33.11 *Châtelier lock, 3 miles from Dinan*

215

33.12   Alongside berths upstream of Châtelier. View from Lyvet on east bank where there is a riverside restaurant and a slipway

33.13   The old port of Dinan with alongside berths on west bank

33.14 The end of the road at Dinan, unless you have a mast-tabernacle, draw less than 1m3 and want to go all the way through the canals to reach the Bay of Biscay between St Nazaire and the Morbihan

Once inside keep within the marked channel. The farther you go the more it tends to favour the W bank.

It is outside the scope of this book to describe every village worth visiting along the way, but St Suliac on the E bank 3½ miles from the barrage is noteworthy for its waterside restaurant. Either anchor off or pick up a mooring (pic 33.6). An alongside berth 1m5 can be found at Mordreuc, where there is another restaurant and fuel. Right opposite is an exquisitely restored small château (la Chêne Verte). Here the river narrows in earnest.

To get through the second lock at Chatelier there needs to be 8m50 above datum. And before getting there a bridge with least clearance of 19m needs to be respected by tall rigs.

Ideally you should set off from the barrage 3h before HW. The lock-keeper at Chatelier can be contacted on tel. (96) 39–55–66 to double check. Only 1m 70 draught can be guaranteed above Chatelier.

Berthing and Facilities Immediately through the lock the village of Lyvet has on the E bank a slipway and an alongside berth, and a yacht anchorage against the W bank.

There are pontoon berths depth 1m6 on the W bank of the canal at Port Dinan, where FW and fuel can be obtained, plus an excellent meal in the Relais Corsaires, and adequate shopping.

The local port authority is on tel. (96) 39–04–67.

Weather See St Malo.

*34 ST BRIAC

Charts: CG 535 (Fr 844 Im C33b BA 3659)

High Water −05h. 15m. Dover 00h. 20m. SP St Helier
Heights above Datum *MHWS 11m2. MLWS 1m3.
MHWN 8m5. MLWN 4m1.*

AT THE MOUTH of the R. Fremur ST BRIAC's holiday homes
among the pine trees and well manicured lawns surround a
sheltered drying harbour of natural beauty and tranquillity –
except for all the other boats and swarms of L-drivers on
sailboards. It lies midway between Cap Frehel and St Malo,
being 6½ miles from the latter by the inshore passage or 8 miles
if you head W from le Grand Jardin. It is an ideal spot for a
picnic afloat, with access normally possible at half-tide. When
the wind is in the NW, give it a miss.

Approaches from the east Close off the Pte de Dinard
either follow the well-marked coast-crawling route to leave
on the Chenal du Décollée on course 314° or head out on the
main channel as far as the new Le Sou E-cardinal buoy and
head W (see the plan of St Malo and approaches on p. 200).
Then pass between the E-cardinal Nerput Bn and a G fairway
buoy close S of it and take a slow swing to port outside the
Île Agot. You can go inside it in settled weather, but the
saving in time is not worth the trouble.

The final approach course is 125° which at night shows W
across only 1° from the Iso WRG 4 s. 12M Lt on the St Briac
shore from a 6m W mast on a hut. There is a 3° R arc to port
and a 3° G arc to starboard of the proper course. Leave the R
pile Bn off the SW corner of Île du Perron close to port and
head straight into the bay between R and G Bns.

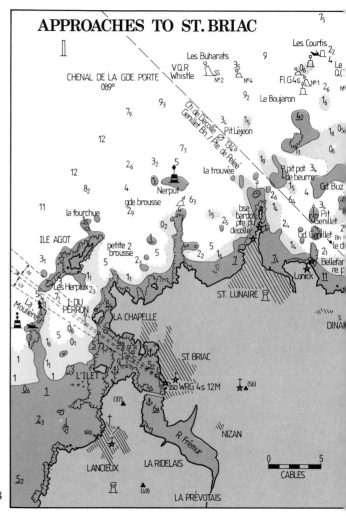

218

34.1   Channel from the north-west leaving Île du Perron and Île Agot (farthest out) to port

34.2   St Briac bay (Le Béchet) at low water facing north from bridge across Le Frémur river bridge (clearance 4m)

Approaches from the west   Pass ½ mile to seaward of St Cast and leave the E-cardinal les Bourdinots to buoy to starboard until picking up the 125° approach described above.

Berths   Depending on weather anchor either side of the prominent little headland just beyond the last R Bn, or pick up one of the 600 moorings in the bay.

Facilities   A local YC and beach café. Shops for essentials, but otherwise everyone relies on Dinard, where the local port authority is to be found.

Charts: *Fr 5646 BA 3659 CG 535, 536 (Im C33b)*

High Water −05h. 15m. Dover −00h. 20m. SP St
Helier
Heights above Datum *Springs MHWS 11m2. MLWS
1m3. MHWN 8m5. MLWN 4m1.*

ST CAST lies 4 miles SE of Cap Fréhel at the head of the
drying-out bay of l'Arguenon and 7 miles WSW of le Grand
Jardin, if sailing from St Malo. It is a fairly classy summer
holiday resort, with a beautiful sweep of beach a mile long

35.2   Conspicuous semaphore station on Pointe de St Cast

*35.1   Cap Fréhel lighthouse 33m grey square tower, 85m above sea-level. As seen from ESE off St Cast. It is often the first landfall
in passage to St Malo from outside the Minquiers. Radio D/F Beacon on 305.7kHz (FÉ ··−· ··−··).*

35.3   *Low-water picture. Suitable for 1m5 draft. Exposed between north-east and south*

running from Pte de St Cast to Pte de la Garde. From the semaphore station there is a breathtaking view of most of the Emerald Coast.

Its attraction for passing yachtsmen is that there is good holding ground in 1m50 and even deeper close in towards the little harbour under the lee of St Cast point, while the quay is dredged to 1m50. Not recommended when the wind is between NE and S.

Even deeper water can be found off the landing at Pte de la Garde where the YC de St Cast is situated.

The town has a monument overlooking it celebrating the day in 1758 when British invaders lost 2,400 killed.

Approach   An E-cardinal BYB unlit buoy $\frac{3}{4}$ mile 070° from Pte de St Cast marks Les Bourdinots rocks and lies in the G sector of the Iso WG 4 s. Lt on a 9m G and W structure at the end of the quay. Its range is 11M in its W sector and 8M in the G.

35.4   *Looking to south-east at half tide*

There is deep water to the S of that buoy; it is easier to leave it to starboard and stay in the W sector 6° either side of 239°. The picture (35.3) shows the Lt structure at the end of the quay and the Bec Rond rocks close to the S; between them is the proper entrance.

If leaving Les Bourdinots to port, simply pass midway between the buoy and Pte de St Cast.

By day a transit on course 216° of Bec Rond rocks and a church steeple on the skyline will bring you straight to the end of the quay. If going on to the anchorage S of Pte de la Garde, hold off until the point with its conspicuous chapel bears due W and close on the echo sounder.

Berthing   Fishermen tend to hog the alongside berths at St Cast quay and have priority for moorings close south of it, but you could be lucky. Otherwise anchor, or pick up a buoy and argue about it later – 12 are reserved for visitors out of 224 laid.

Facilities   There are shops and cafés at the inshore end of St Cast quay which offer most things a visitor might need. The HO is there (tel. (96) 41–88–34).

FW available at the quayside.

There is a local boatyard and chandlery.

The YC at Pointe de la Garde (tel. (96) 41–05–77) also runs a sailing school, but only functions in the summer holidays.

Weather   Forecasts from the semaphore station above Pte de St Cast (tel. (96) 41–88–34). Area 11 Manche ouest.

*36 ERQUY

Charts: BA 3672 Im C33b Fr 5724 (CG 536)

High Water −05h. 20m. Dover −00h. 20m. SP St Helier
Heights above Datum MHWS 11m2. MLWS 1m3. MHWN 8m5. MLWN 3m8.

ERQUY is an active fishing port facing due W 8 miles beyond Cap Fréhel. It dries out completely and offers little protection from the prevailing seas except close inshore between the two breakwaters, where it is always packed out by fishing boats. It affords good shelter from the E.

Approach The approach is from due W bringing the ends of the two breakwaters in transit. By night it will lie in the 10M W sector of the Oc (2 + 1) WRG 12 s. Lt on the 10m high W Tr R top at the pierhead (pic 36.2). The rear Lt is FL R 2.5 s on a 10m R and W Tr, range 3M.

Unless you're planning a brief visit on one tide or to dry out on an open beach with legs and walk ashore, Erquy is not recommended.

Facilities These are no great shakes, being geared to the needs of commercial fishermen. The HM is at the fish quay (tel. (96) 72–19–32). There are two slips. The local YC opens only in July and August.

Weather Posted at the HO or on tape (96) 20–01–92. Area 11 Manche ouest.

36.1 *Fish warehouse and slip inside outer breakwater. No yachts*

36.2 *Inner breakwater. Most yachts take the bottom on legs off picture to the left*

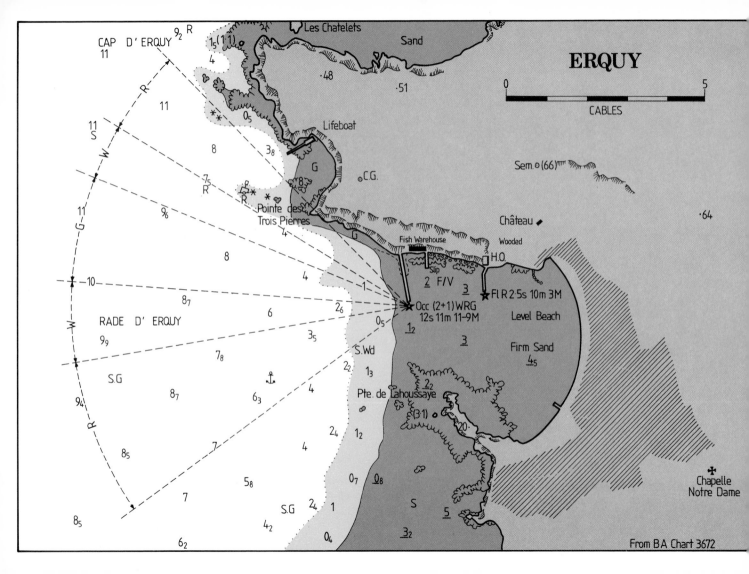

ERQUY

CAP D'ERQUY
11

Les Chatelets

Sand

1_5 (1 1)

9₂ R
R

$\cdot$ 48

$\cdot$ 51

R
S
W
R
G
R
W
R

11

11

8

3_8

0_5

Lifeboat

G

8_3

R

R

Pointe des
Trois Pierres

G

7_5

9_6

8

4

1

8_7

8₇

3_5

6

2_6

0_5

RADE D'ERQUY

9_9

S.G

8_7

6_3

7_8

4

2_2

1_3

S.Wd

Pte. de Lahoussaye

9_4

8_5

7

2_4

1_2

4

8_5

5_8

2_4

1

0_7

0_8

S.G

4_2

0_4

6_2

C.G.

Sem. $\circ$ (66)

Château

$\cdot$ 64

Fish Warehouse

Wooded

H.Q.

Slip

2 F/V

3

Occ (2+1) WRG
12s 11m 11–9M

1_2

3

2_2

(3·1)

S

3_2

5

20

Fl R 2·5s 10m 3M

Level Beach

Firm Sand

4_5

Chapelle
Notre Dame

0
CABLES
5

From BA Chart 3672

PART FIVE

NORTH-WEST BRITTANY

St Brieuc – Brest

Soundings and heights in metres

Bearings and courses in degrees true

Distances at sea in nautical miles or cables

The coast is wild and rugged and utterly beautiful . . . Most of the North Brittany coast is impenetrable to anything but the smallest craft, and then only in good weather, for the coast is defended by a great barrier of natural hazards.

. . . most of the perils lie near the surface, sharp reefs marked only by breaking water. These dangers reach out sometimes 12 miles from the land.

The coast is no friend to the sailor. Only those familiar with its dangers dare approach it with impunity.

Clare Francis in her novel *Night Sky*, writing about
wartime operations with few navigation aids functioning.

SAFE NAVIGABLE DISTANCES BETWEEN YACHT BERTHS, OUTSIDE ÎLE DE BRÉHAT AND ÎLE DE BATZ (in nautical miles)

	ST MALO	BINIC	PAIMPOL	TRÉGUIER	PERROS-GUIREC	MORLAIX	ROSCOFF	L'ABER-WRAC'H	LE CONQUET	BREST
ST MALO										
BINIC	33									
PAIMPOL	38	19								
TRÉGUIER	57	39	26							
PERROS-GUIREC	62	43	31	20						
MORLAIX	92	71	59	48	32					
ROSCOFF	85	64	52	41	26	13				
L'ABER-WRAC'H	117	96	84	73	58	46	33			
LE CONQUET	133	112	100	89	74	61	48	23		
BREST	150	129	117	106	91	78	65	40	17	

Charts: CG 536 Fr 833 (Im C33b BA 2668)

High Water   −05h. 25m. Dover   −00h. 25m. SP St Helier

Heights above Datum   *MHWS 11m2. MLWS 1m3. MHWN 8m5. MLWN 3m8.*

DAHOUET is a charming unspoilt little fishing port with a totally enclosed natural harbour. Unhappily it dries out 5m at the entrance, which is dangerous in strong winds from the NW or N. It is only 1 mile SW of the Pte de Pleneuf and Le Val André, which is a good enough reason for a visit, since the Restaurant Le Cotriade alongside the harbour mole is as good as any on the Emerald Coast. (Tel. (96) 72–20–26.)

Approaches   From any direction it is necessary to find the N-cardinal La Dahouet buoy just under a mile NW of the entrance. It lies in the 32° W sector of the 10M Lt on the 17m G-topped W Bn la Petite Muette slap in the entrance. The light is Oc WRG 4 s., with R to port and G to starboard.

The approach course is 133° with the Lt Bn just open to the right of a pagoda on the N arm of the town (see pic 37.1). When just short of the G and W Bn, side-step to port around it and then come back on to the approach course leaving an R pillar Bn just off the shore (La Mine d'Or) to port.

Berthing   The first quay on your port hand is reserved for fishing-boats, but you should be able to go alongside the Vieux Quai in the N corner of the harbour. The quay on the S bank is unsuitable.

Facilities   Lots of busy waterfront bistros and a YC on the quayside with the HO near at hand (tel. (96) 72–83–20).

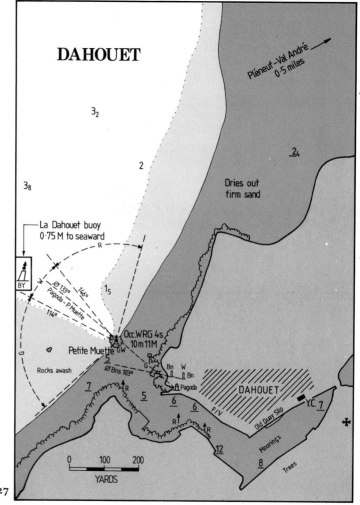

37.1   View to seaward. Note pagoda on headland to the right. Fishing boats only berth on Quai Neuf (right). No alongside berths to the left

37.2   Farther up-harbour, yachts can get alongside Vieux Quai (left) near yacht club in white shed on quayside

*38 LE LÉGUÉ (ST BRIEUC)

Charts: Fr 5725 Im C34 (CG 536)

High Water −05h. 30m. *Dover* −00h. 30m. *SP St Helier*
Heights above Datum *MHWS 11m2. MLWS 1m3. MHWN 8m5. MLWN 4m1.*

LE LÉGUÉ is the commercial port of the cathedral town and provincial capital St Brieuc. Its aproaches dry out 2 miles to seaward and can be nasty during strong onshore winds. The port is mainly for fishermen and coasters serving the industrial complex on the outskirts of St Brieuc, but determined yachtsmen can find good shelter once locked inside.

Approaches At the southern end of the Baie de St Brieuc between Erquy and Binic is Le Légué RW whistle buoy with an Iso R 4 s. Lt. Point à l'Aigle is 210° − 2.5 miles where there is a Lt Ho with a 14m W tower and G top on the N side of

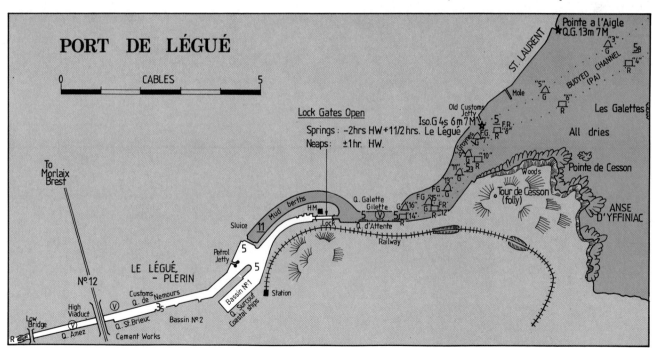

PORT DE LÉGUÉ

38.1   Pointe À l'aigle lighthouse showing folly on left bank (Lt.-Com. O.M. de Las Casas)

38.2   Lock-gates at Le Légué (Lt.-Com. O.M. de Las Casas)

the entrance to Rue du Légué (Q G 13m 7M). Its arc of visibility is 160°–070°. The channel from the offshore buoy is marked by R and G unlit buoys. It has a depth of 3m at MHW Neaps. There is a prominent folly on the wooded headland forming the S side of the estuary. The Old Customs jetty opposite has an Iso G 4 s. Lt on a 9m W Tr marking the start of the final approach to the locks $\frac{1}{2}$ mile on.

Entrance, Berthing and Facilities Yachts should pass through the commercial lock which opens ± 1$\frac{1}{2}$h. HW, rather less at Neaps. Waiting for the locks to open you can secure alongside the Quai d'Attente port side to immediately outside the gates. The HM has his office alongside the N side of the lock. No. 1 basin is only for commercial traffic, so yachts must go on to No. 2 basin and berth where available immediately upstream, probably on the Quai Nemours, where there are Customs and all the replenishment and repair facilities a boat could wish for, although the surroundings are not particularly agreeable. There is a least depth of 3m in the basin.

The HM is on (96) 33–35–41. He also has VHF on Ch 16 and 12. Customs are on (96) 33–33–03.

Weather On (96) 20–01–92. Area 11 Manche ouest.

38.3 Downstream view of berths at Le Légué under the N.12 viaduct

*39 BINIC

Charts: Fr 5725 Im C33b (CG 536) (BA 2669)

High Water −05h. 25m. Dover −00h. 30m. SP St
Helier
Heights above Datum *MHWS 11m2. MLWS 1m3.*
MHWN 7m4. MLWN 4m1.

BINIC, 7 miles NW of St Brieuc, is another popular summer
resort with glorious beaches, where the yachtsmen have all
but elbowed the fishermen out since lock-gates have been
installed and pontoons providing 100 berths, with as many
again in the Avant-Port or alongside the quays. Outside the
harbour it dries at LW to a distance of ¾ mile. Normally the
port can be approached any time during the top half of the
tide, but operation of the lock is normally confined to the
hour before HW. It is as well to check beforehand, especially
around Neaps (tel. (96) 73–61–86).

Approach First find Le Rohein Tr 8 miles to the ENE
in the middle of the Bay of St Brieuc about 4 miles NW of
Pte de Pléneuf. It is a 15m high Y Tr with a B band and the
topmark of a W-cardinal mark. Pass clear to the W and head
WSW in the W sector of the VQ (9) WRG 10 s. Lt with a
range of 10 miles.

Four miles WSW of Le Rohein leave well clear to starboard
the E-cardinal buoy marking the Caffa bank. There's plenty
of water to the S, so hold on until the 12m W Tr at the seaward
end of Penthièvre mole (Oc (3) W 12 s. 12m 12M) can be seen
and brought into line with the church steeple on 275° (see
aerial pic 39.1). Then go for it. Two miles short of the harbour
the W-cardinal buoy La Roselière will be left 1 mile to star-

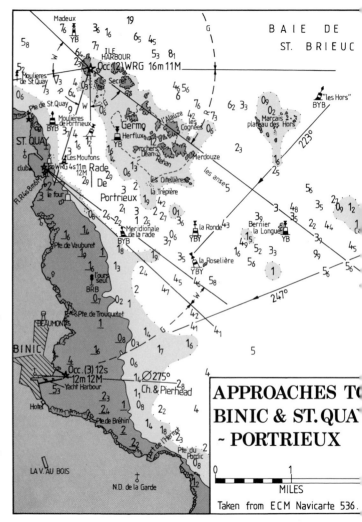

APPROACHES TO
BINIC & ST.QUA
~ PORTRIEUX

0   1
MILES
Taken from ECM Navicarte 536.

Ø 275°

39.1   *(A) Outer harbour accessible in top three hours of each tide.   (B) Lock-gates.   (C) Yacht club.   (D) Public launching slipway*

233

39.2   From harbour entrance. Lock open – bridge down

39.3   Anvil-shaped yacht club and slipway into outer harbour

39.4   *Bridge retracted to allow yacht to enter*

board as a check on the stream running at 2 knots parallel to the coast, turning NW at local HW.

Coming from the W there is a narrow passage close inshore through the Rade de Portrieux bringing one to a pt 2 miles NNW of Binic, but it is easier on the ulcer to go E-about the off-lying rocks, leaving the E-cardinal les Hors buoy to starboard. It lies 2 miles NNW of the Caffa buoy described above and is also unlit.

Once inside the breakwaters, hang about for the lock or take a temporary alongside berth, bearing in mind that it dries up to 6m.

On the left of the lock is the YC with a wide slipway on its seaward side. On the right is the small lock-keeper's hut just across the quayside from the little shack which is occasionally manned as the Bureau du Port. The Simplified Code is used to control traffic: G Lt to enter; R to leave. There is no VHF. The gate is usually open when the tide is 9m.

Berthing   Visitors take their chance on finding a spare slot on a pontoon. Or berth alongside the quay and find the HM. There is ample water inside, reputedly 5m5.

Facilities   Besides the Club Nautique de Binic's small modern clubhouse, the town has everything on hand right along the quayside facing the pontoons.

FW and fuel available.

Customs are at St Quay-Portrieux.

There are two more slipways at the western end of the harbour.

Weather   Posted at the YC and the Bureau du Port. Area 11 Manche ouest. Or call Bréhat on (96) 20–01–92.

235

39.5   *Harbour Office alongside locks*

39.6   *Yacht harbour seen from yacht club. Note town quay is reserved for fishing boats*

*40   ST QUAY-PORTRIEUX

Charts: BA 3672 Fr 5725 Im C33b (CG 536)

High Water −05h. 20m. Dover −00h. 30m. SP St
Helier
Heights above Datum MHWS 12m2. MLWS 1m3.
MHWN 8m5. MLWN 4m1.

THREE miles north of Binic is the popular seaside resort and
home port of lobster fishermen of St Quay, with its drying-
out harbour of Portrieux at its SE end. It has lovely beaches,
smart restaurants, a casino for holidaymakers and a string of
reefs and rocky islets 2½ miles long outside the front door for
those hauling crustaceans.

Approaches Between the rocks (Roches de St Quay) and
the harbour is a narrow but well-marked channel running
parallel to the coast. At its SE end it forms the Rade de
Portrieux. The current runs through this channel at over 2
knots at Springs, starting to the NW at local HW (−05h.
15m. Dover) and turning SE'ly 6h. later at local LW.

From the S follow the directions given for Binic until the
unlit W-cardinal La Roselière buoy is 2–3 cables abeam on
course 320°. This will bring you towards the E-cardinal Les
Moutons buoy 2 miles to the NW at which point it should be
left to starboard, as course is altered to 260° for the harbour
entrance 3 cables away.

From the N it is desirable to make for a point about a mile
offshore on a SSE'ly course, leaving the W-cardinal Bn Tr on
the Madeux rocks to port. A mile farther S there is a promi-

40.1   *Facing to seaward at low water*

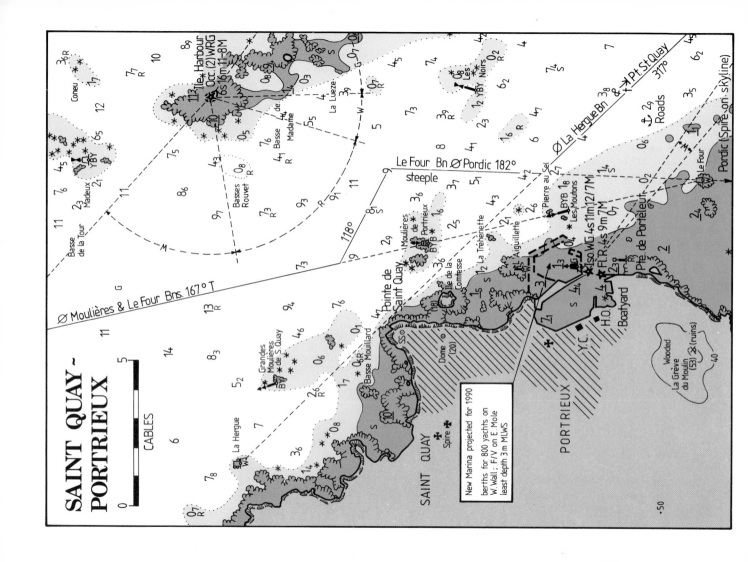

SAINT QUAY ~ PORTRIEUX

CABLES

0 5

New Marina projected for 1990
berths for 800 yachts on
W.Wall; F/V on E. Mole
least depth 3 m MLWS

SAINT QUAY

PORTRIEUX

Pointe de Saint Quay

Spire

Ø Moulières & Le Four Bns. 167° T

Le Four Bn Ø Pordic 182°
steeple

La Hergue Bn

Pt.St.Quay
317°

Pordic (Spire on skyline)

Roads

Pte. de Portrieux

La Grève
du Moulin
(53) (ruins)

Le Four

Boatyard

Y.C.

H.O.

Dome (20)

Basse Mouillard

Grandes
Moulières
de S.Quay

La Hergue

Île Harbour
Occ. (2)WRG
16s 16m 11·8M

Basse de
Madame

Basses
Rouvet

Basse de la Tour

Madeux

Coneu

Les
Noirs

La Lueze

Pierre au Sel

Les Moutons

L'Aiguillette

La Tréhenette

Moulières
de Portrieux

Moulières
de la
Comtesse

Iso.WG.4s11m12/7M

Fl.R.4s 9m 7M

40.2   Why St Quay is planning a deep-water yacht harbour outside (Lt.-Com. O.M. de Las Casas)

40.3   One hour before high water. Dinghies stacked vertically ashore (1) are outside Harbour Office and yacht club

prominent E-cardinal Bn to be left to starboard – Les Moul-ières de Portrieux. From there it is ½ mile to les Moutons and the long N–S breakwater which gives the harbour its protection from most directions except the SE.

There are lights to point the way, but they should only be relied on in settled weather and after some local knowledge has been acquired. The NW end of the Roches de St Quay at Île Harbour has a 13m W square tower with R top and a Lt Oc (2) WRG 6 s. The W sector from 080°–133° is visible at 12M and covers the safe water in the NW entrance to the channel. Its 8M, G sector covers NW–E.

The seaward end of the main breakwater has an Iso WG 4 s. Lt from a prominent octagonal W tower with G top 12m above sea level. Its 12-mile W sector 3° either side of 309° marks the fairway from immediately inshore of La Roselière buoy to the harbour entrance, with an R sector to the E and G to the W. The head of the S mole has a 7M Lt Fl R 4 s. from a 9m mast with an R top.

Berthing and Facilities   The whole harbour dries out at least 3m5 above MLWS. Fishing boats and local pleasure craft have priority for alongside berths, so you must be prepared to take the ground. There are several slips, those on the W side of the harbour for the considerable racing dinghy fleet attached to local YC. The HM is at the NW end of the harbour on Boulevard Marechal Foch, tel. (96) 70–42–27. The HO is at the head of the slipway on the W wall directly opposite the harbour entrance.

Fuel, water and provisions can all be obtained alongside. There are repair facilities and a 1.5-ton crane.

A new outer harbour for 600 yachts and most of the fishing fleet with a least depth of 3m0 and free access at any state of the tide is planned to be built outside the NE breakwater with reclaimed land for a YC. When it happens it will transform St Quay-Portrieux as an attraction for visiting yachtsmen, but it may not be completed until 1990.)

Weather   See Binic.

*41 PAIMPOL

Charts: *Fr 3670 BA 3673 Im C34 CG 537 Stan C16*

High Water −o5h. 25m. Dover −ooh. 30m. SP St
Helier
Heights above Datum MHWS 10m3. MLWS 0m5.
MHWN 7m8. MLWN 3m2.

PAIMPOL is another former home port for those who used to
bring cod back from distant waters. Now only local fishing
and oyster dredgers remain, while yachts increasingly take
over the two basins behind the lock-gates.

The Bay dries out to a distance of 2 miles to the E, so it is
essential to time one's arrival just before HW.

The town is 3 miles S of the Île de Bréhat, a 10m. ferry
crossing from Pointe de l'Arcouest, 6km N of Paimpol.

Approach To position oneself for the correct approach
on the Chenal de la Jument on course 260° it is desirable to
be on the right track 4 miles to seaward by picking up the
BYB E-cardinal les Charpentiers Bn. It lies 1 mile NNE of
the Lost-Pic Lt Ho, a 20m W square Tr with an R top (Oc
WR 4 s). Its W sector has a 10M range 16° either side of 237°
from seaward. You should close on a WSW course in the W
sector, but will be in the 7-mile R sector as you bring Les
Charpentiers Bn abeam to starboard.

If the wind is not NE–SE it is safe to drop the hook ½ mile
inshore of the R buoy la Gueule, bearing in mind that the tide
runs SE–NW up to 2 knots. Unfortunately all the channel
buoys are unlit. The charted transit by day is the Pointe
Brividic (½ mile E of the breakwater) in line with the church
Tr on 260°. But a more easily identifiable transit is the W

41.1 (A) *Bassin No. 1 with a few berths for yachts over 10m*
(top right). (B) Bassin No. 2. (C) Chandlery and
boatyards. Oyster dredgers on the mud (right fore-
ground)

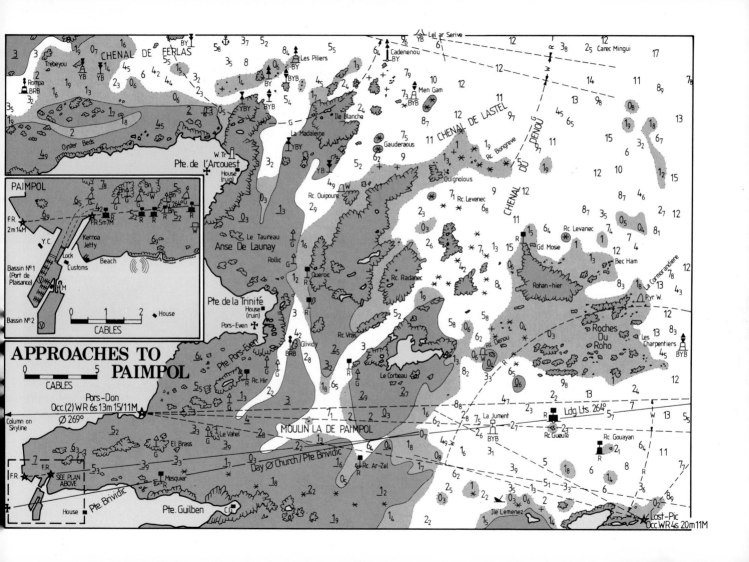

41.2   *Lock-gates from outside*

41.3   *Shabby Harbour Office between Bassin No. 2 and open lock to Bassin No. 1*

41.4   Old lock leading into Bassin No. 1. Now dismantled

house on Pte Porz-Don on the northern shore in line with a high column on the skyline on 269°. Porz-Don has a light Oc (2) WR 6 s. with a narrow 3° W sector 269°–272° and R to the left 272°–279°.

Approaching from the direction of Bréhat, it is wise to use the Chenal du Denou, as shown on the plan. But in fair weather and on the top half of the tide the Chenal de Lastel from the Men Gam Bn to the Ouipoure W Tr Bn leads close inshore between conspicuous G and R pile Bns on course 185° along deep water to a point 1 mile E of Porz-Don. There is the isolated danger mark on Glividy rock in the middle of the fairway which should be left close to port.

The final leading marks on 264° are the W hut with an R top at the seaward end of the main breakwater (Kernoa) in line with a 9m-high W lattice Tr with R top on the shore beyond. Both have fixed R Lts. The rear one is intensified $2\frac{1}{2}$° either side of the correct transit of 264°. This clears all dangers from La Gueule inward. The channel is clearly marked by R and G perches with topmarks or small buoys all the way.

The final approach inside Kernoa Jetty dries to 4m (aerial pic 41.1).

Normally the lock will open $\pm 1\frac{1}{2}$h. HW, but at or near Neaps it is nearer ± 30min or may not open at all. If in doubt, consult the HO, tel. (96) 20–84–30. There is no VHF radio watch.

41.5   Corner of Bassin No. 1 reserved for bigger boats

Berthing   The lock can handle craft with 3m draught at Neaps.

It is possible to dry out on the N side of the Kernoa breakwater while waiting, where it dries 5.5m. The two pontoons on the inner basin (No. 1) reached through a dismantled lock are reserved for deep-draught yachts over 10m in length. The rest of it is for commercial traffic. Coasters up to 1,000 tons call from time to time.

The remaining yachts berth in No. 2 basin alongside the quays or at any of the 230 pontoon berths, of which a few are reserved for visitors.

The HO is on Quai Neuf dividing the two basins (pic 41.3)

to which visiting yachts should report.

Facilities   There are showers and heads near the local station of the Glénans Sailing School at the NE corner of No. 2 basin. FW available at the quays.

The fuelling point is just to seaward of the lock-gate on the Kernoa breakwater.

There are several boatyards, a sailmaker and an excellent chandlery, all on the S side of the locks.

Good shopping and restaurants.

Weather   Broadcast on VHF Ch 84 at 0633 and 1133. Also posted at the HO, the YC and some chandlers. Area 11 Manche ouest.

*42   ÎLE DE BRÉHAT

Charts: *BA 3673 Im C34 Fr 882 CG 537 Stan 16*

High Water   −05h. 25m. Dover   −00h. 25m. SP St Helier

Heights above Datum   *MHWS 10m4. MLWS 1m1. MHWN 8m0. MLWN 3m6.*

BRÉHAT is a group of small rocky islands with tropical vegetation, very popular with day-trippers, artists and owners of twin-keeled yachts. It is a navigator's nightmare, with sluicing tides running all round the islands. Perhaps it is better known as a hazard to avoid when making the mouth of the Pontrieux river on the way to Lézardrieux.

However, given settled weather, it is well worth a short visit, especially if you like walking and want to get away from motor cars: none is allowed on the island.

Approach and Anchorages   The approach from the Roches Douvres 17 miles to the NW is better explained in the chapter on Lézardrieux, which describes the longer-range navigational aids in the area. La Chambre and Port Clos are anchorages on the southern end of the main island. They are best approached from the E.

Coming from the N, shape 1 mile E of the Le Paon Lt Ho a 12m Y framework Tr at 22m elevation FWRG and leave the E-cardinal Guarine buoy close to starboard on course 168°. This is the Chenal de Bréhat. A mile farther the BY N-cardinal Cain ar Monse buoy will be ahead. Two cables short of it, alter towards the left-hand edge of land and pick up the S-cardinal pillar off Logodoc island. Between it and the main island of Bréhat is the most secure anchorage – La Chambre

(pic 42.2). It is marked by R and G perches with topmarks. Depending on space, you can anchor at the entrance in deep water and there is a landing.

Port Clos (aerial pic 42.1)   dries out to its entrance. It is the terminal for the vedettes which run at a similar frequency to the Gosport ferry. One can be seen alongside the LW jetty on the western side. Just to seaward of it is the G-topped Bn marking Les Pierres Noires. Out of the picture 3 cables to the E is the YB W-cardinal Bn Men-Joliquet with an Iso WRG 4 s. Lt at 8m elevation.

Coming from the S it is best to leave Les Charpentiers Bn (see Paimpol) and the W Cormorandière Bn clear to port on a N'ly course until sighting the Cain ar Monse buoy (see above) and altering between the N-cardinal BY Cadenonou Bn and the S-cardinal YB Lel-ar-Serive pillar buoy in towards La Chambre or Port Clos.

If making the trip from Lézardrieux, go downstream for 2½ miles until Levrét Rock immediately W of the little drying-out port at Loguivy is abeam. A course of 085° for just a mile should pass you close S of the BRB Rompa Bn. Le Ferlas channel (shown on the plan of the Approaches to Paimpol, p.241) is thereafter well marked by S-cardinal perches until reaching the relatively open water S of Port Clos. The tide runs to the E +01h. 05m. after HW Dover; turns W at −05h. 10m. before HW Dover at a Spring rate of 3¾ knots.

Port de la Corderie   lies to the NW of the island. It is approached along the main channel to the Pontrieux River (225° or 045°) until the prominent R la Corderie Bn is found off the westernmost point of Bréhat at the white Rosedo pyramid daymark. Head in towards this pyramid until the G Men-Robin perch is identified and left well clear to starboard on a SSE'ly course. Observe the R and G Bns until in the jaws of the bay, where deep water can be found N of the Kaler Bn. But it is necessary to tuck into the bay to get away from

42.1   Port Clos at south end of Island off the Ferlas channel.   (A) Ferry from L'Arcouest using low-water landing.   (B) Les Pierres Noires Beacon.   (C) La Madeleine porthand beacon.   (D) Men-ar-Gouille red beacon to be left to port.   (E) Mid-tide ferry landing – hotel beyond

42.2 (A) Entrance to La Chambre, Bréhat's only deep anchorage, marked by red and green piles. (B) Men-Joliguet light beacon. (C) Port Clos

the strong tides running down Le Kerpont channel to the W. A good afloat anchorage at Neaps.

Berthing and Facilities There are no alongside berths for yachts on the islands. Nor is there an HM.

The YC at Guerzido, E of Port Clos, is the CN de Bréhat.

An ideal spot to go ashore for a walk or even a picnic, but not for too long unless you keep your boat in sight. There are two small hotels, one of them in Port Clos by the HW vedette landing.

The usual amenities one would expect on a remote little beauty spot which dies in the winter – somewhere between Chausey and Arran in this respect.

Weather On (96) 20–01–92.

42.3   *Port Clos entrance eastern side with Men-Joliguet light beacon on right*

42.4   *Le Chambre anchorage. Porthand pillar on left*

Charts: BA 3673 Fr 2845 Im C34 CG 537 Stan 16

High water   *05h. 10m. Dover   − 00h. 30m. SP St Helier*
Heights above Datum   *MHWS 10m0 MLWS 0m9.*
MHWN 7m5. MLWN 3m4.

LÉZARDRIEUX's great attraction for visiting yachts from the South Coast is that it provides an alongside berth in perfect shelter accessible from the open sea at all states of the tide and in bad visibility, provided you hit off one of the outlying buoys. If it is your first visit, a night approach in clear visibility is easiest. Thereafter it is straightforward, since the channel Bns are at short intervals. I once came from St Malo in visibility under 150 yards, happened upon the N Horaine spar buoy and thereafter had no problems. The market town is perched on a high bluff overlooking the Pontrieux River (more frequently referred to simply as 'Trieux') on its western bank. It has a first-class hotel and gourmet restaurant, Relais Brenner, but these are a long uphill walk from the 220-berth marina just downstream. The town itself is of no special interest.

Approach   Coming from the S Coast or the Channel Islands you will find there are several off-lying roadsigns for checking that one is on course. The first and most prominent of these are the Roches Douvres (pic 43.1) whose 70-mile range Rdo Bn on 298.8kHz callsign 'RD' booms out in the same group as Start Point and the Casquets. Its Lt (Fl 5 s.) has a range of 28M, more than enough to cover the 15 miles to the entrance of the Trieux River on a SW'ly course after leaving the Lt to starboard. The structure is a 60m pink Tr on a G-roofed house. It also has a siren ev 60 s.

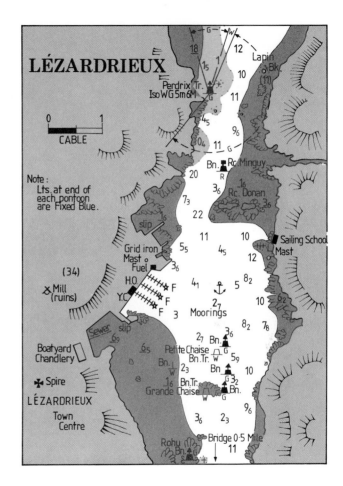

43.1 *Roches Douvres lighthouse, fifteen miles north-west of entrance to Pontrieux river on course from the Channel Islands*

In good visibility and after taking a careful look at the state of the tide and currents, it is all right to head 210° to pass 1½ miles W of Barnonic an octagonal BY Lt Tr 19m high with an E-cardinal topmark and a Lt VQ (3) 5 s. range 8 miles. It lies 5 miles due S of Roches Douvres. If in doubt, for example in heavy weather or fog, stand a mile farther to the west until clear to leave the next mark to port.

A mile farther on is the W-cardinal YBY Roches Gautier whistle buoy (VQ (9) 10 s.) which lies 6 miles NNE of the first of the local buoys marking the Plateau de la Horaine 3 miles NE of the low-lying Île de Bréhat.

By night one is already well within the coverage of another four lighthouses:

La Horaine   A 20m B octagonal Tr, Fl (3) 12 s. with a range of 11 miles. It lies 1 mile S of the N-cardinal BY spar buoy marking the northern limit of that danger.

Rosedo   Lt on the NE corner of Bréhat, a 13m W tower at 29m elevation. The Lt is Fl 5 s. with a range of 20 miles. It also has a rather feeble Rdo Bn (callsign 'DO' on 294.3kHz, the same as le Grand Jardin off St Malo). I have never been able to pick it up. Its notional range is 10 miles.

Les Heaux de Bréhat   off the mouth of the Tréguier River and 4 miles W of the approach course to Trieux. It consists of the very conspicuous 57m-high Grey Tr with a Lt Oc (3) WRG 12 s. Closing the coast one will first be in the W sector at 15 miles. As you come into the G sector (10 miles) the end of the runway is right there. It is best to arrive on the E-setting flood stream (+01h. 35m. on HW Dover).

Le Paon   at the NE corner of Île de Bréhat, demolished by some over-zealous German defender in 1944 but since rebuilt as a Y square Tr. Lt FWRG with a range of 12 miles in the narrow W sector only 7° either side of 188°.

There is also a 50-mile AeroBn inland to the W of Tréguier on 345.5kHz, callsign 'LN'.

43.2　*Les Heaux lighthouse 57m high on rocks two miles offshore, midway between the mouths of the Tréguier and Pontrieux rivers*

43.3　*Le Paon lighthouse, a 12m high square yellow tower, 22m above the sea. The northernmost point of Ile de Bréhat, on the eastern side of the approach to Rive Pontrieux*

43.4   *Rosedo pyramid with the Chapel of St Michael on Bréhat to its right. Close to the entrance of La Corderie anchorage. On a 159° transit they form La Moisie channel from the north-west*

43.5   *Le Croix light beacon on east side of the estuary. The fairway is with it in transit with Bodic (see 43.8) on 225°*

43.6   *Le Vincre red beacon half a mile beyond Le Croix*

43.7 *Conspicuous Bodic lighthouse on the west bank of the river*

43.8 *La Vielle de Loguivy marks the junction between the fairway to Lézardrieux and the Ferlas channel heading east towards Port Clos*

Leaving la Horaine Lt Ho one mile to port one should be on 225° with the R can-topped Bn les Echaudes ½ mile to port. The Grand Chenal leading marks are La Croix Bn due W of the southernmost point of Bréhat (a W structure with R top and Lt Oc 4 s.) lined up with a W house (Bodic) with a G roof 2 miles upstream on the W bank. Its Lt is Q W, range 21 miles.

The Lts are intensified either side of 225° as follows:

Front (la Croix):   10°
Rear (Bodic):   4°

From here on it is quite straightforward, between R and G prominent Bns. Half a mile upstream of la Croix Bn there is the R Vincre Tr and then the Vieille de Loguivy YBY W-cardinal Bn marking the western approach to Bréhat (Le Ferlas Channel). Here course is adjusted to 219° on to another transit of two W-gabled houses on the W bank. The front one is Coatmer at 16m elevation with F RG 9M Lt; the rear one

only 3 cables farther on is 50m above sea level. Both have narrow F R Lts sectors when you are on course: the front one, ±25°, the rear one ±22½°.

Abreast of these marks a further alteration to port is needed to negotiate les Perdrix, a prominent G Bn on an elbow on the W-bank. It has an Iso W G 5m 6M Lt with a 5° W sector covering the 200° course required.

At les Perdrix point, adjust course so as to leave the prominent Donan rocks to port (aerial pic 43.9).

Berthing   One can anchor almost anywhere off the fairway in the lower stretch of the river, but the marina has 220 berths with least depths of 1.8m up to 2.5m.

It is administered from the HO in the hospitable little YC (YC du Trieux), tel. (96) 20–14–22. They listen on Ch 9. There are also some visitors' buoys reserved in the middle of the river.

43.9 *(A) Les Perdrix light with 5° intensified white sector downstream. (B) Roches Donan. (C) Naval school. (D) Trieux Yacht Club and pontoons. (E) Fuel pontoon*

254

43.10 *Trieux Yacht Club*

Facilities The YC and a local waterfront bistro will look after most of your needs without walking up to the town. The Créperie de Gallet just beyond the boatyard is worth a call. FW and fuel are available at the pontoons. The commercial quay next to the marina has a 6-ton crane, a gridiron and a slipway.

Almost next door is Trieux Marine, a boatyard and chandlery which can handle most repairs. Customs are on (96) 20–81–87.

Weather Forecasts obtainable by phone: (96) 20–01–92. Area 11 Manche ouest.

*PONTRIEUX Six miles farther inland from the bridge across the river at Lézardrieux (clearance indicated by tide gauge, but never less than 18m) there is the small market town of Pontrieux with an unexpected industrial complex supplied

43.11 *Pontoon berths off the yacht club looking upstream*

43.12   Fuel pontoon outside new Harbour Office at Lézardrieux

43.13   Pontrieux locks with gates open

If you want a peaceful diversion there are deep alongside berths (minimum 3m2) on the quay along the E bank (pic 43.14).

The lock-gates are 1 mile downstream from the town. The channel up from Lézardrieux winds its way through lonely countryside reminiscent of the upper reaches of the Dart. It is intermittently marked by perches. Since it nearly dries out, obviously one should time one's trip in the last 2h. of the flood. About 4m at Springs and 3m at MHWN.

It would be advisable to enquire first at the YC du Trieux or the HO. They will give you the times of opening of the lock (usually ± 1h. HW) and probably give warning of any shipping movements due.

Berthing and Facilities   Berth alongside the quay as far upstream as possible.

FW and fuel are available.

There is a local YC on the quayside, but not as smart as those one is accustomed to in the new French Yacht Hbrs.

There is a restaurant near the YC, but a brief walk into the old town centre will give a wider choice and all kinds of shops, banks and a main PO.

43.14   *Plenty of water alongside at the 'Port'. The white shed is the yacht club*

43.15   *The nevigable channel ends just around the bend seen in 43.14*

44 TRÉGUIER

Charts: BA 3672 Fr 973 Im C34 CG 537 Stan 17

High Water −05h. 40m. *Dover* −00h. 55m. *SP St Helier*
Heights above Datum *MHWS 9m7. MLWS 0m9. MHWN 7m4. MLWN 3m3.*

TRÉGUIER, like Lézardrieux, is accessible from the open sea at any state of the tide at the end of a well-marked 7-mile passage from the off-lying dangers. But this town is much larger and more interesting. It features a huge cathedral dating back to the thirteenth century, named after St Tugdual. Here lies the tomb of St Yves, the patron saint of lawyers and protector of the poor and persecuted since he was born in Tréguier in 1253. 'Monsieur St Yves' is how he is referred to even nowadays.

Approach On passage from the S Coast or Channel Islands the course to make good after leaving the Roches Douvres to port is 230° − 18 miles to the landfall buoy (La Jument, a N-cardinal BY bell buoy VQ flash). One should be in the W sector of Les Heaux de Bréhat light (Oc (3) 12 s. 48m 12M) for most of the way, although if you are too close to the Roches Gautier the R sector may show briefly. Coming from the NNE the mouth of the river may first be seen to the left of Les Heaux Lt Ho. On the skyline to the SSW the spire at the right hand end of Plougrescant church is conspic. from afar.

Some 2½ miles SW of La Jument buoy is the prominent Crublent R buoy, a whistler Fl (2) R 6 s. with a 5-mile range. Leave it on the starboard bow and shape up for Grande Passe leading marks and Lts on course 137°. This part is easier by night as the leading marks are all but impossible to identify by day. They are on the E side of the estuary 3–4 miles distant, as follows:

Front   Port de la Châine, a W house at 12m elevation Oc 4 s. 12 miles

Rear   Ste Antoine, another W house with R roof at 34m elevation. Its Lt is Oc R 4 s. 15M which is intensified ± 3 either side of 137°.

By day be sure to pass between R and G unlit channel buoys on the transit, exactly 1 mile to the G Penar Guezec buoy, also unlit. Then course is altered to 215° towards La Corne Lt Bn 14m high, a pepper-grinder W tower with a R base. Its Lt is Oc (2) WRG 12 s. range 11/8 miles – the narrow (7°) W sector brings you safely along the first 1½ miles of the river entrance. R means you are too far to the E; G to the W of track (i.e. to starboard going in).

A W Bn Tr (Skeiviec) 4 cables farther upstream should be kept just open to the right of La Corne.

From the unlit G channel buoy just past La Corne, take a ½ mile hitch on 235°. At night this will be another narrow W sector of La Corne Lt, with R on either side of it, which can be confusing.

Just beyond the Fl R Guarvinou buoy at the next port-hand buoy (No. 2 Fl R) alter to 192° with 3½ miles to go to the Yacht Hbr alongside the town. From there on, the channel is well marked with R and G buoys and Bns. The port-hand R buoys all the way to No. 12 have dim R Fl Lts, while the starboard-hand G Fl are numbered 1–11.

At night the final approach calls for a 2-cable SW'ly leg from the last lit buoy, then a hitch to the SE towards the E bank of the river opposite the marina. A light with a strong beam is essential.

The least depth is 2m6 in the channel.

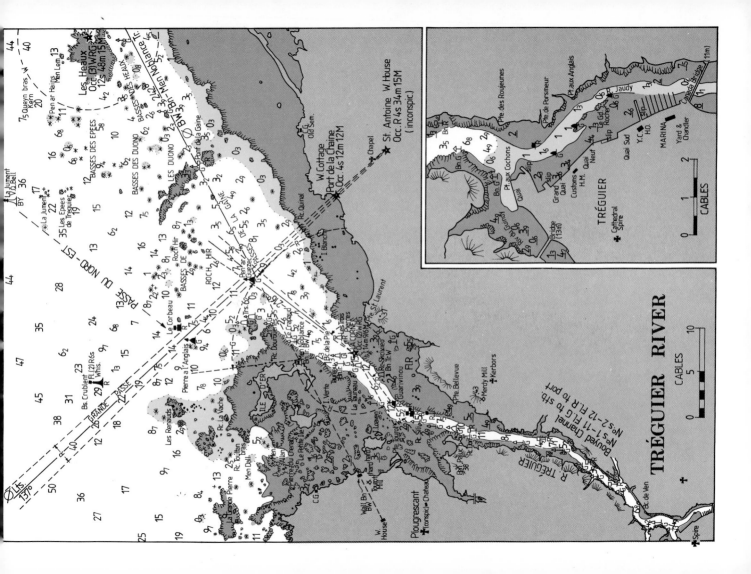

TRÉGUIER RIVER

CABLES

TRÉGUIER

CABLES

44.1   *Plougrescant Church with its spire at the righthand edge is a conspicuous mark by day when approaching from any direction*

44.2   *(A) Men Noblance, front mark for 242° transit with   (B) white wall with black vertical stripe to navigate passe de la Gaine*
        inside Les Heaux   (C) is Plougrescant Church

44.3   La Corne light beacon half a mile upstream from Men Noblance at the narrowest part of the channel

44.4   Roche Skciviec half a mile upstream beyond La Corne

Inshore NE channel – Passe de la Gaine   If coming from Bréhat or Lézardrieux in good visibility by day about $1\frac{1}{2}$ miles can be saved by using the Passe de la Gaine, the inshore passage inside Les Heaux de Bréhat on course 242°. A glance at the chart will show that it is very tight and passes over a om3 patch at MLWS. However it is a possible alternative suitable when outward bound, given close attention to the chart, benign weather and preferably Neapish tides. The astern leading marks are the Grande Maison and the BW wall Bn on the skyline in transit the conspicuous BW Tr Bn to the W of the channel (Men Noblance) on 062°. This is now flood-lit. The Plougrescant church and steeple will be open to the left of the transit just clear of a clump of trees on the skyline.

Berthing   The long quays at the foot of the town are clearly set aside for commercial traffic. Just upstream are the five pontoons of the Club Nautique de Trégor (CNT). There are 300 alongside berths in an average depth of 2m at LW. Visitors should make for the first two pontoons beyond the slipway (pic 44.6). Remember that the streams run through these berths at up to $2\frac{1}{2}$ knots, so great care is necessary in manoeuvring in or out not to get tangled up with other boats. You must berth head to the stream. It is advisable to leave at or near slack water. There is a luxurious clubhouse on the shore end of these pontoons also housing the HO (tel. (96) 92–42–37). There are also moorings on the E side of the river near the bridge, beyond the old low-level viaduct, now mostly demolished.

Facilities   The clubhouse has everything the visitor could wish for. The Restaurant St Bernard 100 yds away is good value (96) 92–20–72.

44.5   *Pen Paluc'h village and slip on west bank, three miles downstream from Tréguier*

FW and fuel available, the latter by hand.

There is a boatbuilder and good heavy chandler at Traou-Meur just across the river, but Marina Sports next to the YC is a well-stocked chandlery with a repair staff.

Besides its cathedral and cloisters, the town has two good hotels and a selection of small restaurants. There is also the usual open market once a week, selling everything from day-old chicks to ten-year-old Calvados.

Weather   Reports at the clubhouse or tel. (96) 20-01-91. Area 11 Manche ouest.

44.6 *(A) Yacht club with Harbour Office. (B) Commercial quay. (C) Last porthand buoy. (D) Starboard-hand buoy. Follow course indicated*

44.7   *Commercial quay downstream from matina. Above is the Cathedral St Tugdual wherein lies St Yves, reputedly patron saint*

44.8   *Yacht club pontoons facing upstream. Note all boats are required to berth in that direction*

Charts: Im C34 CG 537 BA 3172 Fr 974

High Water − 05h. 50m. Dover   SP St Helier
Heights above Datum   MHWS 9m4. MLWS 1mo.
MHWN 7mo. MLWN 3m2.

PORT BLANC is an attractive natural anchorage surrounded by rocky islets in between sandy beaches and woodlands on the mainland. It lies midway between the entrance to the R. Treguier and Perros-Guirec. The local lifeboat and a few fishing-boats remain afloat in a pool inside the entrance and to the W of the transit.

There is a quay which can be reached at the top end of the tide, but it is scarcely worth going ashore, for there are few local amenities, but it remains an outstandingly beautiful harbour. Unfortunately it is exposed to winds from the NW round to the N.

Approaches   Position yourself 0.5 miles NE of the R. Gauzer whistle buoy (see Perros-Guirec) and you'll be 1.2 miles to seaward on the 150° transit course. Le Voleur is a 12m high W Lt Ho almost totally surrounded by trees 100 yards inshore of the little quay. The light is Fl WRG 4s. out to a range of 14/11 miles. Its W sector is ±2° on 150° with a 4° G sector to starboard and 4° R to port.

By day head for the gap between the prominent W pyramid on the Île du Chateau Neuf and an R Bn with topmark on the Roche Ruz to port.

Berths   The harbour dries 3 cables to seaward from the end of the quay, but in gentle weather you can anchor near the lifeboat, as described above.

Weather   See Perros-Guirec.

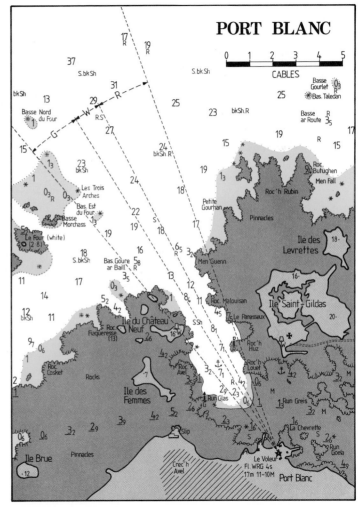

45.1   *White day mark on Ile du Château Neuf marks approach from seaward on 150°. Deep water anchorage off Run Glas on left*

45.2   *Ile St Gildas affords protection from the north off slipway*

45.3   *Dried out alongside quay at Port Bago*

266

Charts: BA 3672 Fr 974 Im C34 CG 537 Stan 17

High Water *05h. 50m. Dover 01h. 05m. SP St Helier*
Heights above Datum *MHWS 9m0. MLWS 0m9.*
MHWN 7m0. MLWN 3m4.

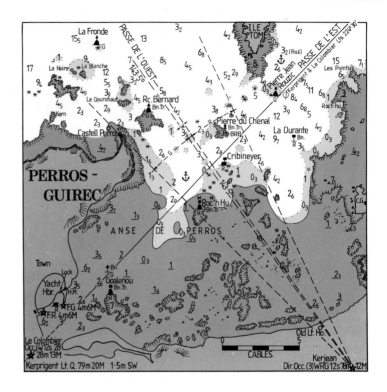

PERROS-GUIREC lies about 10 miles W of the entrance to
Tréguier R. and is a major summer resort with wonderful
beaches. Since the artificial Yacht Hbr has been built, the
town's discos, pubs and sportsgear shops have proliferated
in the marina area, while the luxury hotels and fashionable
restaurants are mostly near the casino, beside the N-facing
beaches some distance away.

The whole bay dries to a mile offshore at LW.

Approaches Before making the run in towards Perros-
Guirec from seaward it is as well to check the times of opening
of the lock-gates unless you are prepared to take the bottom
exposed to the E or lie alongside the Linkin Jetty which
protects the marina from the NE–SE. Here it dries at least
4m.

As a rule the lock will be open at Springs from 2h. before
to 1h. after HW, while at ordinary Neaps it will only open
during the hour before HW. At bad Neap tides it may not
open at all. So check first with the HM near the lock-gates,
tel. (96) 23–19–03. Or call on Ch 9 or 16.

From the NE (Passe de l'est) Two miles NW of Port Blanc
is the R buoy Roche Gauzer. Left to port on course 224° it is
a 5-mile run-in from there, the first 3 miles being in deep
water until passing S of the Île Tomé and leaving the G Pierre
Jean Rouzic buoy close to starboard.

At this point the leading marks ashore should be clearly
visible, certainly by night since they have ranges of 16 and 13
miles respectively, as follow:

Front   Le Colombier a W gabled house 28m above sea
        level with a Lt Oc (4) 12 s. intensified 5° either side
        of the leading line, precisely 224½°.

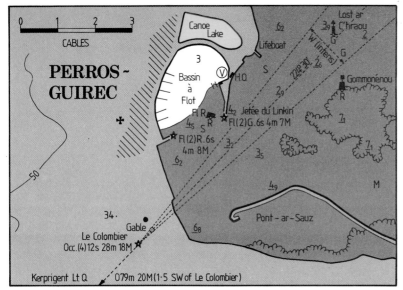

PERROS-GUIREC

46.1 *Linkin Jetty at low water with lock shut up to the 3m5 level of the containing sill which keeps all yachts afloat inside*

Rear   1½ miles farther inland on the transit is the W Kerprigent Tr 79m above sea level with a Q Lt with a 7° intensified arc either side of the leading course.
Half a mile farther the BRB isolated danger Bn Pierre du Chenal is left to starboard, before the last 1½ miles to the head of the Linkin breakwater (Fl (2) G 6 s.) and the lock-gates after a sharp turn to starboard round its end (pics 46.2 and 46.3).
From the NW (Passe de l'Ouest)   A mile NE of Ploumanac'h put the Lt on the westernmost of les Sept Îles astern on a course of 143° to pass between the Île Tomé and the pt of Castell Perros. Leave the R Tr Petit Bilzic to port and two further G channel markers to starboard (the second being the G Bn Roches Bernard just off Castell Perros) before joining the Passe de l'Est SW of Pierre du Chenal (see above).

At night it is easier. There is a directional Lt of 78m elevation at Kerjean (Oc (3) WRG) with less than 1° W sector at 12-miles range.
By day the disused Lt Ho on the foreshore at Nantouar can be brought in line with Kerjean lighthouse on the skyline.
Berthing   Once locked into the Bassin à Flot you will find there are 650 berths on the pontoons, 40 of them reserved for visitors. The least depth is 2m. One can also anchor to the E of the pontoons. The HO by the locks will direct visitors: tel. (96) 23–19–03.
Facilities   There is a fuelling berth just inside the lock-gates.
The Yacht Hbr is in the middle of town with everything on tap. There is a slipway at its northern end.

46.2   Lock-gates, Harbour Office and fuel dock are all at lefthand end of Linkin Jetty

46.3   Some of the 650 berths in the heart of town beyond lock gates

46.4   The inward channel at low water with two red porthand beacon towers: Goalenou (A) and Roc'h Hu (B)

The YC – Société Nautique de Perros-Guirec at Plou-manac'h (SNP) – has a clubhouse by the Yacht Hbr and another (for dinghies and sailboards) at Trestraou beach on the northern side of town.

Chandlery and light repairs are readily available.

Weather   Posted at the Bureau du Port or a taped message can be obtained on tel. (96) 20–01–92. Area 11 Manche ouest.

*47 PLOUMANAC'H

Charts: CG 538 Fr 974 (Fr 967 Im C34 BA 3669)

High Water −06h. 00m. *Dover* −01h. 05m. *SP St Helier*
Heights above Datum *MHWS 8m8. MLWS 0m9. MHWN 6m6. MLWN 2m9.*

PLOUMANAC'H is one of the most spectacularly beautiful small harbours in N. Brittany, lurking inside an entrance guarded on one side by rose granite boulders (the Breton Corniche) looking like a haphazard pile of Henry Moore sculptures; opposite is the elegant mini-Chateau Costaeres standing on its own wooded rocky islet. It is almost a suburb of Perros-Guirec, being 3 miles by road, but 6 by sea.

Its interest to visiting yachtsmen has been enhanced by a new sill fitted at the narrowest part of the entrance (see pic 47.4), which gives boats in the centre of the harbour 1m5 at all times. Locals have most of them. Enter or leave 2h. either side of HW.

Approaches Halfway through the channel between les Sept Îles on its S side there is the prominent Pte de Méan Ruz with its square pink Lt Tr 15m high perched on the edge of the cliff. It is Oc WR 4s. 26m 13/10M. The W sector is ±8° on the approach course of 234°. If coming from the W there is no reason why you should not head straight for the Lt Ho on a SE'ly course. Coming from Perros-Guirec leave the G Roche Bernard Bn and the N.-cardinal La Horaine Bn to port on a NW'ly course until picking up the Méan Ruz Lt Ho. Once beyond that point come on to 214° and pick up the line of R and G Bns until altering to 190° at No. 8. Up to this

point there is always water for a boat drawing 1m5. If you don't fancy going on, or have to wait for the tide, turn to port off the fairway and drop the hook in the little Grève de St Guirec.

When you reach No. 5 Bn, come to port to 150° to pass into the harbour – provided there is enough water over the sill.

Facilities Go ashore on the N side near the Quai Padel. A block in from the beach there is a delightful square with everything a visiting yachtsman looks for, including a garage that does boat repairs. For advance advice on availability of moorings or to check tides over the sill, enquire at Perros-Guirec.

Weather See Perros-Guirec.

47.1 *Square pink light tower Mean Ruz set on pink boulders 26m above the entrance (left)*

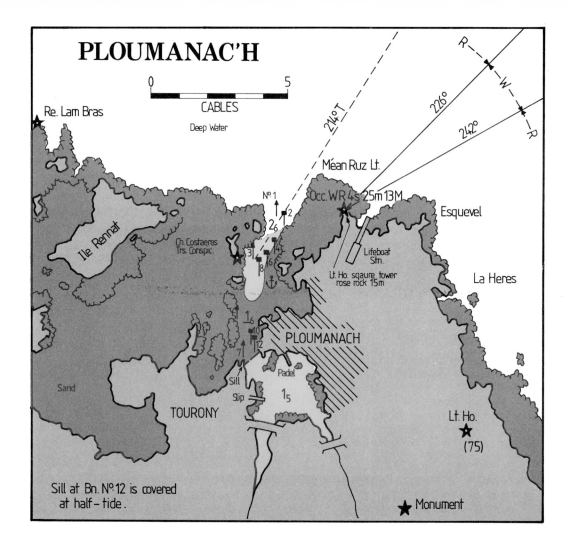

PLOUMANAC'H

0 ⸺ 5
CABLES

Deep Water

Re. Lam Bras

Ile Rennat

24.0°T

226°

242°

R

W

R

Méan Ruz Lt.

Esquevel

Nº 1
2

2 6

Occ. WR 4s 25m 13M

Ch. Costaeres
Trs. Conspic.

3
8
6

Lifeboat
Stn.

Lt. Ho. sqaure tower
rose rock 15m

La Heres

1 6

10
12

PLOUMANACH

Padel

7

Sill

Slip

1 5

TOURONY

Sand

Lt. Ho.

(75)

Sill at Bn. Nº 12 is covered
at half-tide.

Monument

47.2 *Entrance on 214° is well marked and not so alarming as it appears here on a calm day. Château Costaères and beacon No.1 on starboard hand*

47.3 *Grève de St Guirec is a small deep anchorage between beacons 6 and 8, sheltered by Château Costaères*

47.4 *Sill at beacon 12 with small cruiser being helped over*

47.5 *Many boats still afloat, thanks to sill. Ploumanac'h town and Padel quay (top right)*

47.6 *View of harbour with boats secured fore-and-aft between buoys. Small boat in foreground same as that in 47.4 with one crew walking home on Crec'h Cavet side (left)*

*48 LANNION

Charts: Im C34 CG 538 (Fr 5950 BA 3669)

High Water − 06h. 05m. *Dover* SP Brest
Heights above Datum (river entrance) *MHWS 9m1.*
MLWS 1m3. MHWN 7m2. MLWN 3m5.

HEADING westward between les Sept Îles and Ploumanac'h (near Perros-Guirec) on the 20-mile passage to Roscoff and the entrance to the Morlaix R., keep well to seaward of yet another rocky, inhospitable headland. Provided the wind is not in the W–NW sector you might be tempted to head 6 miles SSW from the Bar ar Gall W-cardinal buoy to take a look at Lannion, a medieval town of some interest 4 miles up the R. Léguer, sometimes referred to as the Lannion R.

Three miles N of the river entrance is the fashionable holiday resort of Trébeurden which has two YC, mainly for shoal-draught cruisers, dinghies and sailboards. It has over 300 moorings, some reserved for visitors, but shelter from the weather is entirely provided by the rocky outcrop which encircles the W-facing beach and hardly invites penetration by a keelboat owner with no previous knowledge.

Approach About 3 miles SW of Trébeurden is Le Crapaud, a W-cardinal YBY buoy. Half a mile S of this buoy come on to the 122° transit of the Lts at Locquémeau. The front structure is a 19m-high W lattice Tr with R top. Its Lt is F R. The rear Lt (Oc (3) R 12 s.) is a W gabled building on high ground (39m). Before reaching the G Locquémeau channel buoy, head due E towards the prominent low W house at Bog-Léguer 60m above sea level, which has an Oc (4) WRG 12 s. Lt – the W sector being 7° either side of the

48.1   *Trebeurden anchorage, a possible stop on the way to Lannion, three miles to the south. Approach is round the north end of Île Milliau (top)*

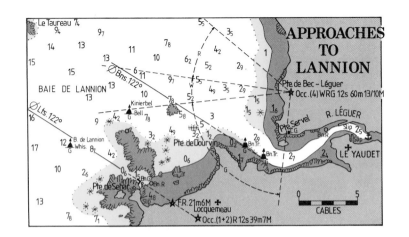

48.2   *Entrance to Lannion River with Le Yaudet Church on skyline conspicuous*

48.3   *View upstream from Beguen slip on north bank. Plenty of room to anchor and land at Le Yaudet pier (mid-right) with road leading up to town*

48.4   Four miles upstream, and hardly worth while. These mud berths at low water are less than half a mile from city centre

correct lead inshore. Two prominent G Bns will be seen on the starboard bow. Alter to 122° to pass close N of both of them. There is 3m of water off them.

Follow the bend in the river round to port for a distance of ¾ mile from the second G Bn. Leave an R Bn to port and you will be off the attractive little village of Le Yaudet on the S bank with its prominent church on the skyline.

Berths   It is preferable to anchor and stay afloat in 2m off Le Yaudet. If you must go on, the next 3 miles up-river should only be attempted in the last 2h. of the flood. Just short of the first bridge (Pont Neuf) it is possible to lie along-side quays on either bank, but the river dries up to 5m at this point and it is not a very attractive spot to stay for any length of time (pic 48.4).

Facilities   There are landing slips on both banks at le Yaudet, where there is an agreeable little hotel/restaurant. The slip on the N bank leads only to private homes. The town centre of Lannion is a tidy walk beyond the mud berths described above, but there are good shops and hotels there.

The HO is at tel. (96) 37–06–52. Customs are on (96) 37–45–32.

The local airfield is only 1½ miles out of town.

Weather   See Morlaix.

*49 MORLAIX

Charts: BA 2745 CG 538 Im C35 Fr 5827 Stan 17

High Water   *−06h. 10m. Dover   +01h. 05m. SP Brest*
Heights above Datum (river entrance)   *MHWS 9m0.*
MLWS 1m3. MHWN 7m0. MLWN 3m5.

MORLAIX is a sixteenth-century town at the head of the river of the same name 7 miles inland from its entrance. An old viaduct above the town dominates the scene, matched by a new one carrying the N12 autoroute to the W. Between the two there is a perfectly sheltered Yacht Hbr (aerial pic 49.5).

In more recent times it has become an important centre of the tobacco industry.

Approach   The most difficult part of the approach is at the river mouth between Carantec on the W side and Térénez

opposite it. Right in the middle is the fort (Château du Taureau) built in 1542 to discourage the British from making further raids up the river (pic 49.1). Once it has been safely left astern there is a well-marked deepwater channel between the oyster beds to the point where the river narrows between Locquénolé and Dourduff, 3 miles downstream from Morlaix.

From seaward   there are two main channels. The Tréguier channel from a point 1½ miles due W of Pte de Primel near the G perch marking the Pierre Noire rocks. It is absolutely straightforward by day any time except within an hour of LW, since there is a ½-mile stretch which all but dries out at Springs. It reaches the deep water midway between the Île Noire and the Château Taureau.

Alternatively, there is the Grand Chenal favoured by commercial traffic, since there is not less than 3m at any state of the tide. This channel starts 3 miles W of Primel, halfway to Roscoff, between the G la Vielle Bn and the R pillar buoy, both unlit, marking the Stolvezen shoal.

Each shares as the inshore end of their leading marks the

49.1   *Île Louet and Château du Taureau seen from the south-west. The Grand Chenal passes between these two*

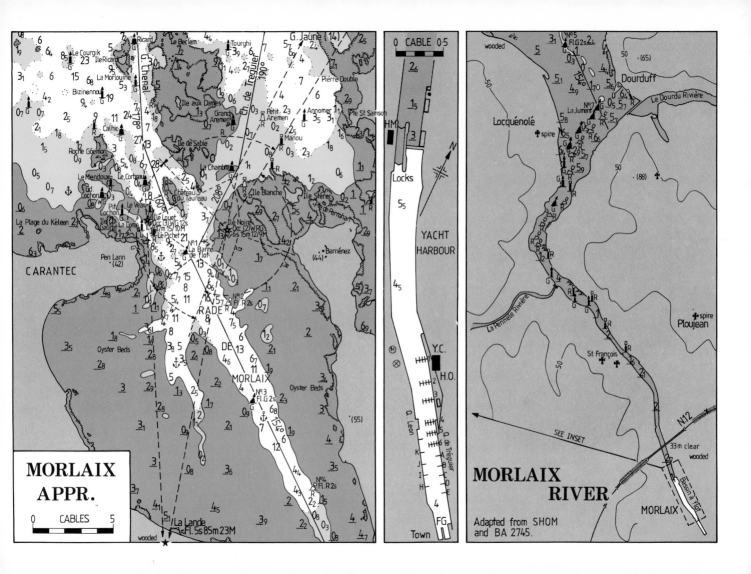

MORLAIX
APPR.

0 CABLES 5

CARANTEC

RADE
DE
MORLAIX

0 CABLE 0·5

Locks

YACHT
HARBOUR

Y.C.
H.O.

Q. Léon

Q. de Tréguier

FG
Town

MORLAIX
RIVER

Adapted from SHOM
and BA 2745.

SEE INSET

Locquénolé

Dourduff

Le Dourdu Rivière

La Jument

La Penneté Rivière

Ploujean

St. François

N12

33m clear
wooded

MORLAIX

49.2　*The alternative channel (Tréguier) leaves Île Noir tower clear to port before joining the main channel. Île Stérec and the last red channel buoy to the left and beyond*

49.3　*Rade de Morlaix facing upstream with Dourduff and viaduct to the east and Locquénolé opposite, where the river begins*

49.4   *Dourduff with La Jument No.7 buoy off the point*

prominent square W Tr la Lande Lt Ho, 19m high at an elevation of 85m a little over 2 miles due S of Château Taureau. This is the strongest Lt in the area with a range of 23 miles. It flashes 5 s.

Grand Chenal lines up La Lande on 176° with the Île Louet 15-mile Lt (Oc (3) WG 12 s.) a square W Tr with B top on an islet off Carantec (pic 49.1); a two-point jink to port has to be made between two prominent R and G Bns immediately to seaward of Château Taureau, on course 160° heading for the G unlit No. 1 channel buoy. Although this is a deepwater channel, it is very narrow, less than a cable wide. From No. 1 buoy (La Barre de flot) the course is 150° down the fairway.

Chenal de Tréguier lines up La Lande on 190° with Île Noire Lt, a 13m high W square with a R top with a Lt Oc (2) WRG 6 s. The channel comes in on the R sector with a range of 9 miles. The shallow water referred to above is between the first pair of prominent but unlit G and R Bns. At La

49.5   *This downstream shot shows Locquenole top centre on the west bank, the N.12 viaduct, lock-gates and Morlaix Yacht Club with its pontoons*

49.6   Upstream from the locks

49.7   Berths on the east bank

Chambre, leave the second G Bn to starboard, alter to 210°
to pick up the main channel at No. 1 channel buoy 3 cables
beyond the Île Noire Lt Ho (pic 49.2). A back bearing of La
Chambre (G) and Petit Aremen (R) Bns in transit will bring
you into the deep channel.

Thereafter the course is 150° with Fl channel buoys until
No. 5 buoy just short of Dourduff. From this point the channel
is clearly marked by channel buoys or perches.

A lot of summer moorings are occupied off Locquénolé and
Dourduff. From this point one's progress should be adjusted

to reach the Morlaix locks while they are open, $1\frac{1}{2}$ h. before
until 1h. after HW, when there will be not less than 2m5 at
the entrance. Lock-master can be contacted on (98) 88–54–
92.

Berthing   There are pontoon berths with not less than
2m0 water for 160 boats, with room for plenty more alongside
the quayside. The HO is on the E bank and keeps watch on
VHF Ch 9.

Alternatively the HM at the lock-side can be contacted on
tel. (98) 88–01–01.

49.8   Sheltered berths right in the heart of town

Visiting yachts should berth anywhere and report to the HO in the YC.

It is a secure, quiet harbour in any weather.

Facilities   The YC de Morlaix (YCM) has everything laid on, tel. (98) 88–25–85.

There are a yacht yard and several chandlery stores. The town centre is $\frac{1}{4}$ mile farther upstream, beyond the first of two town bridges which have no more than head room for inflatables or dinghies. Customs are on (98) 88–06–31.

There are several luxurious old hotels, plenty of restaurants, including some specializing in oriental food.

There is a local airfield at Ploujean and only 28km by fast road to Roscoff and the Brittany Ferries' connection to Plymouth. Although not the quietest or most picturesque of marinas, I rate Morlaix as an ideal place to leave one's boat if sharing its use with another crew or wanting to park it with complete confidence for a few weeks between spells of cruising. It is only 60 miles to the northern end of the Chenal du Four.

Weather   Available on (98) 88–34–04. Area Manche ouest.

Charts: BA 2745 CG 538 Im C35 Fr 5828

High Water − 06h. 05m. Dover + 01h. 00m. SP Brest
Heights above Datum MHWS 8m9. MLWS 1m3.
MHWN 7m0. MLWN 3m5.

ROSCOFF nowadays is best known for the RO/RO Plymouth
ferry terminal at Port de Bloscon, 7 cables E of the old
harbour. It is firmly out-of-bounds to yachts, in spite of its
tempting deep water close inshore.

It is the departure point for Johnny Breton on his bike,
festooned with strings of onions, once a regular feature of
our S Coast lanes. Recently its reciprocal trade from British
farmers has been less welcome.

It is also whence the local ferry sails on its 15min trip to
the Île de Batz close to the N. The whole area is embraced by
the Gulf Stream with concomitant sub-tropical vegetation. It
is surrounded by unfriendly rocks, which are equally famous
for their lobsters and shipwrecks. The sixteenth-century
church is worth a visit. Apart from any other attraction, it is
close to an outstanding restaurant which deserves, but does
not get, a nod from the *Guide Michelin*.

The harbour dries out completely and the approach is hair-
raising, but Roscoff is a neat, friendly little town which should
not lightly be left out of one's cruise plan if the tides work out
and it is not blowing from the NE.

Approaches

From the NE One's ETA should be planned during the
last 2h. before HW, since the inner harbour dries 5m0 and
many of the off-lying rocks are a menace at half-tide (aerial

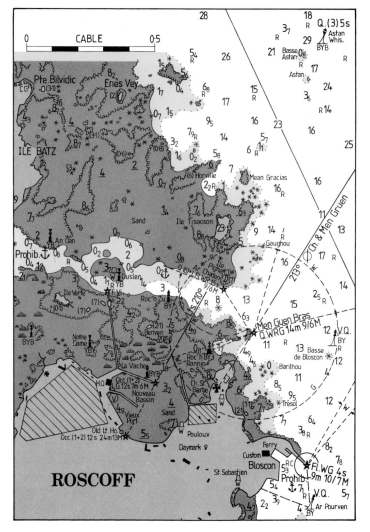

Ø 210°

50.1   *From the north-east almost on the leading line for harbour entry (see line from old lighthouse at the head of the harbour). Note rocks well outside the two beacons on the left (Men Guen Bras and Roch Rannic). Ar-Chaden light tower bottom right*

50.2   *Old lighthouse*

pic 50.1). There is Rdo Bn at the RO/RO ferry terminal –
callsign 'BC' on 287.3kHz with a range of 10 miles – but that
is only marginally helpful.

Keeping clear to the N of the Plateau des Duons on a transit
of 256° Men Guen Bras Lt Tr in line with the bell Tr of the
church near the right-hand edge of Roscoff, it is necessary to
find the other Lt Tr which pairs off with Men Gruen Bras to
mark the front door at 5 cables from the harbour entrance:

Men Gruen Bras is a YB tower with N-cardinal topmark,
20m high and a 9-mile Lt Q WRG. Keep in the W sector.

Ar-Chaden just 2 cables NW of Men Gruen Bras is equally
prominent and the same height. It is YB with S-cardinal
top-mark and a 9-mile Lt Q (6) + LFl WR 15 s.

If on the transit with Roscoff church it is necessary to alter
to starboard to go close to Ar-Chaden Lt as the aerial picture

50.3   *Nouveau Bassin. Berths reserved for commercial craft*

286

50.4   Yachts dry out in the Bassin du Vieux Port

(50.1) shows. Then pick up the transit of the Lt on the 7m W column G top at the seaward end of the main breakwater with the prominent square 24m Tr Lt Ho on the waterfront on course 210°. Their characteristics are:

Breakwater light   Oc (3) G 12 s. 7m 6M.
Shore lighthouse   Oc (3) W 12 s. 24m 15M.

From the West   On passage from the sea buoy off L'Aber-Wrac'h it is 31 miles to Roscoff by passing north of the Île de Batz, as against 28 miles if one takes the inshore passage between the island and Roscoff. The latter is a 3-mile passage with not much sea-room in the event of a sudden drop in visibility in tides running up to $3\frac{1}{2}$ knots. I should never attempt it unless everything was set fair.

However, if bound to the W the Île de Batz channel is fairly straightforward in settled conditions. Ideally it is best attempted in the last hour of the flood, so that navigation can be conducted in relatively slow time. The tide turns to the W at 1h. after HW Brest (−06h. on Dover) so an hour before HW Brest would be a good time to go. The channel is well

marked but has the advantage of presenting its trickiest problems in the first mile after leaving Roscoff harbour on the back-transit of 210°/030° used for entry. Just short of Ar-Chaden alter to 280°, then shape to pass close N of the BY N-cardinal Roch Zu Bn before clearing the end of the 600ft-long pier used by the Île de Batz ferry when the tide water in the harbour is insufficient.

Here course should be altered to starboard to 290° to leave to port the BY Per Roch BY Bn with N-cardinal topmark. A mile farther, on 265°, pass between YB S-cardinal Roche la Croix and N-cardinal BY l'Oignon Bns. A further mile of 285° should leave the N-cardinal BY Basse Plats to port, whence you are in deep water and can go for L'Aber-Wrac'h, the Chenal du Four or the Scillies, as may be desired.

Berthing   It is tempting to berth alongside the outer mole in the Nouveau Bassin, but don't count on staying there. Fishermen and the vedette to the Île de Batz take – indeed enforce – their priority. So it is best to take the ground after finding a spot alongside the inner mole in the Vieux Port. Anchoring S of the ferry terminal outside the prohibited area at Bloscon provides good holding ground, but once ashore it's a long walk to anywhere.

Facilities   There are a boatyard and all kinds of mostly touristy shops. Plenty of good little hotels and restaurants.

The HO is near the Vieux Port on tel. (98) 69–19–59. Customs are at the RO/RO ferry terminal at Bloscon (98) 61–27–86.

The local YC is Société de Régates de Roscoff on (98) 69–75–16.

For a change of scene an outing up the R. Penze to visit Carentac and the Île Callot is recommended – in a dinghy and outboard.

Weather   Posted at the local YC and the HO. Area 11 Manche ouest. Or call Île de Batz on tel. (98) 88–34–04.

51 L'ABER-WRAC'H

Charts: BA 1432 Fr 964, 5772, Im C35 CG 539 Stan 17
High Water +05h. 40m. Dover +00h. 25m. SP Brest
Heights above Datum *MHWS 8m0. MLWS 1m1.
MHWN 6m1. MLWN 2m9.*

OF THE three river-mouths at the NW corner of Finisterre – Aber-Wrac'h, Aber-Benoit and Aber-Ildut – the first named is best known to visiting yachts from the UK. It is easy to find and straightforward to enter in anything but NW'ly gales. The amenities ashore are limited, but the estuary forms a lovely tranquil setting only 15 miles from the Chenal du Four – like Balham, the Gateway to the S.

Approach Just 3 miles ENE of the sea buoy of L'Aber-Wrac'h is the Île Vierge, a massive landmark with its 83m Lt Ho Fl 5 s. 27M and 70-mile Rdo Bn on 298.8kHz, callsign 'VG'. It is in the same group as Roches Douvres and the Lizard but, maddeningly not as Ushant (308.0kHz callsign 'CA'). The Lt is Fl 5 s. and can be picked up at 28 miles, or two-thirds of the way from the Lizard. It also has a foghorn ev 60 s.

Although charts show leading lines along the Chenal de la Pendante and the Chenal de la Malouine, and both are feasible in good weather by day, it is simplest to hold on the W beyond Île Vierge until the W-cardinal YBY Le Libenter whistle buoy is picked up. It has a Lt Q (9) 15 s. 8m 8M. Leave it to port on a southerly heading until picking up the Grand Chenal on course 100°. This will bring into transit the W square Tr R top on the Île Vrac'h (Q R elevation 19m and 7-miles range) with the very conspicuous Lanvaon Lt Ho 2 miles farther inshore.

51.1 *(A) Île Vrac'h is in transit for the Grand Chenal de l'Aber-Wrac'h (B) Breac'h Ver is a green tower beacon on starboard side of main fairway (C) L'Aber-Wrac'h. Chenal de la Pendante on 136° leaves Grand Pot de Beurre and Petit Pot, both red beacons, to starboard. Grand Chenal leaves both to port on 100°. Petit Chanel de la Malouine on 176° joins the others at Petit Pot de Beurre*

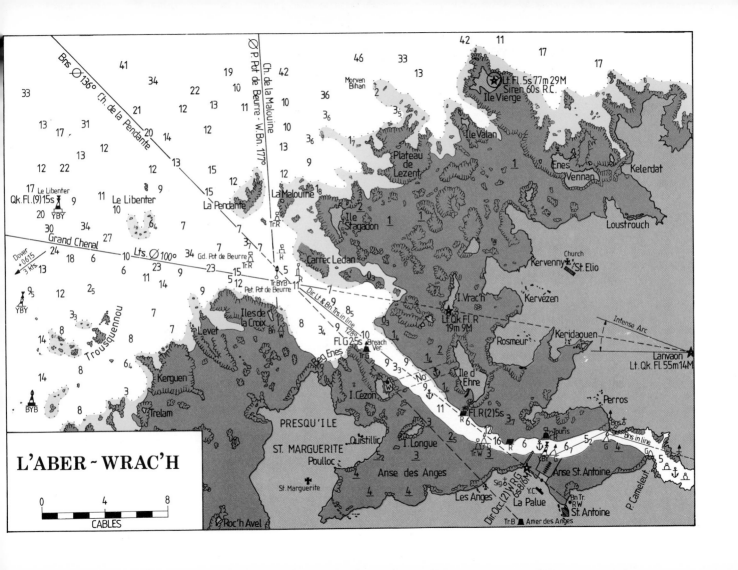

L'ABER - WRAC'H

Brs ⌀136° Ch. de la Pendante

Ch. de la Malouine

⌀ P. Pot de Beurre - W Bn. 177°

41
34
33
21   20
13   17   31
13
12   22   13   12
17   Le Libenter
Qk.Fl.(9)15s   9
20   YBY
30   34
Grand Chenal   27
24   18   6   10   Lts ⌀ 100°   34   Gd. Pot de Beurre
13
Dover
+0615
3 kts
9₅
12   2₅
YBY
3₃   8
14   8
8   6₄
14   Trousquennou
14
BYB

19   42
22   10
13   11
12
13   12
12   15
12   La Pendante
15
12
7
7   3₇   7
Tr.R
Tr.R
6   11   23   15   23   15
9   5   12   11
Tr.BYB   14
Pet. Pot de Beurre
9
7   3₄
Levet   Bn
Iles de   W
la Croix
8
Beg Enes   FLG2.5s
9   3₃
I. Cezon   W
Kerguen   Trelam   PRESQU'ILE
Quistillic
ST. MARGUERITE
Poulloc   I. Longue
St. Marguerite   Anse des Anges
Roc'h Avel

42   11
46   33
Morven   13   17   17
Bihan   2
36   3₅   Ile Valan   Enes   Kelerdat
3₆   Plateau   Vennan
1₇   de
Lezent   1   Loustrouch
La Malouine   1   1
1₈
Ile   1   1
Stagadon   1

Carrec Ledan   0₃
7   7
Dir.Lt & Bn.Trs in line   128°   8₅
1₄   10
Breach
Ver.   Church
Tr.G   Kervenny   St. Elio
0₃   I.Vrac'h
Ile d   Lt.Qk.Fl.R   Kervezen
Ehre   19m 9M
No   Rosmeur   Keridaouen   Infense Arc
9   Lanvaon
11   Lt.Qk. Fl. 55m14M
Fl.R(2)5s   Perros
R 6   3₇
12   Touris   Brs in line
16   R   6   5   G   G
3   YBY   6   7   5₂   G
Tr.W   3   Anse St. Antoine
Les Anges   Y.C.   P. Camelaut
Sig.0   St. Antoine
Dir.Occ.(2)WRG   Bn Tr.
6s87.6m   R.W
La Palue
Tr.B   Amer des Anges

0   4   8
CABLES

51.2   *L'Aber-Wrac'h lifeboat slips downstream from yacht club and pontoon berths. Green and white beacons marking Roche aux Moines are bottom right. Quieter anchorage may be found farther upstream*

51.3   Low water at slipway next to yacht club

Its 27m square Tr is 55m above sea level and painted W on its western side. Its Q Lt has a range of 10 miles. The Lt is intensified 10° either side of the transit of 100°.

About 1½ miles from the Libenter buoy there are the R Bn Tr Grand Pot de Buerre and the E-cardinal Petit Pot de Beurre BYB Bn both to be left close to port.

At this point, alter to starboad to 128° to follow the main channel after 8 cables leaving the G Bn Breac'h Ver (Fl G 2.5 s.) close to starboard; thereafter leading straight for the point of land on the western bank where the village of L'Aber-Wrac'h is situated. The lifeboat shed and slip are prominent, almost right ahead. Alongside is a Lt Oc (2) WRG 6 s. on a W concrete Tr. The W sector is only ¾ of a degree either side of the 128° glide path, with a 1½° G sector indicating off course to starboard and 1½° R when off to port. By day the Lt Tr lines up with two RW unlit Bns beyond it. From the G Breac'h Ver Bn it is 1½ miles to go, but there is a least depth of 3m5 at LW if you leave the G Bns to starboard and R to port.

Approaching from the E in good visibility, 2 miles can be saved by taking the Chenal de la Malouine. Keep ½ mile offshore from the Île Vierge until you have identified the R

Grand Pot de Buerre Tr. Then bring the Petit Pot de Beurre E-cardinal Tr in transit with a conspicuous W obelisk on the Île de la Croix on course 176°. Hold that course to leave the Petit Pot close to port when you are in the Chenal de la Pendante described above.

Berthing and Facilities   Just beyond the prominent lifeboat house and its launching slip is the sumptuous new YC presiding over a single pontoon with berths for 90 yachts. There are moorings for many more offshore and a dinghy slip. Contact on VHF Ch 9.

In stormy weather go another mile upstream and find excellent shelter beyond Pte Camelent, where you should find a buoy or room to anchor.

The clubhouse is also the home of the HO: tel. (98) 04–91–62.

There are limited shops, but one memorable local restaurant near at hand.

Bonded stores can be obtained here.

FW and fuel are available.

Weather   Posted at the HO. Area Manche ouest. Tel. (98) 84–60–64.

*52   LE CONQUET

Charts: BA 3345 Fr 5287 Im C36 CG 540

High Water *+05h. 35m. Dover   As for SP Brest*
Heights above Datum *MHWS 7m2. MLWS 1m4.*
MHWN 5m6. MLWN 2m9.

LE CONQUET is a pretty little fishing port at the southern end of the Chenal du Four between the group of islands which include Ushant and the western tip of Brittany. The channel is famous not only for its sluicing tides running up to 5 knots at Springs, but also because it provided the German battle-cruisers *Scharnhorst* and *Gneisenau* with their escape route from Brest, when the RAF's surveillance suffered from defective radar and the 'tin ring' of our submarines failed to make contact, in spite of ignoring the Admiralty Sailing Directions' caution that the area off Pte St Mathieu 'is prohibited to submerged submarines'.

We always assumed that we lost two of our submarines there, until one of them was found in 1983 just off the Isle of Wight.

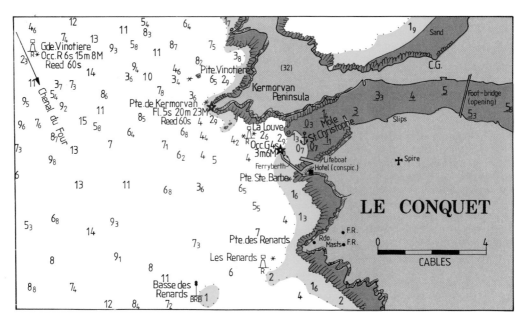

52.1   Approach from north-west leaving Kermovan lighthouse and La Louve beacon to port. Note ferry is alongside outer breakwater and room left for it to turn

293

*52.2 Ferry jetty unoccupied. Lifeboat Station and hotel domi-
nate middle of picture*

Le Conquet is a useful port of refuge if you just miss the
tide all the way through and don't want to divert 17 miles to
the new Yacht Hbr E of Brest.

Approach From the sea buoy off L'Aber-Wrac'h it is just
20 miles to Le Conquet. The Chenal du Four is a deep-ship
channel and marked accordingly. Give Le Four Lt a fair bit
of sea room, especially if the tide is still flooding (up to 1h.
before HW Dover) when it will be setting you onshore. The
Lt is a Grey Tr 28m high, Fl (5) 15 s. to a range of 20 miles.
It has a siren (5 ev 75 s.). Thereafter head 3 miles SSW for
the Chenal du Four. On course 159° pass between the Lt Bns
marking Les Plâtresses and La Valbelle 2½ miles NW of Pte
de Corsen. Les Plâtresses is a 23m W Tr Fl RG 4 s. range 6
miles. La Valbelle is a R whistle buoy Oc R 6 s.

*52.3 Kermovan light looking to seaward with Grande Vino-
tière beacon on the Chenal du Four beyond*

Then pick up the main transit on 159° aligning Pte de
Kermorvan at Le Conquet (a W square Tr – pic 52.3 – 20m
above the sea, Fl 5 s. to a range of 23 miles) with the prominent
Pte St Mathieu (Fl W 15 s. 56m 29M) on a 37m W Tr with
R top. It also has an intensified F W Lt 1° either side of 158½°.

This will bring you straight to the end of the new outer
breakwater with an Oc G 4 s. Lt at its northern end. There is
an unlit R Bn to be left to port at the entrance.

Berthing There are no readily-available alongside berths,
although the new ferry dock just inside the breakwater may
be tempting. The vedettes run back and forth to Ushant, and
they swoop round the corner, confident that they won't find
a visiting British yacht secured there.

52.4   Moorings in outer harbour

52.5   Slipway in old (inner) harbour, which dries

There is over 2m water off the ferry berth, and the shoal water, which dries out, is a cable farther inshore. You could pick up a buoy there or anchor close NE of the breakwater if the weather is settled. Allow room for the ferry to back off and slew round to starboard.

Otherwise you must be prepared to take the ground beyond the inner mole (St Christophe), which is the fish dock, and land there or at the slipway beyond.

Facilities   The local harbour authority is at Rue A-Lucas, tel. (98) 89–00–05.

A local garage can provide an electrician or a mechanic.

FW and fuel available.

There is a spectacular hotel hanging on the edge of the cliff, facing due W. It is a favourite with businessmen from Brest (24km by road) for lunch, or coachloads of Gallic grockles and wedding parties at the weekends.

The town itself is unspoilt but has the usual crêperies and Breton pubs decorated with fishnets and old lobster pots.

Weather   Posted on the quayside. Brest–Le Conquet weather broadcasts are on 1673kHz at 07.33, 16.33 and 21.53. The general weather on Radio France (1071kHz) is put out at 07.25 and 18.50. Area 12 Ouest Bretagne.

53 BREST (PORT DU MOULIN BLANC)

Charts: Fr 6542 BA 3427 Im C36 CG 542 Stan 17

High Water *+05h. 10m. Dover SP Brest*
Heights above Datum *MHWS 7m5. MLWS 3m0. MHWN 5m9. MLWN 1m4.*

BREST is a major naval base and commercial centre of 250,000 inhabitants. It lies on the N shore of the spectacular natural setting of Brest Roads, which provide over 40 square miles of sheltered water, ideal for day cruising.

There are numerous little coves where one can anchor along the 10-mile approach from Pte St Mathieu (4km S of Le Conquet). But the massive artificial harbour in the heart of the city does not welcome or accommodate yachts, which must carry on a further 2 miles to the E to the new Yacht Hbr at Moulin Blanc.

In any case it is to be preferred to berthing in the main port, which is a bit like taking a yacht into Liverpool or Marseilles.

Brest figures in the history books, mostly due to disagreements with the British going back to the fourteenth century when it was swapped for one of Charles VI's daughters.

Its most troubled times were more recently. As a German naval base on the edge of the North Atlantic, it was pounded to pieces by Anglo-American air raids. When it was finally liberated, three months after D-Day, we acquired a heap of rubble. Hence the wide range of new buildings which form the city centre today. It is also the headquarters of the French Hydrographic Service (SHOM).

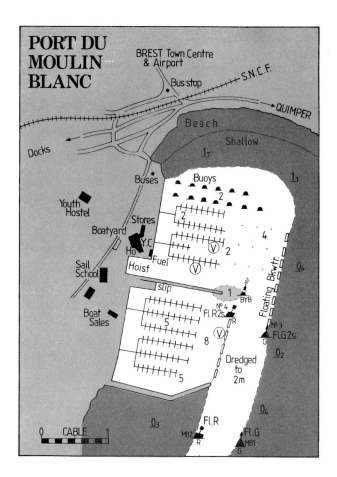

53.1   Pointe St Mathieu marking the point to head east for Brest. Lighthouse is built out of an old ruin

Approach   Pte St Mathieu is the equivalent of Cape St Vincent (pic 53.1). At St Mathieu you turn 90° to port to run along the coast to Brest. It is deep water all the way and very well marked. The Lt Ho at Pte St Mathieu is unforgettable: a 37m W Tr with an R top built out of the ruins of an old abbey. It is 56m above sea level (Fl 15 s. range 29 miles). It has a Rdo Bn on 289.6kHz, callsign 'SM' with a range of 20 miles.

There is a secondary light with a lesser range Q WRG 14/10/9 miles. When you are in the 22° G sector it is time to

53.2   *Looking eastwards over Point du Portzic with naval port nearer and commercial harbour beyond. (A) is the A-Louppe bridge. Port du Moulin Blanc is round the corner at (B)*

53.3   *Rounding floating breakwater to enter the yacht harbour*

53.4   *Some of the 730 pontoon berths*

53.5   The yacht club, surrounded by stores, agencies and boatyards

start altering to the E and leave Les Vieux Moines Lt (Oc R 4 s.) to port – another octagonal Tr.

The rest of the approach is straightforward. Leave the naval and commercial harbours to port and head 065° towards the Pont Albert Louppe carrying the N165 highway southward towards Quimper. No. 2 and 4 R fairway buoys should be left to port. Their lights are Fl (2) R 6 s. and Oc R 4 s. The next buoy is S-cardinal (Q (6) + LFl 15 s.). A mile beyond it is the R Moulin Blanc buoy (Oc (2) R 6 s.). Here alter slowly to port until you can lay 005° to pass between MB1 and MB2 buoys which mark the final short 3-cables channel to the new Yacht Hbr at Port du Moulin Blanc. They have Fl G and Fl R lights, while MB3 is Fl G 2 s. and MB4 is at the end of the floating breakwater, showing Fl R 2 s.

Berthing and Facilities Entering on a N'ly course between two lines of floating pontoon breakwaters there is an E-cardinal buoy to be left to port before going straight to the visitors' berths on the first two pontoons in the N Basin, right in front of the stylish clubhouse, which also accommodates the HO. Call on VHF Ch 9 or 16, tel. (98) 02–20–02.

There is a minimum of 2m water in the N Basin. Altogether there are 800 berths, 730 of them alongside pontoons.

FW and fuel readily available. A 14-ton travel-lift. The YC – Société des Régates de Brest (SRB) – is right there, with an excellent restaurant and every facility a visiting yacht can wish for. There is a supermarket near by. If you don't like your boat, there is a large stock of new ones to choose from.

Brest is on the main SNCF railway line and has an airport at Guipavas only 10 minutes from the marina.

Weather Forecasts on (98) 84–60–64. Also, see Le Conquet. Area 12 Ouest Bretagne.

APPENDIX
Where to buy charts and publications

French Navy Charts (Fr)   published by le Service Hydrographique et Océanographique de la Marine (SHOM). By post from:

À l'établissement Principal du SHOM, Section deliverance, B.P. 426, 29275 Brest Cedex. (tel. (98) 03–09–17)

Main agent in Northern France: Heilmann, Port des Yachts, Bd. Clémenceau, 76600 Le Havre (next to the Yacht Club at Le Havre. They also hold a stock of British Admiralty charts).

Main agent in UK: Kelvin Hughes, 145 Minories, LONDON EC3N 1NH.

Nearly every chandlery carries a selection of SHOM charts. The following are in the area covered by this book:

Dunkerque
Weizsaeker et Carrère
30, rue du Leughenaer
59140 Dunkerque
(28) 66–64–00

Dekyspotter M.R.
14, rue des Fusiliers-Marins,
B.P. 1049 59375 Dunkerque
(28) 65–98–33

St Valéry-sur-Somme
Hall Nautique de la Baie
de Somme 80230 St-Valéry-
sur-Somme
(22) 27–53–64

Rouen
Papeterie du Port
68, quai du Havre
76000 Rouen
(35) 71–45–82

Le Havre
Heilmann (voir agent
distributeur)
Nautic-Service
23–27, rue A. Barbes
76600 Le Havre
(35) 26–40–40

Ouistreham
Accastillage Diffusion
Port de plaisance
14150 Ouistreham
(31) 96–07–75

Caen
Caen Marine
9, boulevard Bertrand
14000 Caen
(31) 85–70–36

Cherbourg
Nicollet
40, rue du Commerce
50100 Cherbourg
(33) 53–11–74

Granville
Roquet
22, rue Le Campion
50400 Granville
(33) 50–09–34

La Marine
2, rue Saint-Sauveur
50400 Granville
(33) 50–71–31

Saint Malo
Back
5, rue Broussais
35402 Saint Malo
(99) 40–91–73

Voilerie Richard
3, rue du Glorioux
35400 Saint Malo
(99) 81–63–81

Sablons Yachting
Port des Bas Sablons
35400 Saint Malo
(99) 56–98–17

Librarie Nautique des
Bas Sablons
26, rue des Bas Sablons
35400 Saint Malo
(99) 83–06–60

L'Ancre de Marine
4, rue Porcon
35400 Saint Malo
(99) 56–78–43

Saint Brieuc
Accastillage diffusion
4, rue Baratoux
22000 Saint-Brieuc
(96) 33–96–36

Plérin
L'Habitat et la Mer
28, rue de la Tour
22190 Plérin
(96) 33–71–68

Binic
Jean Bart Marine
quai Jean Bart, BP 15
22520 Binic
(96) 73–75–28

Paimpol
Le Corre L
rue de Romsey
22500 Paimpol
(96) 20–85–17

Perros-Guirec
Ponant Loisirs
La Rade
22700 Perros-Guirec
(96) 23–18–38

Lannion
Lesbleiz S.A.
Route de Guingamp
22300 Lannion
(96) 37–09–12

Morlaix
Jegou Ritz
10, place des Otages
B.P. 186
29204 Morlaix
(98) 88–04–15

Brest
Jouanneau
75, rue de Siam
29200 Brest
(98) 80–17–07

Berra Michel
6, rue Porstrein
29200 Brest
(98) 80–49–74

Belmar
quai Commandant
Malbert   29200 Brest
(98) 44–39–61

Fonderies Phocéennes
4, rue Amiral Troude
29200 Brest
(98) 44–84–69

Carte Guide (CG)   Navicarte Éditions Cartographique Maritimes are available at any Librarie Maritime and at all chandleries, including those listed above. For corrections or further details, write to:
Navicarte E.C.M., 9 quai d'Artois, 94170 Le Perreux-sur-Marne

Admiralty charts (BA)   are sold through agents listed on pages 259–65 of the Shell Pilot to the English Channel Part 1. They are also published quarterly in the Small Craft edition of *Admiralty Notice to Mariners*.

Imray Yachting Charts (Im)   are available at most outlets carrying BA charts. Some of their stockists are listed below:

Great Britain

Bath
Anchor Marine
1 Sussex Place
Widcombe   BA2 4LA

Bournemouth
A.H.F. Marine Ltd
934 Wimborne Road
BH9 2DH

Burnham-on-Crouch
Kelvin Aqua
The Quay
Essex   CM0 8AT

Brighton
Marina Watersports
Brighton Marina
BN2 5UP

Bristol
Tratmen & Ladyline Ltd
Berkeley Place
Clifton
BS8 1EH

Chichester
Yacht & Sports Gear Ltd
13 The Hornet
PO19 4JL

Christchurch
Rossiter Yacht Builders Ltd
Bridge Street
BH23 1DZ

Clacton-on-Sea
Anglo Marine Services
Forse Lane Ind. Est.
Essex   CO15 4LT

Cowes
Groves & Guttridge
Chandlery Ltd
127 High Street
PO31 7AY

Pascall Atkey & Son Ltd
29–30 High Street
PO31 7RX

Dartmouth
The Bosun's Locker
24 Lower Street
Cobbold Marine
The Quay

Dartmouth Chandlers
24 Foss Street
TQ6 9DR

Harbour Bookshop
Fairfax Place   TQ6 9AE

Dover
Dover Marine Supplies
158–160 Snargate Street
CT17 9BZ

East Looe
Jack Bray & Son
The Quay   Cornwall

Emsworth
The Bookshop
The Square
PO10 7EJ

Wheelhouse Chandlery
51 High Street
PO10 7AN

Exeter
Devon Boats Ltd
Haven Road
EX2 8DP

Eland Bros
22 Bedford Street
EX1 1LE

Falmouth
Bosun's Locker
Upton Slip
Church Street   TR11

Falmouth Yacht Marina
North Parade
TR11 2TD

Marine Instruments
79 Killigrew Street
TR11 3HL

M & P Miller
15 Arwenack Street
TT11 3JH

Folkestone
Forepeak
Fishmarket
Kent

Fowey
Guerniers
3 Station Road
Cornwall

Guernsey
David Bowker
Castle Emplacement
St Peter Port

303

Channel Island Yacht
Services
Old Harbour
St Helier

Marquand Bros Ltd
North Quay
St Peter Port

Navigation & Marine
Supplies
North Plantation
St Peter Port

Gosport
Hardway Marine
95–99 Priory Road
Hardway
PO12 4LF

Hayling Island
Dinghy Den Ltd
Regal Precinct
Mengham Road
PO11 9BS

Sparkes Boatyard Co Ltd
38 Wittering Road
Sandy Point
PO11 9SR

Havant
West Havant Marine
43 West Street
PO9 1LA

Ipswich
Ancient House Bookshop
25–27 Upper Brook Street
IP4 1ED

Ipswich Marina Ltd
The Strand
Wherstead   IP2 8NJ

Itchenor
H.C. Darley & Son
Chichester
PO20 7AU

Jersey
Gorey Yacht Service
Gorey Pier
South Pier Shipyard
St Helier

Kingston-upon-Thames
The Boat Shop Ltd
Kingston Bridge
Hampton Wick
KT1 4BZ

Lancing
Compass Marine Services
145 South Street
BN15 8BD

Littlehampton
Britannia Watersports
Fisherman's Quay

London
Arthur Beal
194 Shaftesbury Avenue
WC2H 8JP

Force 4 Chandlery
30 Bressenden Place
Buckingham Palace Road
SW1E 5DB

Greenwich Marine Ltd
22 College Approach SE10

Ivory Marine
Eastgate House
St Katharine's Dock   E1

London Yacht Centre
13 Artillery Lane
E1 7LP

Kelvin Hughes Ltd
145 Minories
EC3N 1NH

Edward Stanford Ltd
12–14 Long Acre
WC2E 9LE

Telesonic Marine Ltd
60/62 Brunswick Centre
Marchmont Street   WC1

Captain O. M. Watts Ltd
48a Albemarle Street
Piccadilly
W1X 4BJ

Lymington
Berthon Boat Co
The Shipyard
Bath Road
Hants
SO4 9YL

The Boathouse
The Quay
The Haven Boatyard
Kings Saltern Road
SO1 9QD

Milford-on-Sea
Tony Redfern Marine
27 High Street
SO4 9QF

Paignton
Torbay Sail & Power Boat
The Harbour
TQ4 6DT

Parkstone
Harbour Chandlers
10 Bournemouth Road
BH14 0EF

Fredk. C. Mitchell & Sons
Sandbanks Road
BH14 8JW

Plymouth
A. E. Monson
Vauxhall Quay
PL4 0DL

Saltash Yacht Services
43 Bretonside

Sutton Marine Ltd
Sutton Harbour
PL4 0DW

Poole
J. Looker
82 High Street
BH15 1DD

J. G. Meakes
P.H.Y.C. Marina
Salterns Way
Lilliput
BH14 8JR

H. Pipler & Son Ltd
The Quay
BH15 1HF

Ramsgate
Laurestine Ltd
Royal Harbour
Stuart Marine Services
50A Harbour Parade

Rye
Sea Cruisers of Rye
Winchelsea Road
TN31 7EL

Salcombe
Offshore Seachest
Union Street
TQ8 8BZ

Salcombe Chandlers
19 Fore Street

Shaldon
Brigantine
The Quay
TQ14 0DL

Mariners Weigh
Fore Street
Devon

Southampton
Kelvin Hughes Ltd
19–23 Canute Road

Southend-on-Sea
Shoreline (Yachtsmen)
Ltd
36 Eastern Esplanade

Southsea
Chris Hornsey Chandlery
Ltd
152/154 Eastney Road

Topsham
The Foc'sle
32 Fore Street
EX3 0HD

Retreat Boatyard Ltd
Exeter Road
EX3 0LS

Totnes
Compass Sailing &
Boating
Centre
71 High Street

Wareham
Barnard Boats
10 South Street

Ridge Wharf Yacht Centre
Ridge
BH20 5BG

Warsash
Warsash Nautical
Bookshop
31 Newtown Road
SO3 6FY

Westcliff-on-Sea
Boatacs
833 London Road
SS0 9SY

West Mersea
Wyatt Yacht Chandlery
128 Waterside Coast Road

France
Paris
Le Yacht
55 Av de la Grande Armée
75116 Paris, 16e

Eire
Cork
Mizen Books
Main Street
Schull
Salters Bar
Baltimore

Dublin
Allweather Marine
(Ireland) Ltd
Grand Canal Quay
(off Pearse St)
Dublin 2

Dublin Boat Centre Ltd
Airport Road
Cloghran

Perry & Co Ltd
114 Lower George's Street
Dun Loaire

Kerry
O'Sullivans Marine Ltd
Rock Street
Tralee

Stanfords Coloured Charts (Stan)   are published by:
Barnacle Marine Ltd, The Wharehouse, 1 Crowhurst Road, Colchester, Essex CO3 3JN
They are generally available at most outlets selling BA or Imray charts.

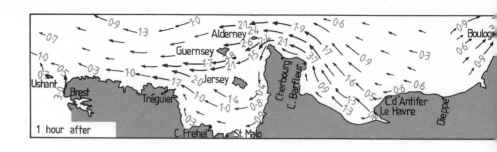

1 hour after

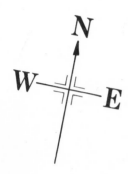

N
W — E

Mean rate of tidal streams in the Channel during the six hours after HW DOVER.

Arrows indicate direction of the stream. The figures give average rate in knots at each point. For Spring rate, add one-third. At Neaps, subtract one-third of the figures shown on each chart.

For greater detail, see Admiralty Tidal Stream Atlases or relevant charts.

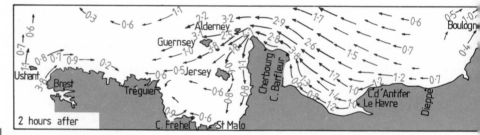

2 hours after

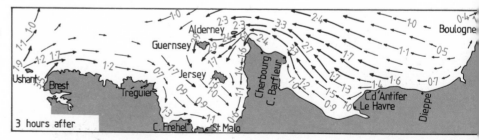

3 hours after